W9-BSJ-780

TEACHING BASIC AND ADVANCED VOCABULARY

A FRAMEWORK FOR DIRECT INSTRUCTION

Robert J. Marzano

HEINLE
CENGAGE Learning

Australia • Brazil • Japan • Korea • Mexico • Singapore • Spain • United Kingdom • United States

HEINLE
CENGAGE Learning

**Teaching Basic and Advanced Vocabulary:
A Framework for Direct Instruction**
Robert J. Marzano

Publisher: Sherrise Roehr

Acquisitions Editor: Tom Jefferies

Associate Development Editor: Catherine Black

Director of Marketing: Jim McDonough

Marketing Manager: Caitlin Driscoll

Content Project Manager: Mark Rzeszutek

Print Buyer: Susan Carroll

Compositor: Macmillan Publishing Solutions

Cover Designer: Lisa Mezikofsky

For product information and technology assistance, contact us at
Cengage Learning Customer & Sales Support, 1-800-354-9706
For permission to use material from this text or product,
submit all requests online at **www.cengage.com/permissions**
Further permissions questions can be emailed to
permissionrequest@cengage.com

Library of Congress Control Number: 2009926192

ISBN-13: 978-1-4240-6713-8

ISBN-10: 1-4240-6713-8

Heinle
20 Channel Center Street
Boston, MA 02210
USA

Cengage Learning is a leading provider of customized learning solutions with office locations around the globe, including Singapore, the United Kingdom, Australia, Mexico, Brazil, and Japan. Locate your local office at **www.cengage.com/global**

Cengage Learning products are represented in Canada by Nelson Education, Ltd.

Visit Heinle online at **elt.heinle.com**
Visit our corporate website at **www.cengage.com**

Printed in the United States of America
2 3 4 5 6   14 13 12 11 10

ED067

To my Jana
Robert J. Marzano

CONTENTS

PREFACE

This book is best thought of as the culminating piece in a series of works on vocabulary development that has spanned almost three decades. Over that time, I have become convinced that direct vocabulary instruction is a necessary and vital component of a robust K–12 curriculum. In 1988, I coauthored a book entitled *A Cluster Approach to Elementary Vocabulary Instruction* (Marzano & Marzano, 1988). There the case was made that vocabulary could be taught more effectively and efficiently if terms were organized in semantic clusters—groups of related words. The advantage to this approach is that when teaching one word, others can also be taught, as they share semantic features with the target word. In such a system, words are not taught in isolation. Rather, they are taught and reinforced in the context of a set of related terms that form a rich semantic network. Many instructional activities are available when words are taught in semantic clusters that are not otherwise available. Most prominently, a wide variety of comparison, classification, analogy, and metaphor activities are easily generated in a semantic cluster approach.

In 2004, I authored a book entitled *Building Background Knowledge for Academic Achievement* (Marzano, 2004). There the case was made that schools and districts should adopt a systematic approach to ensuring that all students have background knowledge of key subject matter terms. The best way to ensure such background knowledge is to teach academic terms in a way that provides students with an initial understanding of the target terms in the context of their personal experiences. To this end, a six-step process to direct vocabulary instruction was provided. Since the publication of that book, the six-step process has been validated in regard to its effectiveness by a number of formal and information studies (see Marzano, 2006a and 2006b; Gifford & Gore, 2008; and Dunn, Bonner, & Huske, 2007). *Building Background Knowledge for Academic Achievement* also identified 7,923 important academic terms from 17 different subject areas. What that book did not address is nonacademic subject matter terms that are important to general literacy. That domain is the focus of this current work.

As its title indicates, *Teaching Basic and Advanced Vocabulary* is focused on providing a framework for direct instruction in basic terms—those words that are critical to understanding and using the English language. To this end, 2,845 basic terms have been identified and listed in the book. These words can be considered absolutely necessary for all students to master if they are to be successful navigating their way through a society that relies on the English language as the primary medium of communication. Although many students will acquire these terms naturally as part of their home environment, many will not. In particular, students who are English Language Learners and students of poverty do not necessarily enter school with a thorough grounding in basic terms. Direct instruction in these terms should be considered a necessary component of their curriculum. As its title indicates, *Teaching Basic and Advanced Vocabulary* also provides a framework for teaching advanced terms. These are words that are critical to general literacy development, an area in which all students can benefit from direct instruction. To this end, *Teaching Basic and Advanced Vocabulary* lists 5,162 advanced terms. The composite list of 8,007 advanced and basic terms (i.e., 2,845 basic terms and 5,162 advanced terms) are organized into 420 semantic clusters—groups of related terms. These semantic clusters are ranked in order of the number and importance of the basic terms they contain. Thus, the first cluster contains the largest number of the most basic terms; the second cluster contains the second largest number of the most basic terms; and so on. To place students on this continuum of semantic clusters, the book provides teachers with a Snapshot Assessment, which is easily administered to individual students. Using this assessment, the most appropriate beginning place for instruction can be readily identified for each student. Additionally, advanced terms can easily be taught in conjunction with the basic terms to maximize the efficiency and effectiveness of direct instruction. The six-step process offered in the book *Building Background Knowledge for Academic Achievement* has been modified to capitalize on the semantic cluster arrangement of basic and advanced terms.

Finally, *Teaching Basic and Advanced Vocabulary* also explains how a district, school, or individual teacher might use the semantic clusters in a whole-class approach to direct instruction that focuses on advanced vocabulary. In summary, the book is intended to provide K–12 educators with frameworks for direct instruction in basic and advanced terms that form the foundation of general literacy development in the United States.

Robert J. Marzano

1

The Need for Instruction
in Basic Vocabulary

In 1997, Congress commissioned the National Institute of Child Health and Human Development (NICHHD) to convene a national panel to conduct a comprehensive review of the research on reading. The panel was known as the National Reading Panel. In April 2000, the panel completed its review and published the *Report of the National Reading Panel: Teaching Children to Read: An Evidenced-Based Assessment of the Scientific Research Literature on Reading and Its Implications for Reading Instruction: Reports of the Subgroups* (NICHHD, 2000). In that report, the following subjects were identified as focus areas for instruction: phonemic awareness, phonics, fluency, vocabulary, and comprehension. Of these, vocabulary was singled out for special consideration. As reported by Kamil and Hiebert:

> Vocabulary holds a special place among these components. Vocabulary is not a developmental skill or one that can be seen as fully mastered. The expansion and elaboration of vocabularies is something that extends across a lifetime. (Kamil & Hiebert, 2005, p. 2)

The importance of vocabulary to literacy in general and reading in particular was recognized long before the National Reading Panel report. Numerous studies have documented the relationship between vocabulary knowledge and academic achievement. As early as 1941, researchers estimated that for students in grades 4 through 12, there was about a 6,000-word gap between students at the 25th and 50th percentiles on standardized tests (see Nagy & Herman, 1984). Using a different method of calculating vocabulary size, Nagy and Herman estimated the difference to be anywhere between 4,500 and 5,400 words for low- versus high-achieving students (1984).

Both research and common sense indicate that it is prudent to increase the vocabulary knowledge of students, but this is not a simple or straightforward task. To understand the challenges involved in vocabulary development, consider that there are a number of types of vocabulary. Kamil and Hiebert (2005) make a distinction between two types: receptive vocabulary and productive vocabulary. Receptive vocabulary includes terms and phrases that an individual recognizes and understands. Productive vocabulary includes terms and phrases that an individual uses. Another distinction made by Kamil and Hiebert is that between oral and written language. These distinctions make for a two-by-two classification of vocabulary, as depicted in Figure 1.1.

	Receptive	Productive
Oral	Listening Vocabulary	Speaking Vocabulary
Written	Reading Vocabulary	Writing Vocabulary

FIGURE 1.1 Types of Vocabulary

As indicated in Figure 1.1, listening vocabulary includes terms and phrases that an individual understands when being spoken to—when listening. Reading vocabulary includes terms that an individual recognizes and understands when reading. Speaking vocabulary includes terms that an individual uses when speaking. Finally, writing vocabulary includes terms that an individual uses when writing. This book focuses on receptive vocabulary, although some activities described are useful for developing expressive vocabulary.

Kamil and Hiebert note that "In general…receptive vocabulary is larger than production vocabulary" (2005, p. 3). It is also reasonable to conclude that in general, oral vocabulary is larger than written vocabulary, because written vocabulary involves a component that oral vocabulary does not—the written symbols for the terms. More pointedly, oral vocabulary can be considered the foundation of written vocabulary. It is true that for literate adults, there might be situations in which there are words and phrases that they can recognize and understand in print but have little or no experience with within oral language; however, for the vast majority of terms, learners will most probably understand a word in the oral language and then use this as a basis to develop their speaking and writing vocabularies.

WHAT IS BASIC VOCABULARY?

As its title indicates, this book focuses on basic vocabulary (although it can also be used to develop a comprehensive program that focuses on advanced vocabulary). There have been a number of attempts to identify basic terms in the English language. Early attempts were made by Ogden (1932) and Dupuy (1974). However, they did not actually generate a list of basic terms. Rather, they simply identified the defining characteristics of basic terms and estimated the number of basic words in the English language. Becker, Dixon, and Anderson-Inman (1980) went a step further. Following the Dupuy criteria, they identified 8,109 words drawn from a list of 25,782 terms that were an updated version of the Thorndike and Lorge (1943) list. Such a list was presumed to have instructional utility, in that teaching 8,109 terms would unlock the meaning to 25,782 terms. Nagy and Anderson (1984), however, challenged the logic of Becker, Dixon, and Anderson-Inman. They concluded that Becker et al.'s 8,109 basic terms were, for the most part, too unrelated semantically to the other words in the 25,782 corpus from which they were drawn to constitute an instructionally meaningful set. In effect, Becker, Dixon, and Anderson-Inman (1980) had identified root words, some (or many) of which were not very useful in unlocking the meaning of other terms. For example, each of the following was identified as one of the 8,109 root words by Becker, Dixon, and Anderson-Inman:

abate	begone	chattel
accede	besmirch	colossus
amalgam	boneset	cutworm

It does not seem likely that a knowledge of *amalgam* or *boneset* (and the others) will provide much help for readers trying to determine the meaning of unknown terms. In short, the Becker, Dixon, and Anderson-Inman list simply did not possess face validity as a list of basic terms that are essential to facility with the English language. Consequently, the search for a list of basic terms continued.

Using a corpus of words drawn from reading material in grades 3 through 9 and referred to as "written school English" (Carroll, Davies, & Richman, 1971), Nagy and Anderson estimated that there are 88,500 words in the reading material taught in grades 3 through 9 alone (1984). They used their estimate as the basis for a logical case against direct vocabulary instruction. They reasoned that because it is impossible to directly teach 88,500 terms, wide reading (as opposed to direct vocabulary instruction) should be the primary vehicle for vocabulary development. Beck, McKeown, and Omanson (1987) offered a qualifier to Nagy and Anderson's position. They conceded that there are far too many terms in the English language to teach all of them directly. However, they noted that about half of the 88,500 terms in Nagy and Anderson's estimation would be encountered only once in the life of an avid reader. Additionally, of the remaining half of the 88,500 terms, about 15,000 would be encountered once in every 10 million running words.

In effect, Beck, McKeown, and Omanson agreed with Nagy and Anderson that there are too many terms in the English language for all of them to be taught directly, but also added that only a small portion of those terms are used frequently enough to be thought of as "basic." To illustrate, consider Figure 1.2.

7.57% (6,700)	1 time or more in 1 year	Tier 1 and Tier 2
9.77% (8,650)	Up to 3 times in 10 years	Tier 2
7.18% (6,350)	Up to 3 times in 100 years	Tier 3
27.80% (24,600)	1 time in 100 years	Tier 3
47.68% (42,200)	Up to 3 times in 10,000 or more years	Tier 3

Computed from data reported in Nagy and Anderson, 1984.

FIGURE 1.2 Frequency of Words Encountered During a Typical Year of Reading*

The information in Figure 1.2 is based on the estimate that an average reader will read about one million words of text per year (Nagy & Anderson, 1984). Figure 1.2 indicates that of the 88,500 terms that form Nagy and Anderson's corpus of written school English, 6,700 will be encountered one time or more in one year of reading; 8,650 will be encountered up to three times in 10 years of reading, and so on. The most striking aspect of Figure 1.2 is that the vast majority of words would be encountered remarkably infrequently in the normal course of reading. For example, 24,600 words (27.80%) would be encountered one time in 100 years of reading and 42,000 words (47.68%) would be encountered three times in 10,000 or more years. Fundamentally, for 75.5% of the terms in the Nagy and Anderson corpus, there is a good chance that students will encounter these terms very infrequently or never throughout their reading lives. Consequently, for some 75% of the words, the question arises as to how important are they for students to learn. Beck and her colleagues proposed an answer.

Beck and McKeown (1985) suggested that vocabulary terms be categorized into three tiers. As described by Beck, McKeown, and Kucan (2002), the first tier includes those terms that are very frequent in the English language—the most basic terms in the language. Tier 1 includes words like *big, clock, walk, baby*, and so on. These are the most basic terms in the first row of Figure 1.2. As described by Beck, McKeown, and Kucan: "Words in this tier rarely require instructional attention to their meanings in school" (2002, p. 8). Tier 2 terms are those that appear infrequently enough that they will probably not be learned in context. These terms probably include all words from the second row of Figure 1.2 and the less-frequent words from the first row of Figure 1.2. Tier 3 words in the Beck schema are subject-matter specific—terms that are important to academic subject areas but are not as frequently found in the general use of the language. Subject-matter terms are found in the last three rows of Figure 1.2. For example, the term *cellular response* might be encountered quite infrequently (or never) in the course of general reading. However, it is a term that has been identified as important to high school science (see Marzano, 2004).

Beck recommends that general vocabulary instruction (instruction in terms that are necessary for general literacy, as opposed to instruction in terms that are specific to academic subjects) should focus on Tier 2 terms. Stated differently, Beck's solution to the problem of 88,500 terms is to not teach all of them. Some will be learned without any formal instruction (Tier 1 words). Some will be addressed in academic subject areas (Tier 3 terms). Some are so infrequently used that they are not worth teaching directly (the words in Tier 3 that are not subject-matter specific). There are a relatively small set of words (i.e., Tier 2 words) that are general in nature and important to the English language. These should be taught directly.

Beck's proposed solution provided great clarity to the debate regarding direct vocabulary instruction. To a great extent, she ended the debate, by conceding that there are too many terms to teach directly, but she also narrowed the focus of instruction to a relatively small set that can be taught directly. Beck's proposal was to teach a relatively small but highly important set of terms. Unfortunately, Beck and her colleagues did not construct a list of Tier 2 words.

In 1991, Marzano, Kendall, and Paynter attempted to identify a list of basic words that should be taught in grades K–6. They identified 6,768 terms. Although this list was a step forward, it still presented problems. First, though many of the terms appear to qualify as basic, in that they are foundational to the English language, some do not. To illustrate, the terms *ankle* and *closet* are on the fourth-grade list. They seem to be basic, in that without knowledge of them, students might have difficulty with the English language—at least in certain contexts. However, the terms *procrastinate* and *trinket* are also on the fourth-grade list. These do not appear as necessary to the English language as do the previous two.

A second problem with the list is the sheer number of terms—6,768 in all. Even if these terms could be evenly distributed across the seven vocabulary levels from grades K–6 (which they could not be, as fewer terms can be taught at lower grade levels), it would still mean that about 987 terms would be taught each year or about 5.5 per day. This, of course, is a task that would probably strain the time and energy resources of most teachers.

In this text, I present a list of 8,007 terms, 2,845 of which are classified as basic and 5,162 of which are classified as advanced. The 2,845 basic terms are those that Beck and colleagues would probably classify as Tier 1 words; the 5,162 advanced terms are those that Beck and colleagues would probably classify as Tier 2 terms. Although Beck and colleagues are accurate in their assertion that basic (i.e., Tier 1) terms do not have to be taught to many students in school, there are some notable exceptions. That is, there are some students for whom instruction in basic terms is vitally important.

WHO NEEDS INSTRUCTION IN BASIC TERMS?

Basic terms are operationally defined in this book as terms that are used across a variety of situations and that are used quite frequently. For example, the term *because* is used in a variety of situations and is quite common in the English language, as is the term *river*. As Beck and colleagues note, these terms will be learned by many students without direct instruction, simply through their interaction with the world and their reading outside of school. However, this is not the case for all students. There are a growing number of students in U.S. schools for whom their experiences outside of school might not provide sufficient access to this basic terminology. There are at least two types of students who are in uniquely precarious situations regarding basic vocabulary development: students from a background of poverty (free and reduced lunch–qualified students, or FRL students) and English Language Learners (ELLs).

Students of Poverty

There is considerable evidence that vocabulary development is highly correlated with family income and socioeconomic status (SES). For example, Nagy and Herman (1984) found a consistent difference in vocabulary knowledge between students at different family income levels. They estimated a 4,700-word difference in vocabulary knowledge between high and low SES students. Similarly, they estimated that mid-SES first graders know about 50 percent more words than do low-SES first graders. Graves and Slater (1987) found that first graders from higher-income backgrounds have about double the vocabulary of those from lower-income backgrounds.

Hart and Risley (1995) found that the differences in vocabulary development due to family economic status start at a very early age. They computed the differences in vocabulary development from age 10 months to 36 months between children from three socioeconomic groups: welfare families, working-class families, and professional families. They found that 36-month-old children from welfare families have about 70 percent of the vocabulary of children from working-class families and only about 45 percent of the vocabulary of children from professional families. Even more disturbing are the differential rates of vocabulary development among children from the three types of families. This means that the differences in vocabulary knowledge will be even greater as the children grow older. As Hart and Risley note: "We saw a widening gap beginning as early as age 24 months" (1995, p. 234). Students of poverty, then, represent one group of students who might benefit from direct instruction in basic terms.

Vocabulary instruction for students of poverty is not a straightforward process, in that few if any generalizations apply to all of these students. Some might require direct instruction in only a few of the basic terms; others might require instruction in a great many basic terms.

English Language Learners (ELLs)

ELLs represent a growing population in U.S. schools. Calderon et al. explain: "Large and growing numbers of students in the United States come from homes where English is not the primary language" (2005, p. 115). According to the National Center for Educational Statistics (2002), in the 2001–2002 school year, the ELL population had increased 105% in U.S. schools since the 1991–1992 school year, whereas the general school population had increased only 12%. By 2002, almost 4,600,000 English language learners were enrolled in U.S. schools, representing 9.6% of the total school enrollment. Calderon et al. note: "However, the schools and, more generally, the educational system have not been adequately prepared to respond to the rapidly changing student demographics" (2005, p. 115).

Biemiller and Slonim (2001) note that the typical ELL student beginning school has already learned from 5,000 to 7,000 words in their first language. Unfortunately, this is not the case in their second language. Second language learners typically do not have a well-developed vocabulary in their second language, regardless of the socioeconomic status of their homes. To illustrate, Umbel, Pearson, Fernandez, and Oller (1992) examined the receptive vocabulary in both English and Spanish of Hispanic ELL students in Miami. They found that even ELL students from middle- and high-SES families had poorly developed vocabularies in their second language.

On a more positive note, McLaughlin, August, Snow, Carlo, Dressler, White, Lively, and Lippman (2000) examined the impact of direct vocabulary instruction in English terms on ELL students and found that by the end of the study, ELL students in the program closed the gap between themselves and native English speakers by 50 percent in measures of vocabulary knowledge and reading comprehension.

Again, vocabulary instruction for ELL students is not a straightforward process. Freeman and Freeman (2009) explain that there are at least three categories of ELL students: those newly arrived in the United States but well prepared in the schools in their homeland; those newly arrived in the United States but not well prepared in the schools in their homeland; and those who have been in the United States for a long time and have succeeded in acquiring basic terminology but require help in academic vocabulary. These differences must be carefully considered when designing a program of direct vocabulary instruction in basic terms.

BUILDING ON PREVIOUS WORK

To a great extent, this text builds on previous work I have done. Indeed, it would be accurate to say that this text "completes" previous work on direct vocabulary instruction. For example, in the book, *Building Background Knowledge for Academic Achievement* (Marzano, 2004), I identified 7,923 academic terms from 17 subject areas. The distribution of terms across subject areas is depicted in Figure 1.3.

Subject Area	(K–2)	(3–5)	(6–8)	(9–12)	Totals
Mathematics	80	190	201	214	685
Science	100	166	225	282	773
English Language Arts	83	245	247	223	798
History					
General History	162	560	319	270	1,311
U.S. History	0	154	123	148	425
World History	0	245	301	297	843
Geography	89	212	258	300	859
Civics	45	145	210	213	613
Economics	29	68	89	155	341
Health	60	68	75	77	280
Physical Education	57	100	50	34	241
The Arts					
Arts (General)	14	36	30	9	89
Dance	18	24	42	37	121
Music	14	83	67	32	196
Theater	5	14	35	13	67
Visual Arts	3	41	24	8	76
Technology	23	47	56	79	205
Totals	782	2,398	2,352	2,391	7,923

From R. J. Marzano (2004). Building Background Knowledge for Academic Achievement, *(p. 115). Alexandria, VA: Association for Supervision and Curriculum Development. Reprinted with permission.*

FIGURE 1.3 Academic Terms in 17 Subject Areas

As shown in Figure 1.3, General History has the most terms (1,311) and Theater has the least (67). The greatest number of academic terms is found in the grade level interval 3–5 (2,398) and the least number of academic terms is found in the grade level interval K–2 (782).

As described in Marzano (2004), these terms were extracted from national standards documents. Since the publication of *Building Background Knowledge for Academic Achievement*, two states—Tennessee and Oklahoma—have constructed their own lists of academic terms based on their state standards, as have a number of school districts. Additionally, the approach to direct instruction in academic terms described in that book has been shown to enhance the academic achievement of students in general and those students classified as qualified for either free and reduced lunch (FRL) and ELL in particular (see Marzano, 2006a and 2006b; Gifford & Gore, 2008; Dunn, Bonner, & Huske, 2007).

Although the results of focusing direct vocabulary instruction in academic terms is encouraging, there is a need to provide direct instruction in basic terms for some ELL students and FRL students and possibly others for the reasons described previously. Additionally, all students might benefit from direct instruction in more advanced general terms. Recall that

Beck and her colleagues (Beck & McKeown, 1985; Beck, McKeown, & Kucan, 2002) argued that all students can benefit from instruction in Tier 2 terms. In effect, this text articulates the Tier 1 words (in which some students are in need of direct instruction) and the Tier 2 words (in which all students might benefit from direct instruction). In this text, Tier 1 words are referred to as "basic terms" and Tier 2 terms are referred to as "advanced terms." Figure 1.4 depicts the distribution of basic and advanced terms.

Category	Basic Index	Numbered Terms	Total Terms in Categories
Basic (Tier 1)	1	222	2,845
	2	993	
	3	1,630	
Advanced (Tier 2)	4	3,638	5,162
	5	1,524	
Total			8,007

FIGURE 1.4 Distribution of Basic and Advanced Terms

As shown in Figure 1.4, there are 2,845 basic terms (Tier 1 terms) and 5,162 advanced terms (Tier 2 terms). Also note the column entitled Basic Index, which has values that range from 1 to 5. This number indicates how basic each term is judged to be. The specifics of how this value was assigned to each term are described in Marzano and Haysted (2009). As shown in Figure 1.4, terms that received a score of 3 or less in the Basic Index were classified as basic. Those with scores of 4 and 5 were classified as advanced. The relationship between basic and advanced terms is described in more depth in Chapter 2.

Here it is useful to note that between this text and *Building Background Knowledge for Academic Achievement* (Marzano, 2004), the corpus of Tier 1, Tier 2, and subject-specific terms has been articulated. One can make a case that if a student had a firm grounding in the 2,845 basic terms and the 5,162 advanced terms listed in this text and the 7,923 subject-matter terms listed in Marzano (2004), he or she would have the foundational knowledge to: (1) develop mastery of the basics of the English language, (2) develop mastery of the content considered important to general literacy, and (3) develop mastery of the content important to 17 subject areas.

SUMMARY

This chapter addressed the nature of and need for direct instruction in basic vocabulary. Basic vocabulary includes high-frequency terms that are critical to an understanding of the English language. Although many students enter school with a firm grasp of these terms, at least two groups of students require direct instruction in these terms: students of poverty (FRL students) and English language learners (ELL students). The chapter also described the basic features of the basic and advanced terms found in this text.

CHAPTER

2

What Are the Basic Terms?

As described in Chapter 1, there have been a number of attempts to identify basic terms (see for example, Ogden, 1932; Dupuy, 1974; Becker, Dixon, & Anderson-Inman, 1980; Marzano, Kendall, & Paynter, 1991). Although each of these efforts has been noteworthy, they all suffer from a common problem. They present terms in order of their frequency of appearance in the English language or in order of the grade level in which they might be addressed. To illustrate, the following is a partial list of terms that are commonly identified for kindergarten students:

a	at	blue
all	away	book
am	back	box
an	ball	boy
and	bell	brown
are	big	but
as	bird	by

A quick review of these terms illustrates the obstacles to instruction created by simply listing basic terms in order of their frequency: namely, each term is presented without any reference to its meaning or use. This practice makes for a list of vastly different types of terms. Some of the terms in the list are articles (*a, an*); some are prepositions (*at, by*); some are conjunctions (*but*); some are adjectives (*big, blue*); some are adverbs (*away*); some are nouns (*book, boy*); and so on. Additionally, there is no indication of the important semantic features that should be emphasized when the term is taught. Is the term *bird* to be taught as a type of animal or a category of animals that has many different types within it? In short, the frequency-based approach to listing basic vocabulary terms provides no instructional guidance for teachers. It also relegates vocabulary instruction to an isolated word-by-word approach. We mentioned in Chapter 1 that this text lists 2,845 basic terms. Although this number is far fewer than that of previous efforts, teaching each word in isolation would still represent a daunting instructional task, especially considering the fact that the basic terms should probably be mastered in the lower elementary grades to prepare students for the more advanced content at high grade levels. For example, if all 2,845 basic terms were addressed in grades 1 through 3, 948 would have to be taught each year. An answer to this problem is to organize terms in semantic clusters.

THE SEMANTIC CLUSTERS

To address the problem of teaching words in isolation, the 2,845 basic terms and the 5,162 advanced terms have been organized into semantic clusters. The specifics of how these terms were identified and classified are articulated in the technical report *Identifying and Classifying Basic and Advanced Terms* (Marzano & Haystead, 2009). Briefly, basic terms are operationally defined as those that are not specific to an academic subject area (e.g., mathematics, science, social studies) and frequent enough in the English language that a student's ability to understand or use the English language is severely limited without knowledge of the term. Advanced terms are operationally defined as those that also are not specific to an academic subject area but are infrequent enough in the English language that they are not considered essential to understanding or using the language. The 8,007 basic and advanced terms are organized into 420 semantic clusters.

To illustrate, consider the following cluster, entitled Bodies of Water:

1. lake	2		18. rapids	4
2. ocean	2		19. strait	4
3. puddle	2		20. surf	4
4. river	2		21. swamp	4
5. sea	2		22. tide	4
6. stream	2		23. tributary	4
7. bay	3		24. waterfall	4
8. creek	3		25. waterline	4
9. pond	3		26. bog	5
10. brook	4		27. eddy	5
11. cove	4		28. estuary	5
12. current	4		29. fjord	5
13. delta	4		30. geyser	5
14. gulf	4		31. headwaters	5
15. inlet	4		32. lagoon	5
16. marsh	4		33. marshland	5
17. outlet	4		34. reef	5

This cluster contains 34 terms, 9 of which are basic (signified by bold font) and 25 of which are advanced.

As explained in Chapter 1, each term is accompanied by a number ranging from 1 to 5. This number indicates how basic each term is. Any term with a rating of 1, 2, or 3 is considered basic. Those with a rating of 4 or 5 are considered advanced. It is important to note that the rating of terms is not an exact science. (For a discussion of the procedure used to rate terms, see Marzano & Haystead, 2009.) Consequently, teachers should feel free to consider some terms rated as level 4 as basic. Additionally, a teacher may wish to teach selected score 4 and score 5 terms (i.e., advanced terms) along with the basic terms. While students are learning basic terms within a semantic cluster, selected advanced terms might be easily addressed.

In Appendix B, the semantic clusters themselves are listed in order of how "basic" they are. In general, only basic terms were considered when ordering semantic clusters. For each cluster, a rank order was assigned that indicates how many basic terms it contains and how basic those terms are. To illustrate, the cluster in the previous example has a rank order of 102 out of 420 clusters. The following cluster, entitled Cause/Effect (Relationship Markers) has a rank order of 10, indicating that it contains more basic terms, and those terms are highly important to understanding and using the English language (i.e., very basic):

1. **because**	1		23. accordingly	5
2. **by**	1		24. as a consequence	5
3. **for**	1		25. as a result	5
4. **from**	1		26. consequently	5
5. **if**	1		27. else	5
6. **since**	1		28. for all that	5
7. **so**	1		29. for as much	5
8. **then**	1		30. for the fact that	5
9. **to**	1		31. hence	5
10. **because of**	2		32. hereby	5
11. if only	4		33. herein	5
12. if…then	4		34. hereupon	5
13. in that case	4		35. herewith	5
14. now that	4		36. in that	5
15. on account of	4		37. lest	5
16. so that	4		38. thereby	5
17. therefore	4		39. whereby	5
18. thus	4		40. wherefore	5
19. until…then	4		41. whereupon	5
20. when…then	4			
21. where…there	4			
22. whereas	4			

Finally, the following cluster, entitled Uncleanliness and Filth, has a rank order of 288, indicating that it contains relatively few basic terms and that those terms themselves are less basic than those in clusters with lower ranks:

1. garbage	3		14. pollute	4
2. junk	3		15. rubbish	4
3. litter	3		16. sewage	4
4. trash	3		17. slop	4
5. bleak	4		18. smear	4
6. clutter	4		19. smudge	4
7. dismal	4		20. streak	4
8. dreary	4		21. contaminate	5
9. filth	4		22. debris	5
10. foul	4		23. dingy	5
11. grime	4		24. eyesore	5
12. infect	4		25. taint	5
13. nasty	4			

The cluster approach allows for a comprehensive and efficient treatment of all 2,845 basic terms (as well as any of the 5,162 advanced terms that the teacher wishes to address). Instead of teaching each term as a separate task, terms are taught in clusters of semantically related terms—420 in all. In effect, the cluster approach shrinks the process of teaching basic (and advanced) terms to 420 instructional tasks, as opposed to 8,007 separate tasks, as would be the case if basic and advanced terms were taught in isolation. The efficacy of using semantic clusters to provide rich instructional activities in new terms has been demonstrated directly and indirectly in a number of studies. (See Marzano & Marzano, 1988; Marzano, 2004; Graves, 2006.)

THE SUPER CLUSTERS

For added instructional flexibility, the 420 clusters are organized into 60 super clusters. These are depicted in Figure 2.1.

Rank	Super Cluster Name	Basic *N*	Advanced *N*	Total *N*
1	Auxiliary and Helping Verbs	29	6	35
2	Pronouns	48	15	63
3	Cause and Effect	17	44	61
4	Physical Location and Orientation	98	92	190
5	Measurement, Size, and Quantity	139	156	295

Rank	Super Cluster Name	Basic N	Advanced N	Total N
6	Time	126	130	256
7	Comparison and Contrast	35	85	120
8	Color	17	35	52
9	Verbal Interaction	97	213	310
10	Animals	131	224	355
11	Importance and Goodness	31	106	137
12	The Human Body	62	98	160
13	Trees and Plants	21	108	129
14	Acquisition and Ownership	25	81	106
15	Parts of Dwellings	61	84	145
16	Vehicles and Transportation	78	91	169
17	Money and Goods	43	86	129
18	Actions Involving Walking and Running	20	43	63
19	Attitudinals	12	28	40
20	Water	62	125	187
21	Sounds and Noises	60	114	173
22	Food and Eating	175	130	305
23	Literary Composition and Writing	80	123	203
24	Arts and Entertainment	27	90	117
25	Seeing and Perceiving	15	48	63
26	Clothing	82	122	204
27	Texture, Durability, and Consistency	10	22	32
28	Movement and Action	137	263	400
29	Structures and Buildings	48	103	151
30	Shapes	50	67	117
31	Contractions	40	6	46
32	Categories of People	88	173	261
33	Places, Land, and Terrain	40	99	139
34	Combustion and Temperature	15	33	48
35	Actions Involving Holding and Touching	28	46	74
36	Mathematical Operations and Quantities	16	37	53
37	Reasoning and Mental Actions	85	150	235
38	Locations and Places Where People Live	17	18	35

Rank	Super Cluster Name	Basic *N*	Advanced *N*	Total *N*
39	Emotions and Attitudes	63	214	277
40	Actions Involving the Face	18	20	38
41	Machines and Tools	97	183	280
42	Games, Sports, and Recreation	45	64	109
43	Containers, Materials, and Building	56	113	169
44	Groups	28	112	140
45	Events	11	39	50
46	Rocks, Metals, and Soil	23	86	109
47	Life, Death, and Survival	11	45	56
48	Weather and Nature	20	35	55
49	Cleanliness	20	49	69
50	Actions that are Helpful or Destructive	31	99	130
51	Danger and Difficulty	10	24	34
52	Occupations	98	211	309
53	Physical Traits of People	23	49	72
54	Language	15	44	59
55	Nonphysical Human Traits	39	137	176
56	Disease and Health	24	92	116
57	Popularity, Familiarity, and Likelihood	16	63	79
58	Light and Darkness	17	62	79
59	Complexity and Conformity	11	39	50
60	Chemicals and Matter	4	29	33

FIGURE 2.1 Super Clusters

Figure 2.1 lists 60 super clusters. A super cluster is basically a "cluster of clusters." To illustrate, consider super cluster 10: Animals, which includes the following clusters:

32 Birds

35 Baby Animals

64 Cats/Dogs

65 Land Animals (General)

70 Sea Animals

82 Reptiles and Mythical Animals

95 Insects

117 Actions Related to Animals

155 Parts of Animals

188 Rodents

189 Dwellings for Animals

194 Animals (General)

309 Shellfish (and Others)

310 Equipment Used with Animals

341 Primates

In the book *A Cluster Approach to Elementary Vocabulary Instruction*, Marzano and Marzano (1988) first developed the concept of clusters organized into super clusters, but did not identify basic words. This book not only identifies basic words and organizes them into clusters and super clusters, but it also lists the clusters in order of their level of "basic-ness." That is, in this book, the clusters (as opposed to the super clusters) are the organization scheme. However, the super cluster organization can also be used, because after each cluster, the name and rank of all related clusters (i.e., all clusters within the same super cluster) are provided.

In Figure 2.1, the super clusters are listed in order of their level of basicness. Thus, the first super cluster, Auxiliary and Helping Verbs, has terms that are the most basic in nature; the second super cluster, Pronouns, has terms that are the second most basic in nature, and so on. Figure 2.1 also reports the number of basic terms in each super cluster (Basic N), the number of advanced terms in each super cluster (Advanced N), and the total number of terms in the super cluster (Total N). Thus, super cluster #1 (Auxiliary/Helping Verbs) contains 35 terms, 29 of which are basic and 6 of which are advanced. Super cluster #2 (Pronouns) contains 63 terms, 48 of which are basic and 15 of which are advanced. Appendix C contains a complete listing of each super cluster and the clusters they contain.

For instructional purposes, a teacher might wish to address all the terms in a super cluster. For example, assume that a teacher has determined that a student has trouble with the basic terms in cluster 32 (Birds). This is the first cluster in super cluster 10 (Animals). Once students have learned the terms in cluster 10, the teacher might then move on to the next cluster in this super cluster. As noted before, in rank order, these clusters are 35, 64, 65, 70, 82, 95, 117, 155, 188, 189, 194, 309, 310, and 341. From this perspective, a teacher might begin with the first super cluster in Figure 2.1 and then move on to the second and so on.

Another perspective on the super clusters is provided in Figure 2.2.

Rank	Super Cluster Name	Basic N	Advanced N	Total N
22	Food and Eating	175	130	305
5	Measurement, Size, and Quantity	139	156	295
28	Movement and Action	137	263	400
10	Animals	131	224	355
6	Time	126	130	256
4	Physical Location and Orientation	98	92	190
52	Occupations	98	211	309
9	Verbal Interaction	97	213	310
41	Machines and Tools	97	183	280
32	Categories of People	88	173	261
37	Reasoning and Mental Actions	85	150	235
26	Clothing	82	122	204
23	Literary Composition and Writing	80	123	203

Rank	Super Cluster Name	Basic N	Advanced N	Total N
16	Vehicles and Transportation	78	91	169
39	Emotions and Attitudes	63	214	277
12	The Human Body	62	98	160
20	Water	62	125	187
15	Parts of Dwellings	61	84	145
21	Sounds and Noises	60	114	173
43	Containers, Materials, and Building	56	113	169
30	Shapes	50	67	117
2	Pronouns	48	15	63
29	Structures and Buildings	48	103	151
42	Games, Sports, and Recreation	45	64	109
17	Money and Goods	43	86	129
31	Contractions	40	6	46
33	Places, Land, and Terrain	40	99	139
55	Nonphysical Human Traits	39	137	176
7	Comparison and Contrast	35	85	120
11	Importance and Goodness	31	106	137
50	Actions that are Helpful or Destructive	31	99	130
1	Auxiliary and Helping Verbs	29	6	35
35	Actions Involving Holding and Touching	28	46	74
44	Groups	28	112	140
24	Arts and Entertainment	27	90	117
14	Acquisition and Ownership	25	81	106
56	Disease and Health	24	92	116
46	Rocks, Metals, and Soil	23	86	109
53	Physical Traits of People	23	49	72
13	Trees and Plants	21	108	129
18	Actions Involving Walking and Running	20	43	63
48	Weather and Nature	20	35	55
49	Cleanliness	20	49	69
40	Actions Involving the Face	18	20	38
3	Cause and Effect	17	44	61
8	Color	17	35	52

Rank	Super Cluster Name	Basic N	Advanced N	Total N
38	Locations and Places Where People Live	17	18	35
58	Light and Darkness	17	62	79
36	Mathematical Operations and Quantities	16	37	53
57	Popularity, Familiarity, and Likelihood	16	63	79
25	Seeing and Perceiving	15	48	63
34	Combustion and Temperature	15	33	48
54	Language	15	44	59
19	Attitudinals	12	28	40
45	Events	11	39	50
47	Life, Death, and Survival	11	45	56
59	Complexity and Conformity	11	39	50
27	Texture, Durability, and Consistency	10	22	32
51	Danger and Difficulty	10	24	34
60	Chemicals and Matter	4	29	33

FIGURE 2.2 Super Clusters Ordered by Basic Terms

In Figure 2.2, the super clusters are listed in order of the number of basic terms they contain. Thus, the super cluster Food and Eating has the most basic terms (175); the super cluster Measurement, Size, and Quantity has the second most basic terms (139), and so on. This is a very different ranking than that provided in Figure 2.1, which is based on the level of basicness of terms in the super clusters. For example, Food and Eating is ranked 22nd from the perspective of how basic the terms are, but first from the perspective of number of basic terms it contains. Figure 2.2 provides another way to use the super clusters. A teacher might wish to move through the super clusters in order of how many basic terms they contain.

SUMMARY

This chapter addressed the manner in which the terms in Appendix B are organized. There are 420 clusters of semantically related terms. Clusters are ordered in terms of the number of basic terms they contain and how basic they are. Each cluster contains basic terms as well as advanced terms. Clusters have also been organized into 60 super clusters, which are clusters of clusters. This allows teachers a number of instructional options when working with students.

3

Determining Where to Begin
with Individual Students

It would be counterproductive if not impossible to begin teaching the basic terms listed in Appendix B by starting with cluster 1 and continuing on until cluster 420. Rather, it is more efficient to identify the cluster on which each student should begin. Recall from the discussion in Chapter 2 that the semantic clusters are listed in order of how basic they are. Clusters with a large number of basic terms that are fundamental to the English language are listed first; clusters that have fewer basic words that are less fundamental to the English language are listed later.

THE SNAPSHOT ASSESSMENT OF BASIC TERMS

To place students on the continuum of clusters of basic terms, a teacher can use the list of 840 "test words" in Appendix A. This list is referred to as the Snapshot Assessment of Basic Terms. The Snapshot Assessment contains two terms per cluster for a total of 840 test words. The first two test words are from the first cluster, the next two terms from the second cluster, and so on. To illustrate, term 1a is *can* and term 1b is *will*. Both are from the first cluster, entitled *Modals*. Term 50a is *moon* and term 50b is *planet*. Both are from the 50th cluster, entitled *Bodies in Space*.

To place a student on the continuum of 420 clusters, the teacher begins with the first two test words from Appendix A. Again, they are *can* and *will*. The teacher asks the student to use each of the two terms in a sentence. For example, the teacher points to the word *can* and pronounces it for the student and then says, "Please use *can* in a sentence." If the answer provided by the student leaves the teacher in doubt regarding the student's understanding of the term, the teacher simply asks the student to use the term in another sentence or to explain the term.

If the student misses both terms for cluster 1, the teacher stops there and begins instruction on the basic words from cluster 1. If the student does not answer both terms correctly, one of two scenarios will play out—one scenario is followed if the student misses one term and another scenario is followed if the student misses both terms. We begin with a student missing one term.

If the student answers one term correctly, then the teacher moves up to cluster 25 and asks the student to use terms 25a and 25b in a sentence. They are *where* and *anywhere*, respectively. If the student misses both these terms, the teacher moves back to cluster 24 (terms 24a and 24b) and asks the student to use these two words in sentences. The teacher keeps moving backwards until he or she reaches the first cluster in the continuum for which the student misses both test terms for the cluster.

The scenario described in this example is based on the assumption that a student demonstrates knowledge of one of the two test terms for a given cluster. Now let's consider what happens when the student demonstrates knowledge of both terms. Again, the teacher begins with terms 1a and 1b from cluster 1. If the student demonstrates knowledge of both terms, the teacher jumps up to terms 50a and 50b. They are *moon* and *planet*. If the student misses one of these terms, we have already seen what to do. The teacher moves up to cluster 75 (terms 75a and 75b). If the student misses both terms for cluster 50, the teacher keeps moving back in the continuum until he or she locates the first cluster in the continuum for which the student misses both terms. It is important to remember that once a student misses two terms after skipping up to the next 25th cluster or 50th cluster, the teacher still has to keep moving back in the continuum until he or she finds the first cluster for which two terms are missed.

Fundamentally, the goal of the assessment process is to find the first cluster for which the student misses both test words. Missing both test terms is an indication that the student probably needs instruction regarding the basic terms (and advanced terms, if the teacher so chooses) in that cluster.

Theoretically, then, a student could know one out of the two test words for every cluster up to cluster 305 (as an example). In this case, the first cluster for which the student missed two test terms would be cluster 305, and this is where instruction would begin. A reasonable question regarding this method of placing students in the continuum of clusters is why not use one missed term as the criterion for working on the terms in a cluster, as opposed to two terms? One reason for this convention is that any single item on an assessment can be missed for a variety of reasons other than the student not knowing the content. For example, a student might not use a test word correctly because he or she initially mistook it for another term, or because the student simply was not paying enough attention to the teacher's query. In a sense, allowing one test word to be missed is providing students with the "benefit of the doubt" regarding their knowledge of the terms in a cluster.

A second reason for using two missed terms as the criterion is that the test terms are representative only of the basic terms in the cluster. For example, the first cluster (Modals) has 10 basic terms in it. *Can* and *will* are two of those 10 basic terms. It might be the case that a particular student knows 9 of the 10 basic terms in this cluster, but it just so happens that the one term he or she doesn't know is one of the two test terms. Again, allowing the student to miss one term before identifying a cluster as the starting point for instruction provides students with the benefit of the doubt.

Finally, it is useful to acknowledge that the most comprehensive way to determine where a student should be placed in the continuum of clusters would be to assess each student on all 2,845 basic terms. Although this method might provide complete diagnostic coverage of the basic terms, it is impractical in terms of the amount of time that would be spent on assessment.

In the same vein, it would provide a more valid picture of a student's placement in the continuum of clusters if students were examined on all 840 test words in Appendix A. Again, the reason for not doing so is that it is impractical in terms of the amount of time that would have to be spent on assessment.

Given all of the qualifications described here regarding the use of the Snapshot Assessment of Basic Terms, teachers should feel free to use information other than the test words in Appendix A to identify instructional needs of students. For example, a student might correctly use both test words for a given cluster. However, in informal conversation the teacher might observe that the student has difficulty with terms in that cluster. This observation would warrant providing the student with instruction regarding the terms in that particular cluster.

WORKING IN THE CLUSTERS

Once the teacher has identified the cluster with which to begin instruction for a given student, the teacher consults Appendix B, which lists all clusters in rank order. To illustrate, assume that a particular student has been placed in cluster 33, which is entitled Size and Weight. This cluster contains the following terms:

1. **big**	1		13. grand	4
2. **giant**	2		14. immense	4
3. **great**	2		15. mammoth	4
4. **huge**	2		16. massive	4
5. **large**	2		17. medium	4
6. **little**	2		18. miniature	4
7. **small**	2		19. monstrous	4
8. **tiny**	2		20. vast	4
9. **enormous**	3		21. compact	5
10. **gigantic**	3		22. petite	5
11. **jumbo**	3		23. wee	5
12. bulk	4			

Again, the basic terms in this cluster are listed in bold; the advanced terms are not. Next to each term is a rating from 1 to 5. All terms with a rating of 3 or below are considered basic. Recall, though, that a teacher might decide to consider some terms with a rating of 4 as basic. For example, after considering the types of content that his or her students are expected to know in school and outside of school, a teacher might decide that the terms *immense* and *massive* should also be considered basic and teach them as such. Additionally, a teacher might decide to include some advanced terms as "challenge" words for students.

Once the terms from cluster 33 have been adequately addressed, the teacher would move on to cluster 34. Once the terms in cluster 34 were adequately addressed, the teacher would move on to cluster 35 and so on. It is important to note that when moving through the clusters, the teacher might find that a student knows the terms in clusters that are "more advanced" than the cluster in which a student began—clusters that have a higher rank than where the student started. This is to be expected. Students can have different experiences in life that will provide them knowledge of clusters that are rated more advanced in Appendix B. Thus, if a student appears to know the terms in a given cluster, the teacher should simply move on to the next cluster.

THE ONLINE SNAPSHOT ASSESSMENT OF BASIC TERMS

If a teacher doesn't wish to use the Snapshot Assessment of Basic Terms (Appendix A), he or she can use an electronic version to place students in the continuum of clusters. The Online Snapshot Assessment of Basic Terms contains two items for each semantic cluster, as does the assessment in Appendix A. For example, the following are the two items for cluster 102, regarding Bodies of Water:

1. Todd liked to fish with his brother. Once a week they went down to the _____ to spend the day fishing.
   a. stadium
   b. lake
   c. grocery store
   d. theater

2. Randy lived several hours from the _____. He hoped to see waves crash into the beach some day.
   a. ocean
   b. amusement park
   c. library
   d. museum

To further illustrate the types of items in the Snapshot Assessment of Basic Terms, the following listed items are for cluster 249, entitled Conclusions:

1. Shane loved music. He wanted to _____ a song about friendship.
   a. forget
   b. compose
   c. confirm
   d. research

2. Sheryl loves to read mysteries. She always tries to _____ the mystery before the main character does.
   a. remember
   b. forget
   c. carry
   d. solve

Just like Appendix A, the Online Snapshot Assessment has 840 items—2 items for each of the 420 clusters, although these items are multiple choice in nature. Also, the items are presented to students orally and in writing, so that students' ability to read will not be a factor in their assessments. The items in the online assessment are ordered in the same fashion as the clusters, beginning with the most basic cluster and ending with the least basic cluster.

The Online Snapshot Assessment works the same way as the assessment in Appendix A. A student progresses through the items until the student is placed on the continuum of clusters. As before, the teacher must be aware of the fact that a student might be quite familiar with terms in more advanced clusters due to his or her background experience. If a student appears to know the basic terms in a given cluster, the teacher simply moves on to the advanced words in the cluster or to the next cluster.

SUMMARY

This chapter described how to place students on the continuum of clusters for instructional purposes. To this end, Appendix A contains the 840 test words for the Snapshot Assessment of Basic Terms. The teacher begins with items 1a and 1b, representing cluster #1. If one item is missed by the student, the teacher moves up to the 25th cluster; if no items are missed by the student, the teacher moves up to the 50th cluster. This pattern continues until a cluster is found for which the student misses both test words, the teacher keeps moving backward in the clusters until the first cluster in the continuum is identified for which the student misses both items. Instruction begins there.

4

The Role of Direct Vocabulary Instruction

This book is about direct instruction in basic and advanced vocabulary with an emphasis on receptive vocabulary—listening and reading vocabularies. Although there are many different ways to think of direct vocabulary instruction, I believe effective instruction for receptive vocabulary is best thought of as involving three general phases, particularly when terms are organized in semantic clusters, as they are in this book. Those phases are: (1) an introductory phase, (2) a comparison phase, and (3) a review and refinement phase.

I should contrast my comments here with previous work I have done on direct vocabulary instruction. Specifically, in the book *Building Background Knowledge for Academic Achievement* (Marzano, 2004) and the book *Building Academic Vocabulary: Teacher's Manual* (Marzano & Pickering, 2005), I described a six-step process for teaching vocabulary. Those steps are:

1. The teacher provides a description, explanation, or example of the new term.

2. Students restate the explanation of the new term in their own words.

3. Students create a nonlinguistic representation of the term.

4. Students periodically engage in activities that help them add to their knowledge of the vocabulary term.

5. Periodically, students are asked to discuss terms with one another.

6. Periodically, students are involved in games that allow them to play with the terms.

The positive effects of this process on student achievement have been demonstrated in a series of studies (Marzano, 2006a, 2006b; Gifford & Gore, 2008; Dunn, Bonner, & Huske, 2007). The six-step process was designed for teaching terms that are *not* organized in semantic clusters. The introduction of semantic clusters as described in this book allows for powerful options that are not available when teaching terms in relative isolation. Although the six steps listed are included in the three phases articulated in this book, the phrases described here capitalize on the semantic relationships between words in semantic clusters.

The *introductory phase* of teaching vocabulary terms involves the first three steps of the six-step process. The purpose of these steps is to help students attach meaning to new terms they are learning. This initial stage of learning involves associating past experiences with a new term. To illustrate, assume that a student is learning the term *sibling*. During the introductory phase, the instructional task is to help the student associate the term *sibling* with the student's experiences. In this case, the teacher's goal is to have students make a connection between the term *sibling* and their brothers and sisters.

During the *comparison phase*, the instructional focus is on helping students develop distinctions between the meaning of the new word and other words they might know or are learning. This is where the semantic clusters come into play. To illustrate, the term *sibling* is found in cluster 94: Family Relationships. The basic terms in that cluster are reported in Figure 4.1.

aunt	2	sister	2
brother	2	son	2
dad	2	uncle	3
family	2	cousin	3
father	2	daughter	3
granny	2	grandparent	3
ma	2	husband	3
mama	2	mammy	3
mom	2	nephew	3
mother	2	niece	3
papa	2	sibling	3
parent	2	wife	3

FIGURE 4.1 Basic Terms in Cluster 94: Family Relationships

By engaging students in tasks in which they examine the similarities and differences between the term *sibling* and terms like *brother, sister, cousin,* and *mother,* the teacher can help students deepen their knowledge of the target term as well as the related terms. Whereas the purpose of the introductory phase is to provide students with an initial understanding of the target term, albeit with little clarity or depth, the purpose of the comparison phase is to help students make distinctions regarding what terms mean and what they do not mean.

During the *review and refinement phase*—the third phase—the instructional task is to expand students' understanding of the term by making multiple and varied linkages. This helps students make refinements in their understanding. For example, a student who has a fair understanding of the term *sibling* might explore the relationship between the term *sibling* and a term like *household*. This is a situation in which the advanced terms associated with a cluster might be used. To illustrate, following are the advanced terms for cluster 94:

Family Relationship.

ancestor	4	offspring	4	maternal	5
bride	4	spouse	4	patriarch	5
groom	4	domo	5	pedigree	5
heir	4	guardian	5	ward	5
household	4				

As students review and refine what they know about the term *sibling*, they can add some of the advanced terms to their knowledge base, as the advanced terms share some semantic features with the basic terms. The goal of the third phase, then, is to expand the number and diversity of linkages between the target term and other terms that are closely related or even tangentially related. The introductory phase provides an initial understanding of the term. The next two phases help students make varied and complex linkages with other terms. Thus, by definition, the second and third phases expand instruction beyond the initial term that was taught.

These three phases are not discrete. Though the introductory phase is first, the comparison phase and the review and refinement phases overlap and can be done at any point. This relationship is depicted in Figure 4.2.

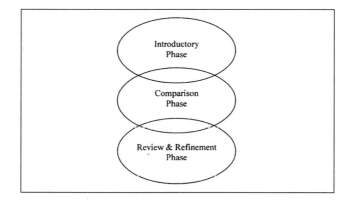

FIGURE 4.2 Phases of Teaching a New Term

As Figure 4.2 indicates, the first phase overlaps with the second and the second overlaps with the third. This means that while focusing instruction on any one phase, a teacher might also employ instructional strategies from another phase. We consider the introductory phase in the remainder of this chapter. In Chapters 5 and 6, we consider the comparison phase and the review and refinement phases, respectively.

STRATEGIES FOR THE INTRODUCTORY PHASE

The purpose of the introductory phase is to provide students with an initial understanding of a new term. It involves two steps: (1) providing descriptions, examples, anecdotes, and illustrations, and (2) having students develop their own descriptions, examples, and illustrations.

Providing Descriptions, Examples, Anecdotes, and Illustrations of the New Term

The first step in the introductory phase is to provide students with descriptions, examples, anecdotes, and illustrations of the new term. While providing a description, the teacher tries to present defining or important characteristics of the new term or examples of the new term used in context. For some words, it might be difficult to provide descriptions of their important characteristics. In this case, examples become very important. For example, it would be relatively easy to provide a description of the important characteristics of the term *automobile* (e.g., another name for a car, most families have one, it's used to go to work and run errands). However, it wouldn't be very easy to describe important characteristics of the term *since*. For this term the teacher might provide examples of how the word is used—examples that clearly demonstrate the meaning and use of the term. While providing descriptions and examples, the teacher might elicit information about the term from the students to help ensure that linkages are made to their background knowledge. Anecdotes can also be provided by the teacher. At some point, the teacher might provide students with a picture or pictorial illustration of the new term. This is particularly important for ELL students, who might not fully understand the teacher's descriptions or examples if this information is not presented in their native language.

The behaviors described do not represent a strict sequence. Different strategies can and should be used, depending on a term's meaning and part of speech (Stahl, 1999). Next, we consider how instruction during the first step of the introductory phase might play out for various parts of speech.

Nouns

About 61% of the basic terms in Appendix B are nouns. When a vocabulary term is a noun, the teacher might provide a brief description that focuses on some of the characteristics of the term. For example, assume that a teacher is introducing the term *sled*, which is from cluster 318. The teacher might begin by describing general characteristics of the noun, such as:

* *A sled is something you use to slide down a hill when it has snowed.*
* *A sled is used to have fun during the winter.*
* *You can have more than one person on a sled if it's long enough.*

The teacher might then elicit input from students about the new term. Students who had background experience with the new term could provide anecdotes about their experiences. To elicit information from students about the term *sled*, the teacher might ask questions like the following:

* *What are some things you have done with a sled?*
* *What are some different types of sleds you have seen or heard of?*

At some point, the teacher might relate a brief anecdote about a time when he or she has gone sledding. The teacher would use the term in a sentence or two, drawing on the input students had provided:

* *I rode the sled down the hill on the slippery snow.*

Finally, to illustrate the term, the teacher might provide a picture that had been downloaded from the Internet and that involves the new term. This is shown in Figure 4.3.

FIGURE 4.3 Sled

If an appropriate picture cannot be found, then the teacher might provide a simple hand-drawn picture, like that in Figure 4.4.

FIGURE 4.4 Sled

Verbs

About 22% of the basic terms in Appendix B are verbs. To illustrate how verbs might be approached, assume that a teacher is introducing the term *discuss*, which is from cluster 105. The teacher might describe important characteristics of the verb by stating the following:

- *Discussing is talking with another person about something you are both interested in.*
- *Discussing is more than just telling someone what you think. It is also listening to the other person, even though you might not agree with them.*

Notice that the examples use the gerund form of the verb. If the gerund form is not familiar to students, the teacher would make sure to provide examples with familiar syntax:

- *I will discuss the movie with you when it's over.*

Next, the teacher might provide students with a brief story about a time when he or she was in a discussion. Afterwards, the teacher would illicit input from students regarding the new term by asking questions like the following:

- *Can anyone tell me about a time when you discussed something?*
- *What are some discussions you have heard?*

Next, the teacher would use the term in a sentence that illustrates some of its characteristics:

- *The man and woman were discussing whether they should buy a new car.*

Finally, the teacher would provide a relevant hand-drawn picture or a picture from the Internet, like that in Figure 4.5.

FIGURE 4.5 Discuss

Adjectives

About 11% of the basic terms in Appendix B are adjectives. To illustrate the use of descriptions, examples, anecdotes, and illustrations with adjectives, assume that a teacher was introducing the adjective *polite*, which is found in cluster 228. The teacher might provide information about the term in the following way:

- *When you are being polite, you are being nice to people.*
- *The man who gave up his seat to a lady on the bus was being polite.*

With adjectives, it is common to provide information about their defining characteristics by providing examples as illustrated in the second bullet. Here the teacher did not describe the characteristic of being polite, but rather simply gave an example depicting a person being polite.

Next, the teacher might elicit examples from the students by asking questions like the following:

* *Tell us about a time when you were being polite or saw someone else being polite.*
* *How would you describe someone who is being polite?*

The teacher might provide an example of *polite* used in a sentence in the following way:

* *The polite policeman helped the little girl cross the busy street.*

This example might be coupled with a brief story from the teacher about a time when someone was polite to him or her.

Finally, the teacher might provide a hand-drawn picture or a picture from the Internet, like that in Figure 4.6.

FIGURE 4.6 Polite

Adverbs

About 3% of the basic terms in Appendix B are adverbs. To illustrate how adverbs might be approached, assume that a teacher is introducing the adverb *away*, which is from cluster 20. To introduce this term, the teacher might provide the following:

* *When I went on vacation, I was away from home.*
* *When you leave someplace, you go away from that place.*

Notice that the first statement is an example of the term that leaves the inference about its characteristics up to students. The second statement is more of a description of the characteristics of *away*. As is the case with adjectives, it can be very challenging to describe defining characteristics of adverbs.

Next, the teacher might provide a brief anecdote about a time when he or she was away from home. Examples from students could be elicited by asking questions like the following:

* *Tell us about a time when you were away from someplace.*
* *Tell us about a time when someone was away from you.*

The teacher might then provide students with the following sentence using *away:*

* *When I went to college I was away from home.*

Finally, the teacher might provide a hand-drawn picture or a picture from the Internet like that in Figure 4.7.

FIGURE 4.7 Away

Conjunctions

About one-half of 1 percent of the basic terms in Appendix B are conjunctions. The purpose of conjunctions is to connect ideas stated in clauses. Thus, their meanings can be fairly abstract. Because of this, it typically takes more explanation to articulate the characteristics of conjunctions than is the case with nouns, verbs, adjectives, and adverbs. For example, a teacher might provide the following when introducing the conjunction *since*, which is from cluster 10:

* *If the reason I couldn't do my homework is that I had to visit my sick grandmother in the hospital, I would say: "Since I was visiting my grandmother in the hospital, I didn't do my homework.*
* *When you use the word "since," you mean about the same thing as the word "because."*

In the first statement, the teacher provides a clear context for which the term *since* would be appropriate. In the second statement, the teacher provides students with a synonym for the term.

Next, the teacher would elicit student input using questions like the following:

* *Describe something that happened to you or someone else where you could have used the term "since."*
* *How have you heard people use the term "since"?*

As students described situations, the teacher would help them phrase their examples in ways that illustrate correct use of the conjunction *since.* Additionally, the teacher might provide students with the following example of the term used in a sentence:

* *Since I was very tired last night, I went to bed early.*

The teacher could elaborate on this example by providing a brief anecdote that accompanies it.

Finally, the teacher would provide a hand-drawn picture or a picture from the Internet like that in Figure 4.8.

FIGURE 4.8 Since

Prepositions

About 2% of the basic terms in Appendix B are prepositions. Prepositions connect information, as do conjunctions. Again, this renders them fairly abstract. Consequently, extra explanation or examples are frequently required when introducing a preposition. To illustrate, assume that a teacher is introducing the preposition *across*, which is from cluster 22. Because it is difficult to describe the meaning of *across*, the teacher might initially provide students with the following two examples of the preposition:

* *Bill yelled across the river.*
* *Bill threw the ball across the river.*

These examples might be highlighted by a brief anecdote that is consistent with one of the examples. The teacher could also provide the following explanation:

* *In the first sentence, the word across tells us where Bill was yelling. In the second sentence the word across tells us where the ball went after Bill threw it.*

The teacher might follow up these examples with a demonstration of the term. For example, the teacher might present the following sentences with accompanying enactments:

* *I am throwing the eraser across the room.*
* *I am walking across the room.*

While providing the first example, the teacher might actually throw an eraser across the room. In the second example, the teacher might walk across the room. Teacher demonstrations like these can also be done with many verbs, adjectives, and adverbs.

To elicit student input, the teacher might provide students with the following prompt:

* *Describe something that happened to you where you could use the term across.*

As students described their situations, the teacher would help them phrase their examples in ways that demonstrated the correct use of the preposition.

Finally the teacher would provide a hand-drawn picture or a picture from the Internet like that in Figure 4.9.

FIGURE 4.9 Across

Interjections

Less than 1 percent of the basic terms in Appendix B are interjections. Interjections are terms that typically depict emotion or convey information that will be said with great emphasis. For example, the term *wow* is an interjection. It is from cluster 14. Interjections are difficult to describe, because they deal more with emphasis than information. Consequently, they are typically introduced by examples. To illustrate, a teacher might provide the following statements to students when introducing *wow*:

* *If I'm excited about winning the lottery, I would say, "Wow!"*
* *If you watch a baseball player hit a home run, you might say, "Wow!"*
* *Wow, class! You got the highest test score in the school on the state's reading test.*

The teacher might elaborate with an anecdote about a time when the term *wow* could be applied to his or her actions.

To elicit input from students, the teacher might ask the following:

* *Describe a time when something happened to you where you could have used the term "wow."*

As students provided their examples, the teacher would help them phrase their comments in ways that correctly illustrate use of the interjection.

Finally, the teacher would provide a hand-drawn picture or a picture from the Internet like that in Figure 4.10.

FIGURE 4.10 Wow!

Pronouns

Pronouns constitute about 2 percent of the basic terms in Appendix B. There are many types of pronouns, including personal pronouns (e.g., *I, me*), interrogative pronouns (e.g., *who, what*), and reflexive pronouns (e.g., *myself, yourself*). Pronouns are function words; consequently, they are very difficult to describe. One of the best ways to introduce them is to provide examples of their use:

* *When I'm explaining something about me I might use the term "myself": "I told Bill a lot about myself."*

With pronouns, it is difficult for students to provide much input regarding their meaning, simply because they are a function more of syntax than of meaning. Consequently, it is useful to provide students with some simple exercises that might give them insight into their meaning and use, such as the following.

Which pronoun would you use in the following sentence?

The car is _____.

* *myself*
* *mine*
* *you*
* *your*
* *the*

After providing a few brief exercises like this to demonstrate use of a specific pronoun, the teacher might use it in a sentence:

* *I believe in myself.*

Again, a brief anecdote that goes with this example might be used to dramatize the use of the term. Finally, the teacher would provide a hand-drawn picture or a picture from the Internet like that in Figure 4.11.

FIGURE 4.11 Myself

Some Special Terms

There are a number of terms that are like pronouns, in that they have more of a syntactic function than a semantic function. Such terms include articles (e.g., *a, an, the*) (found in cluster 13) and auxiliary verbs (e.g., *could, would, should*) (found in cluster 1). Articles are found in cluster 13, entitled Specifiers (e.g., *each, every*). Together, these types of "special terms" make up less than 1 percent of the basic terms in Appendix B.

To introduce specifiers like *each* and *every*, the teacher might employ some concrete props like five blocks of wood. While pointing to each block individually, the teacher would say:

* *I am pointing to each block.*

Next, the teacher would open his or her palms in a way that includes all five blocks and then say:

* *Now I'm including all the blocks.*

Here the teacher has used a comparison of the specifiers *each* and *all* to demonstrate their meaning. The same basic comparative approach could be used with auxiliary verbs. The teacher would start by providing students with the following statements:

* *I can ski.*
* *I should ski.*

The teacher would then explain the differences in the following way:

* *The first sentence, using "can," means that I know how to ski. The second sentence, using "should," means that it would be good for me to ski but it doesn't mean that I know how to ski right now.*

Again, short exercises might next be provided to students:

I like _____ person in class.

- *each*
- *none*
- *all*

I _____ be at school on time.

- *am*
- *are*
- *should*

After a few simple exercises have been presented to students, the teacher would again use the new terms in sample sentences:

- *I know the name of each student in class.*
- *I should always be nice to the teachers in school.*

Finally, the teacher would provide a hand-drawn picture or a picture from the Internet like that in Figure 4.12 depicting the term *each*.

FIGURE 4.12 Each

HAVING STUDENTS DEVELOP THEIR OWN DESCRIPTIONS, EXAMPLES, AND ILLUSTRATIONS

The second step of the introductory phase involves student descriptions, examples, and illustrations. That is, after the teacher has introduced a new term, students use their own experiential base to generate descriptions, examples, and illustrations. Again, it is useful to consider how this might be done with specific types of terms.

Nouns

After the teacher has introduced the noun *sled*, the teacher might say:

* *Now you try to explain what you think a sled is. If you have trouble describing a sled, then use it in a sentence in a way that will help you remember what it means later on. Also draw a picture that shows what you think the term means.*

Notice that the teacher has provided students with two options: one in which they try to describe a sled or explain what it does, and the other in which they simply use the term in a sentence in a way that will remind them what it means.

One student might write the following and accompany it with the picture in Figure 4.13:

* *A sled is something you use in the winter to have fun with.*

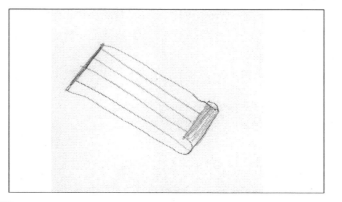

FIGURE 4.13 Sled

Another student might write the following and accompany it with the picture in Figure 4.14:

* *I had fun riding the sled at my grandfather's house last year.*

FIGURE 4.14 Sled

Following are samples of the types of descriptions, examples, and illustrations that two students might provide for terms that exemplify the various parts of speech described previously. For all parts of speech, the teacher's directions would be the same. Students are invited to explain or describe the target term or use it in a way that demonstrates its meaning. Students are also asked to draw a picture or pictograph illustrating the meaning of the term. In the following samples, student descriptions, examples, and illustrations are provided for the remaining parts of speech without further comment.

Verbs

Target term: *discuss*.

First student's example and illustration:

- *When you discuss something, you talk a lot about it.*

FIGURE 4.15 Discuss

Second student's example and illustration:

- *I discuss important things with my big brother.*

FIGURE 4.16 Discuss

Adjectives

Target term: *polite*.

First student's example and illustration:

- *I am being polite when I say please.*

FIGURE 4.17 Polite

Second student's example and illustration:

- *My teacher was polite when she met my parents. She said nice things about me.*

FIGURE 4.18 Polite

Adverbs

Target term: *away*.

First student's example and illustration:

- *My brother is away in the army.*

FIGURE 4.19 Away

Second student's example and illustration:

◈ *When you throw something away, you don't want it anymore.*

FIGURE 4.20 Away

Conjunctions

Target term: *since*.

First student's example and illustration:

◈ *Since I first decided to be a professional basketball player, I have practiced every day.*

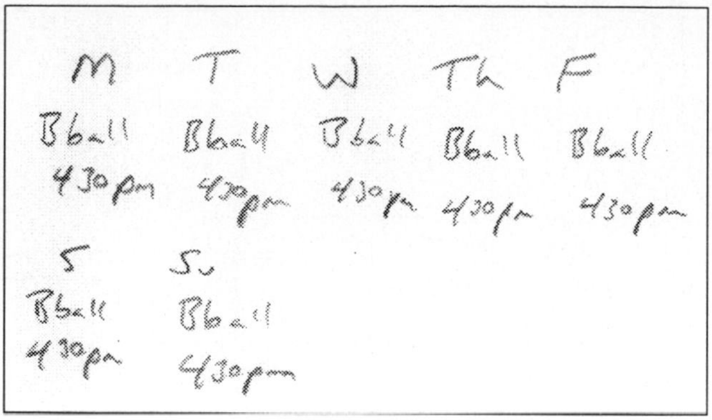

FIGURE 4.21 Since

Second student's example and illustration:

* Since *means the same thing as* because *means.*

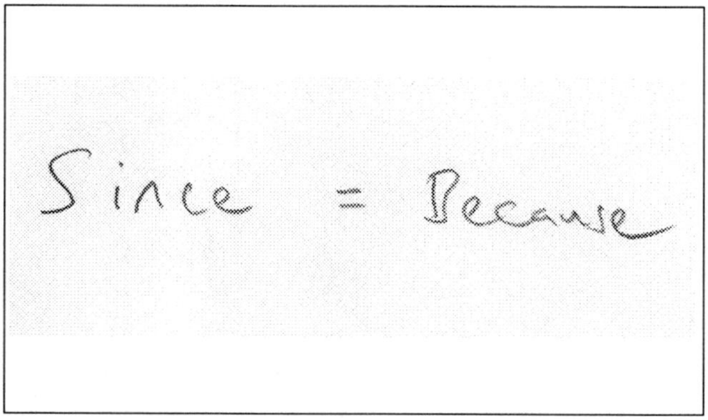

FIGURE 4.22 Since

Prepositions

Target term: *across.*

First student's example and illustration:

* *Every day I walk across the park to get to school.*

FIGURE 4.23 Across

Second student's example and illustration:

❋ *When you say "across," you mean something is far away.*

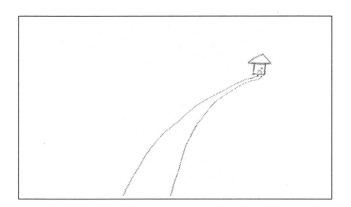

FIGURE 4.24 Across

Interjections

Target term: *wow*.

First student's example and illustration:

❋ *I said, "Wow!" when I got my birthday present from my parents.*

FIGURE 4.25 Wow

Second student's example and illustration:

* *"Wow" means that you are really excited.*

FIGURE 4.26 Wow

Pronouns

Target term: *myself.*

First student's example and illustration:

* *You use "myself" like you would use "I."*

FIGURE 4.27 Myself

Second student's example and illustration:

- *I talk about myself a lot.*

FIGURE 4.28 Myself

Some Special Terms

Target term: *each*.

First student's example and illustration:

- *I like all the students in my class, but each one is different.*

FIGURE 4.29 Each

Second student's example and illustration:

● *"Each" means you're talking about specific things one by one.*

FIGURE 4.30 Each

Target term: *should.*
First student's example and illustration:

● *I should brush my teeth every night, but I don't.*

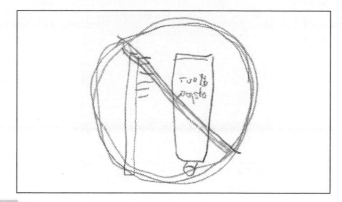

FIGURE 4.31 Should

Second student's example and illustration:

● *"Should" and "could" kind of mean the opposite of each other.*

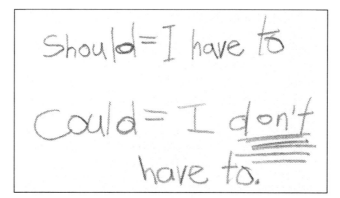

FIGURE 4.32 Should

SUMMARY

This chapter has addressed the introductory phase of teaching a new term. This phase involves two steps:

1. Providing descriptions, examples, anecdotes, and illustrations.
2. Having students develop their own descriptions, examples, and illustrations.

During the first step of the introductory phase, the teacher provides students with information and experiences that help them attain a general understanding of the term. During the second step of the introductory phase, students use their own experiential base to generate personalized descriptions, examples, and illustrations.

5

Strategies for
the Comparison Phase

Chapter 4 addressed the introductory phase of teaching a new term. The purpose of that phase is to provide students with an initial understanding of a new term. This initial understanding might be quite superficial and even contain some misconceptions. This chapter addresses the comparison phase. Its purpose is to deepen students' understanding of a new term and help students clear up misconceptions.

It is during the comparison phase that related terms within a semantic cluster can be used to increase the number of basic and advanced terms with which a student is familiar. As you will see in Chapter 7, it is most helpful for students to maintain a vocabulary notebook in which they record their entries during the introductory phase and the comparison phase. In that chapter, we will also consider how a teacher might schedule or pace instructional activities for the comparison phase. In this chapter, we focus on specific instructional strategies for this second phase.

It is important to note that the term *comparison* is being used here in a very generic way. Comparing, as used in this text, refers to a variety of ways to help students examine similarities and differences between terms. Using the terms *comparing* and *contrasting*, Graves (2006) attests to the potentially powerful affects of activities that involve identification of similarities and differences:

> Not only is instruction that involves activating prior knowledge and comparing and contrasting word meanings a powerful approach to teaching word meaning, but such instruction has also been shown to improve comprehension of selections containing the words taught. (p. 21)

Graves (2006) cites studies that demonstrate the effectiveness of a wide range of strategies involving comparison and contrast (Heimlich & Pittelman, 1986; Pittelman, Heimlich, Berglund, & French, 1991; Anders, Bos, & Filip, 1984). A summary of a variety of studies of the effects of comparison activities can be found at http://www.marzanoresearch.com.

It is during the comparison phase that the cluster approach to organizing terms used in this book serves as a powerful tool. For any term that is the target of instruction, terms to be used for comparison activities can be drawn from a cluster or the super cluster to which a specific cluster belongs. To illustrate, consider the term *sled* from cluster 318. The other words in this cluster are:

sleigh	2	bobsled	4
snowplow	3	toboggan	4

Any or all of these terms are good candidates to be used in the comparison phase. Also recall that cluster 318 belongs to a super cluster. In this case, it is super cluster 16, entitled Vehicles and Transportation. Other clusters in this super cluster are:

93	Things You Traveled on	159	Vehicles (Sea Transportation)
97	Vehicles (Actions/Characteristics)	234	Parts of Vehicles
120	Vehicles (Air Transportation)	331	Vehicles (Work Related)
128	Transportation (Types)		

A teacher can also examine terms from these related clusters to use in comparison activities. In short, the clusters and super clusters in Appendix B make it easy for teachers to identify related terms to be used during the comparison phase.

It is important to note that comparison activities can be quite elaborate and complex. With terms for which students have little experiential base, it is useful to have students engage in these activities in their native language. That is, if at all possible, ELL students should be allowed to complete comparison activities in their language of choice. This can be facilitated by grouping monolingual ELL students with bilingual ELL students.

In the remainder of this chapter, we consider seven basic types of comparison activities: (1) similar terms, (2) sentence stems, (3) the Venn diagram, (4) the double bubble, (5) the comparison matrix, (6) classifying activities, and (7) metaphors and analogies.

SIMILAR TERMS

The most straightforward use of the clusters and super clusters is to help students make linkages between words that have been initially introduced and words that have not been introduced. For example, assume that the term *sled* has been introduced to students and entered in their vocabulary notebooks. As we have seen, the other terms in that cluster are:

sleigh	2	bobsled	4
snowplow	3	toboggan	4

Shortly after *sled* had been introduced, the teacher might select a highly related term like *sleigh*. The teacher might simply explain that some people use the terms *sled* and *sleigh* to mean the same things. The teacher might also note that sleighs are usually pulled by horses and sleds are ridden downhill by people. After this brief discussion, the teacher would ask students to enter the term *sleigh* in their vocabulary notebooks in the same section as the term *sled*. This is depicted in Figure 5.1.

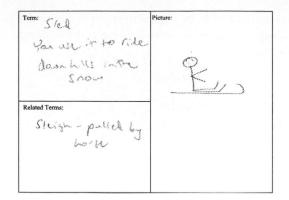

FIGURE 5.1   Student Notebook Entry for *Sled*

Again, we address the role of vocabulary notebooks in depth in Chapter 7, but Figure 5.1 illustrates the general format for notebooks. Each term has room for the student's description or explanation of the term. It also has a place for the student's illustrations of the term. What is most pertinent to the current discussion is the section called "related terms." Note that the student has entered the term *sleigh*, with the brief explanation that it is "pulled by horses."

The simplest type of comparison activity, then, is to introduce related terms for terms that have already been introduced using the clusters and super clusters as the source for the terms. Additionally, students should be encouraged to do this on their own. As they encounter terms that are related in their mind to terms that they have already entered in their notebooks, students add them to the related terms section of their vocabulary notebooks, along with a phrase, picture, or symbol that reminds them of how the terms are related. In this way, each new term that is taught becomes a framework on which other new terms can be hung, thus increasing the number of terms in students' receptive vocabularies without having to use direct instruction with each term.

SENTENCE STEMS

Sentence stems begin with providing students with prompts like the following:

_____ and _____ are alike because _____.

_____ and _____ are different because _____.

To illustrate how sentence stems might be used, consider the terms *sled* and *snowplow* both from cluster 318. Also assume that both terms have been introduced to students and both have been entered in students' vocabulary notebooks. The first part of the sentence stem asks students to articulate how *sled* and *snowplow* are similar. The teacher might lead the whole class in a discussion of their similarities. As a result of this discussion, the following characteristics might be identified and written on the whiteboard:

- Both are used in snow.
- Both have people riding in them.

Students would then be organized into small groups to identify how the terms are different. Each group would generate some possible differences. For example, one group of students might generate the following differences:

- *Sleds* are used for play but *snowplows* are used for work.
- *Sleds* are much smaller than *snowplows*.

Differences generated by each group would be listed on the board and discussed. After this discussion, students would be asked to examine the entries for *sled* and *snowplow* in their notebooks to determine whether there are things that they want to change regarding their initial entries or things they want to add. Based on the comparison activity, one student might realize that she was slightly inaccurate in what she said about snowplows and make the necessary changes. Another student might add information to what he had initially recorded about sleds.

This example involves two terms that have already been introduced to students and recorded in their academic notebooks. Sentence stems can also be used to introduce new terms. For example, assume that students have been introduced to the term *sled* but not the term *toboggan*. The teacher might provide a brief description of a toboggan along with a picture. The teacher would then immediately move into a whole class sentence stem activity involving the terms *sled* and *toboggan*. Given that *toboggan* was a new term, the teacher might provide a great deal of input and guidance regarding how the terms are similar and different. He or she would also draw heavily from the students in class who were familiar with the term *toboggan*. At the end of the whole class comparison activity, students could either enter the term *toboggan* as a related term to *sled* or record the term as an entirely new entry in their vocabulary notebooks.

THE VENN DIAGRAM

Variations of the Venn diagram have been used by educators for years to engage students in comparison activities. A Venn diagram is depicted in Figure 5.2 for the nouns *sled* and *snowplow*.

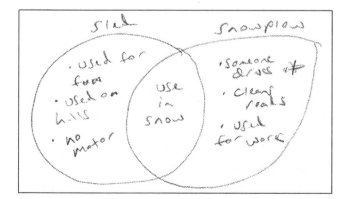

FIGURE 5.2 Venn Diagram

As depicted in Figure 5.2, the similar characteristics are placed in the intersecting part of the Venn diagram; characteristics that are unique to each item are placed in their respective unique parts of the circles.

As before, if both terms have been entered into their notebooks, students would be responsible for generating the similar elements (that go into the intersecting portion of the Venn diagram) and the unique elements for each term (that go into the nonoverlapping sections of the Venn diagram). If one of the terms is being introduced for the first time, the teacher would provide necessary descriptions, examples, anecdotes, and illustrations, such that the class as a whole could generate the common and unique characteristics.

THE DOUBLE BUBBLE

The double bubble was popularized by Hyerle (1996; 2009). It has a format illustrated in Figure 5.3.

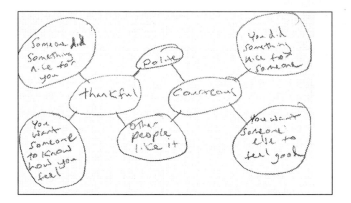

FIGURE 5.3 Generic Format of Double Bubble

Figure 5.3 depicts a double bubble for the adjectives *thankful* and *courteous*, both of which are basic words from cluster 228: Goodness and Kindness. With the double bubble, similarities are placed in the bubbles between the items; unique characteristics are placed to the outside of each item's bubble. In this case, the similar characteristics are:

* Polite
* Other people like it

The unique characteristics for *thankful* are:

* Someone did something nice for you
* You want someone to know how you feel

The unique characteristics for *courteous* are:

* You do something nice for someone else
* You want someone else to feel good

THE COMPARISON MATRIX

The comparison matrix provides a great deal of flexibility to teachers. More than two terms can be addressed at once and various types of conclusions can be generated for terms that are being studied. Figure 5.4 contains a comparison matrix for the terms *duck*, *rooster*, and *owl*, all of which are basic terms from cluster 32: Birds.

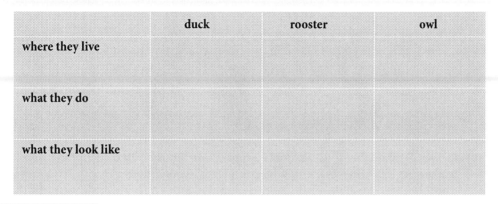

	duck	rooster	owl
where they live			
what they do			
what they look like			

FIGURE 5.4 Comparison Matrix

The three terms to be compared are listed in the columns of Figure 5.4. The characteristics on which they are to be compared are listed in the rows. In this case, those characteristics are: where they live, what they do, and what they look like.

CLASSIFYING ACTIVITIES

Classifying activities require students to organize terms into like categories. To engage students in these tasks, a teacher might present students with terms from two or more related clusters. This situation is where the super clusters can be very useful. To illustrate, consider cluster 32: Birds. This cluster belongs to super cluster 10, entitled Animals. As mentioned in Chapter 2, that super cluster contains the following clusters:

32	Birds	155	Parts of Animals
35	Baby Animals	188	Rodents
64	Cats/Dogs	189	Dwellings for Animals
65	Land Animals (General)	194	Animals (General)
70	Sea Animals	309	Shellfish (and Others)
82	Reptiles and Mythical Animals	310	Equipment Used with Animals
95	Insects	341	Primates
117	Actions Related to Animals		

To create a classification activity, the teacher might select terms from two or more of the clusters in this super cluster. For example, the teacher might present students with the following terms:

chicken	*pup*	*lion*
bunny	*fox*	*robin*
wolf	*owl*	*kitten*
crow	*calf*	*collie*

Students would be asked to sort the terms into three categories: birds, baby animals, and cats/dogs. A very different type of classifying activity would require students to generate and defend their own categories instead of using those provided by the teacher.

METAPHORS AND ANALOGIES

Metaphors can be thought of as abstract comparisons between two seemingly unrelated terms. For example, the following would be considered a metaphor:

* *Discussing* is *building a new house*.

Obviously, at a literal level, the term *discussing* is not synonymous with building a new house. However, at an abstract level, there are similarities between the act of discussing and the act of building a new house. For example, when done well, both result in something new. Building a new house results in a new dwelling. A good discussion results in new knowledge on the part of all parties involved. Another abstract similarity between *discussing* and building a new house is that both require good foundations. A house needs a strong concrete foundation to stand over the years. A good discussion requires a foundation in terms of the content that is being discussed. It is these abstract linkages that create the metaphoric linkage between the term *discussing* and the act of building a new house.

When creating and explaining metaphors, it is helpful if students make the abstract relationships as explicit as possible. This is depicted in Figure 5.5.

	Something new is made	
Discussing	Both need a foundation	Building a new house
	Both need a structure	

FIGURE 5.5 Explicit Metaphors

When students explicitly describe the relationships inherent in a metaphor, they address subtle shades of similarities and differences between terms. Metaphor activities are most easily designed for nouns, adjectives, and adverbs. The same can be said for analogies.

Analogies are commonly confused with metaphors, but they are quite different and have a specific form:

* *A* is to *B* as *C* is to *D*.

To illustrate, consider the following:

* *Discussing* is to *arguing* as *dancing* is to *wrestling*.

Here *discussing* and *arguing* are similar, in that they deal with people communicating verbally; however, *arguing* is a much more violent and aggressive form of communication than is *discussing*. *Dancing* and *wrestling* are similar, in that they deal with two people doing something together physically; however, *wrestling* is a much more violent and aggressive form of people doing something physical than is *dancing*.

One way to structure analogy activities with students is to provide them with the complete analogy as in the previous example and ask them to explain the relationship. Another option is to provide students with a partially completed analogy, like the following:

* *Discussing* is to *arguing* as _____ is to _____.

Here students must supply the second set of terms as well as explain the relationship.

SUMMARY

This chapter addressed the comparison phase of teaching a new term. The purpose of this phase is to help deepen students' understanding of new terms that have been presented during the introductory phase. This phase can also be used to introduce new terms that are similar to terms that have been introduced previously. It is during the comparison phase that the cluster approach used in this text is of particular use. Seven types of activities were presented: similar terms, sentence stems, the Venn diagram, the double bubble, the comparison matrix, classifying activities, and metaphor and analogy activities.

6

Strategies for the Review and Refinement Phase

As its name implies, the purpose of the third phase of teaching a new term is to provide a platform for students to review what they have learned and further refine their knowledge of specific terms. There are three general categories of activities that might be employed during the review and refinement phase: (1) give-one, get-one activities, (2) use of roots and affixes, and (3) games. We discuss each in this chapter; however, before doing so, it is important to note that after each review or refinement activity, students should be asked to make changes in their vocabulary notebook. The basic purpose of these activities is to allow students to make corrections in their initial surface-level understanding of new terms. Systematic review of the entries in their academic notebooks allows students to capture their developing knowledge of basic and advanced terms.

GIVE-ONE, GET-ONE ACTIVITIES

Give-one, get-one activities are easy to set up. They are best done in pairs. Here, student pairs examine their partner's vocabulary notebooks to do the following: identify information they have in common, identify information they have that is different, and identify questions they share. To illustrate, assume that a teacher has organized students in pairs and asked them to review the term *court*, which had been entered in their vocabulary notebooks. This term is from cluster 190: Places Related to Sports/Entertainment. In pairs, students would examine each other's notebook entries for this term by first looking for information on which they agreed. One student might have written the following: "A place where you play tennis." The second student might have written: "The basketball court on the playground." Both students would agree that a court is where you play something, but by examining each other's entries, one student would now have added the information that basketball is played on courts; the other student would have added the information that tennis is played on courts. Pairs of students would also be invited to come up with a question they have about the meaning of the term. One pair might ask the question: "Is court also a place you go if you get into trouble?" These questions would be posed to the entire class. Each pair would ask their question and the teacher would respond so that all could hear, inviting answers and comments from the class. After the whole class interaction, students would be invited again to add information to their vocabulary notebooks. As the example of the term *court* illustrates, give-one, get-one activities are perfect opportunities for students to discover and explore multiple meanings for words.

USE OF ROOTS AND AFFIXES

Teaching roots and affixes has long been an integral part of vocabulary instruction. The general idea behind teaching roots and affixes is that if students understand these basic components of the language, they will be able to unlock the meaning of a large number of words. For example, if students know that the Latin root *act* means *do*, then they can more easily discover the meaning of words like *react* and *transact*. Figure 6.1 lists some common Greek and Latin roots that might be used to enhance students' vocabulary development.

Greek Root	Meaning	Examples
ast	star	astronomy, disaster
cycl	circle, ring	cyclone, cycle
gram	letter, written	telegram, diagram
graph	write	telegraph, autograph
meter	measure	thermometer, centimeter
phon	sound	symphony, telephone
photo	light	photograph, photosynthesis
scop	see	microscope, periscope
therm	heat	thermometer, thermal
Latin Root	**Meaning**	**Examples**
act	do	react, transact
ang	bend	angle, angular
aud	hear	audience, audible
credit	believe	discredit, incredible
dict	speak	contradict, dictate
duc, duct	lead	aqueduct, educate
fac	make	factory manufacture
loc	place	location, allocate

Latin Root	Meaning	Examples
man	hand	manuscript, manipulate
migr	move	immigrant, migratory
miss	send	dismiss, missionary
mob	move	automobile, mobile
mot	move	motion, motor
ped	foot	pedal, pedestrian
pop	people	population, popular
port	carry	import, portable
rupt	break	erupt, rupture
sign	mark	signature, signal
spec	see	inspect, spectator
tract	pull, drag	tractor, attraction
urb	city	urban, suburb
vac	empty	vacant, vacuum
vid	see	video, evidence
volv	roll	revolver, revolution

Adapted from Marzano, 2004, p. 79.

FIGURE 6.1 Common Greek and Latin Roots

When teaching a new term, the teacher might identify a root that is a critical part of the term. For example, assume that the teacher is introducing the term *photographer*, from cluster 264. To teach this term, the teacher might introduce students to the Latin root *photo*, which means *light*. After examining the relationship between the root and the meaning of photographer, the students and teacher might explore other terms that contain the same root, like *photograph*.

Affixes can be used in ways similar to roots to deepen students' understanding of new terms. Affixes include prefixes and suffixes. Prefixes commonly add to the meaning of a word. For example, when the prefix *intra* is added to the word *vein* to form the term *intravenous*, it changes the meaning of the term. By itself, *vein* means a tube in the body through which blood flows. *Intravenous* signifies something inserted into a vein. Suffixes typically do not change the meaning of a term, but do change the part of speech of the term. For example, when the suffix *ly* is added to the adjective *quiet*, the result is the adverb *quietly*.

Although there are many lists of affixes a teacher might use, these lists contain so many affixes that it is difficult to know where to begin. Fortunately, White, Sowell, and Yanagihara (1989) have identified the most common prefixes and suffixes. About prefixes, they note:

What is striking about these data is that a handful of prefixes account for a large percentage of the prefixed words. The prefix *un-* alone accounts for 26% of the total. More than half (51%) of the total is explained by the top three prefixes, *un-*, *re-*, and *in-* "not". And with just four prefixes, *un-*, *re-*, *in-*, "not", and *dis-*, one could cover approximately three-fifths of the prefixed words (58%). (pp. 302–303)

They recommend a sequence of six lessons when teaching prefixes. The focus of the first lesson is to help students understand the difference between genuine prefixed words like *unkind* and *refill* and words like *uncle* and *reason* that contain the combination of letters associated with a prefix, but for which these letters are not additions to the front of an existing word. During this first lesson, White and colleagues recommend presenting students with examples and nonexamples of prefixed words. Once students are able to discriminate genuine prefixed words, then the class as a whole develops a working definition of prefixes. The second lesson addresses the negative meaning of the prefixes *un-* and *dis* . The third lesson addresses the negative meaning of the prefixes *in-*, *im-*, *ir-*, and *non-*. During the fourth lesson, the teacher exemplifies the two meanings of *re-* ("again" and "back"). The fifth lesson deals with the less common meanings of *un-* and *dis-* ("do the opposite") and the less common meaning of *in-* and *im-* ("in or into"). The sixth lesson addresses the meanings of *en-*, *em-*, *over-*, and *mis-*.

White and colleagues reported the same findings for affixes as they did for prefixes:

> It is plain...that the distribution of suffixes, too, is not unknown. The first 10 suffixes listed comprise 85% of the sample. Plural and/or third person singular *-s/-es* alone account for about a third (31%) of the sample. Three inflectional suffixes *-s/ -es, -ed*, and *–ing*, account for 65%. In light of this, a middle elementary teacher would do well to concentrate on *-s/-es, -ed*, and *–ing*. (1989, p. 303)

Again, they recommend a series of lessons that address the common suffixes. During the first lesson, the teacher introduces the concept of a suffix by providing clear examples and nonexamples. The next two lessons are devoted to words that do not require a spelling change when a suffix is added: *blows, boxes, talking, faster, lasted, sweetly, comical, rainy*. Next, from one to three lessons are devoted to the three major kinds of spelling changes that occur when a suffix is added to word: (1) consonant doubling (*thinner, swimming, begged, funny*); (2) changing *y* to *i* (*worried, flies, busily, reliable, loneliness*); and (3) deleted silent *e* (*baking, saved, rider, believable, refusal, breezy*). Finally, a number of lessons are devoted to three inflectional endings (*-s/-es, -ed, -ing*) and the following derivational suffixes: *-ly, -er, -ion, -able, -al, -y, -ness*.

GAMES

Games are a powerful way to help students review and refine their understanding of new terms. Here we consider four games described by Marzano (2007) that can be used with new vocabulary terms: (1) Talk a Mile a Minute, (2) What Is the Question?, (3) Classroom Feud, and (4) Which Word Doesn't Fit?.

Talk a Mile a Minute

In this game, teams of students are given a list of seven terms from a cluster. For example, Figure 6.2 lists seven words from cluster 32: Birds. To play a round, each team designates a "talker," who is provided with the list of seven words. The talker first tells his or her teammates the name of the cluster (in this case, Birds) and then tries to get the team to say each of the words by quickly describing them. For example, for the term *chicken*, a particular talker might say "This is the bird that the store next to the school sells fried." The talker is allowed to say anything about the terms while "talking a mile a minute," but may not spell words or use any rhyming words. The talker keeps talking until the team members identify all seven terms in the cluster. If members of the team are having difficulty with a particular term, the talker skips it and comes back to it later. The first team to identify all seven terms wins the game.

Types of Birds
chicken
crow
eagle
goose
owl
parrot
robin

FIGURE 6.2   Terms from Cluster 32: Birds

With this game and all others, it is important that the teacher asks students to review the vocabulary terms after the game is played with an emphasis on refining students' knowledge of the terms. To do so, the teacher might simply ask students which words were difficult to provide clues for and which words were easy to provide clues for. When a particularly good clue is offered by students, the teacher uses the opportunity to discuss the meaning of the difficult terms. Students are then invited to make changes in their vocabulary notebooks.

One way to make games highly energizing to students is to use what Marzano (2007) refers to as "inconsequential competition." As its name implies, inconsequential competition means that students compete in the spirit of fun. To use inconsequential competition, the teacher assigns students to small groups for a set period of time, such as two weeks. Group membership is systemically changed, so that students who are more familiar with new terms are matched with those are not. In this way, over time, every student will probably be on a winning team and every student will probably be on a losing team. As games are played, the team or teams finishing must quickly receive "team points." At the end of the unit, team points are totaled and the two (or more) teams with the highest points are singled out for some minimal reward such as coupons for fruit drinks from the cafeteria.

What Is the Question?

Just like the popular game show *Jeopardy!*, this game requires a simple matrix, like the one in Figure 6.3. The columns in the matrix are cluster names (or super cluster names). A teacher can use a white board, an overhead transparency, or presentation software such as Microsoft PowerPoint to create the game matrix. Initially, all cells are covered either by slips of paper or using software animation. In each cell is a term from the cluster (or super cluster) indicated by the title of the column. For example, for the column entitled Performers and Entertainers (cluster 167) the term *clown* might be listed for 100 points; *dancer* for 200 points;

actress for 300 points; *comic* for 400 points; and *ventriloquist* for 500 points. Terms that are more difficult to describe or explain are associated with more points. The game is played in the same fashion as the popular game show. A member from each of two teams comes to the front of the room. The member from the team that won the last round selects the cluster and the points for the next round. For example, if Performers and Entertainers is selected for 300 points, the term *actress* is revealed. The two representatives then race to press a ringer if they believe they know the meaning of the term. The student who has pressed the ringer first then has the opportunity to describe the term. The teacher decides whether the student's explanation is acceptable. If it is, the winning student gets to select the next category and the level of points. If not, the other student has an opportunity to describe the word. When the game is completed, students make changes and additions to the entries in their vocabulary notebooks.

Points	Public Officials	Writers and Reporters	Performers and Entertainers	People Who Clean Up
100				
200				
300				
400				
500				

FIGURE 6.3 "What Is the Question" Matrix

Classroom Feud

This game is modeled after the popular television quiz show *Family Feud*. The game can be played with teams that are put together "on the spot" by randomly organizing students into two teams or by teams that have been set up for an extended period of time such as an entire unit. To prepare the game, the teacher selects terms that have already been introduced and entered into student vocabulary notebooks. Enough terms should be selected for each member of each team. The teacher judges whether students' descriptions of terms are acceptable.

One student from each team serves as the responder for the group. Students on each team take turns being responder in some systematic fashion. The teacher presents a term to the responder for a team. The responder then turns to his or her team members and shares with them the description of the term that he or she thinks is correct or tells the team that he or she doesn't know the meaning of the term. Team members either agree with the responder and provide support for his or her description or offer suggestions as to the correct description. The responder has 15 seconds to decide which description to offer. When the description is offered, the teacher determines whether it is acceptable. If acceptable, the team receives a point. If the description is unacceptable, the other team is given an opportunity to provide a description. The last responder for that team again acts as responder for the group. He or she has 15 seconds to come up with an alternative description of the term, again, taking suggestions from his team. If the description is correct, the other team gets the point and is presented with the next term. If a correct description is not offered by the challenging team, no point is awarded. When every student on both teams has acted as the responder, the team with the most points wins. When the game is complete, students review the entries in their vocabulary notebooks to make changes and additions.

Which Word Doesn't Fit?

This game is particularly easy to construct. The teacher simply selects three words from a specific cluster. For example, the teacher might select the following three words from cluster 318: *sled, sleigh,* and *snowplow.* The teacher would also identify a fourth term from another cluster like *automobile.* The four terms would then be presented to students as a set:

sled	*sleigh*
automobile	*snowplow*

Students must identify which term doesn't fit and explain why it doesn't fit.

SUMMARY

This chapter addressed the review and refinement phase of direct vocabulary instruction. The purpose of this phase is to continue deepening students' understanding of new terms. Three categories of instructional strategies were discussed. Give-one, get-one activities require students to examine their understanding of specific terms in light of other students' understandings of the same terms. Activities involving roots and affixes help students understand words more deeply by examining the meanings of various parts of words. Popular games can be adapted to provide students with multiple exposures to new terms in highly engaging ways.

7

The Role of Vocabulary Notebooks

One vitally important tool to effective direct vocabulary instruction for basic and advanced words is a written record of students' vocabulary development. To this end, I strongly recommend that every student have a vocabulary notebook. The reason for vocabulary notebooks is that they allow students to continually revisit their understanding of new terms. Stated differently, vocabulary notebooks allow for "multiple exposures" to new terms. The benefits of multiple exposures make sense from an intuitive perspective: the more time students re-examine their understanding of new terms, the more chances they have to correct misconceptions and add new insights. The benefits of multiple exposures are also supported by the research literature (for a review see Marzano, 2004). Also, the use of academic notebooks has been shown to positively affect student achievement (Marzano, 2006a, 2006b; Gifford & Gore, 2008; Dunn, Bonner, & Huske, 2007).

Multiple exposures are inherent in the three instructional phases described in Chapters 4, 5, and 6: the introductory phase, the comparison phase, and the review and refinement phase. Obviously, these three phases do not occur in a single lesson. A teacher might introduce a few new terms in one lesson. A few days later, the teacher might engage students in some comparison activity. A few days after that, the teacher might play a game with students that relates to some of the terms that have been taught. As described in the last two chapters, after each of these activities, students would be invited to make changes in their vocabulary notebooks. Vocabulary notebooks, then, are a critical component of a systematic approach to multiple exposures.

THE FORMAT FOR VOCABULARY NOTEBOOKS

Every page of a vocabulary notebook should provide adequate space for students to record and add to their understanding of terms. One possible format is depicted in Figure 7.1.

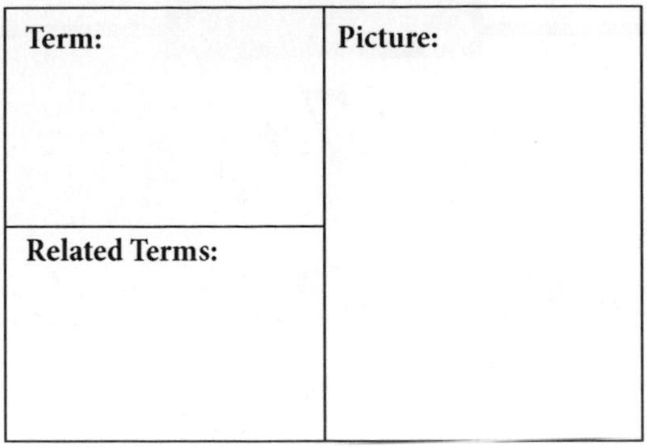

FIGURE 7.1 Format for Vocabulary Notebooks

At the top of Figure 7.1 is a space for the new term, along with the student's initial description of the term. A space on the right is available for students to record their pictures or representations of the new terms. A space at the bottom is reserved for students to list related terms. For lower elementary students, each page of the notebook should probably allow for only two terms, because elementary students have difficulty writing in small spaces. For upper elementary or secondary students, each page of the notebook can allow for three or four terms.

The sections at the top left and right of Figure 7.1 are filled in during the introductory phase. After the teacher has provided a description, example, anecdote, and illustration for a new term, students record their own description or explanation at the top left and their illustration at the right.

During the comparison phase, students make additions and changes to their vocabulary notebooks. They also add terms to the rectangle at the bottom as they make linkages with other terms. During the review and refinement phase, students again make additions and changes to their initial descriptions of new terms or their representation of new terms. They also add to the list of related terms. Figure 7.2 provides an illustration of what one entry in a vocabulary notebook might look like after the comparison phase and the review and refinement phase.

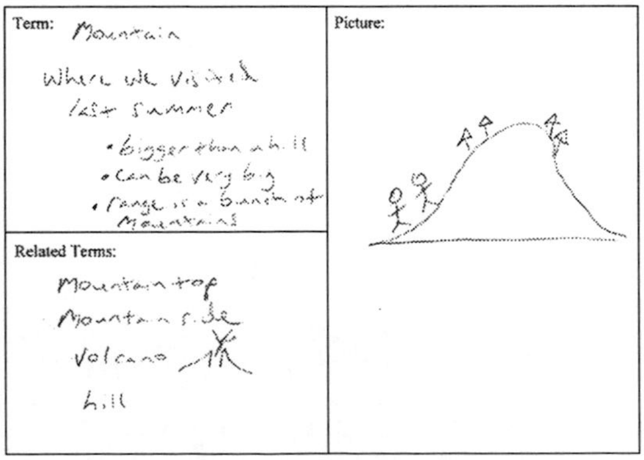

FIGURE 7.2 Revised Entry in a Vocabulary Notebook

Figure 7.2 depicts an entry in a specific student's notebook for the term *mountain* after the three phases of direct instruction. This term is from cluster 168. As shown, the student described a mountain as "where we visited last summer." However, over time, the student added other entries in the rectangle reserved for his or her description:

- Bigger than a hill
- They can be very big
- A range is a group of mountains

Also, over the three phases of instruction, the student has entered the following terms in the rectangle at the bottom for related terms:

- *mountaintop*
- *mountainside*
- *volcano*
- *hill*

Over time, the student would continue to add information as his or her knowledge of the term *mountain* deepened.

ORGANIZING NOTEBOOKS USING THE CLUSTERS

To facilitate student learning, the vocabulary notebooks should be organized according to the clusters that are being studied. For example, assume that based on taking the Snapshot Assessment of Basic Terms, a particular student began instruction on cluster 95: Insects. Thus, the first pages in the vocabulary notebook would all be devoted to words from this cluster. The name Insects would be written at the top of each page devoted to that cluster. When instruction in the terms from this cluster was completed, the student would begin on cluster 96, and so on. Recall from the discussion in Chapter 3 that a teacher might decide that a particular student does not require instruction in the next cluster in order. The teacher would skip ahead in the clusters until he or she found one for which the student exhibited a need.

To help students keep track of the location of clusters in their vocabulary notebooks, it is useful for them to reserve a page of their academic notebooks for a table of contents, as depicted in Figure 7.3.

Cluster	Page
Land Animals (General)	1
Sea Animals	4
Reptiles and Mythical Animals	8
Actions Related to Animals	10

FIGURE 7.3 Table of Contents for a Student's Vocabulary Notebook

The table of contents makes it relatively easy for students to identify exactly where in their notebook clusters begin and end. Some teachers like to have students use three-ring binders with tabs for their vocabulary notebooks. Each tab is devoted to a specific cluster. This makes identification of the location of clusters even easier. Students can locate clusters using the table of contents or the tabs with the cluster names written on them.

AN INDIVIDUAL AND SMALL GROUP EMPHASIS

One issue to keep in mind when planning a vocabulary development program is that teaching basic terms is probably best accomplished in an individual or a small group setting. Recall from the discussion in Chapter 2 that basic terms are typically mastered by native English speakers without direct instruction. However, if a child is not a native English speaker or is a child of poverty, he or she very will probably not have mastered many of these critical terms. Given the importance of basic terms, it makes sense that extraordinary efforts should be made to teach the terms as quickly and efficiently as possible for students in need. Students requiring instruction in basic terms should be identified in a school as quickly as possible and direct instruction provided.

If an individual approach is taken, students would receive one-on-one instruction in the basic terms. Each student is placed on the continuum of clusters using the Snapshot Assessment and instruction is begun with the appropriate cluster. Individualized instruction might be provided for the identified students before school, after school, or during times in the school day that do not interfere with scheduled instruction in core subject areas.

Although an individual approach would certainly require exceptional resources in terms of personnel to provide one-on-one instruction, the expense would certainly be worth the potential benefits for ELL students and FRL students. Additionally, one-to-one instruction in basic terminology might not have to be provided by credentialed teachers. Rather, paraprofessionals or even adult volunteers might be able to provide the instruction, thus decreasing the cost of an individualized approach.

If one-on-one instruction cannot be provided, then a small group approach might be used. Small groups of students can be assembled during the week to receive focused instruction in basic vocabulary. For example, if a school has an extended block of time for language arts, students in need of instruction in basic vocabulary might be pulled together two or more times per week. Students would be placed in small groups based on their entry point in the continuum of clusters. For example, students who begin instruction in clusters 1 through 50 would be grouped together, as would students who begin in clusters 51 through 100 and so on. Within each small group, students would still receive instruction in the terms for their particular starting cluster. However, students in each small group would also receive instruction in terms from a cluster or clusters for which all students need instruction. For example, if a group of students is placed together because all are beginning instruction below cluster 30, the teacher might select words from cluster 30 for instruction with the entire group. Thus, each student in the group would receive instruction in the particular cluster that is their entry point in the continuum of clusters. Additionally, each student would receive instruction in a cluster that is the common focus for the group.

FOCUSING ON THE ADVANCED WORDS

As stated in Chapter 1, the focus of this book is on basic terms, many of which are already known by native English speakers who come from homes where these words are learned through informal exposure. Appendix B contains 2,845 basic terms. However, the text also lists 5,162 advanced terms that might be appropriate for all students in a whole class setting. If advanced terms are to be the focus of instruction in a whole class setting, there is no need to place students in the continuum of clusters. Rather, it is better to systematically work through the super clusters.

As noted previously, there are 60 super clusters, each of which contains basic terms and advanced terms. Appendix C lists each super cluster, along with its related clusters. Figure 7.4 lists the super clusters in order of how many advanced terms they contain.

Rank	Super Cluster Name	Basic *N*	Advanced *N*	Total *N*
28	Movement and Action	137	263	400
10	Animals	131	224	355
39	Emotions and Attitudes	63	214	277
9	Verbal Interaction	97	213	310
52	Occupations	98	211	309
41	Machines and Tools	97	183	280
32	Categories of People	88	173	261
5	Measurement, Size, and Quantity	139	156	295
37	Reasoning and Mental Actions	85	150	235
55	Nonphysical Human Traits	39	137	176
22	Food and Eating	175	130	305
6	Time	126	130	256
20	Water	62	125	187
23	Literary Composition and Writing	80	123	203
26	Clothing	82	122	204
21	Sounds and Noises	60	114	173
43	Containers, Materials, and Building	56	113	169
44	Groups	28	112	140
13	Trees and Plants	21	108	129
11	Importance and Goodness	31	106	137
29	Structures and Buildings	48	103	151
33	Places, Land, and Terrain	40	99	139
50	Actions that are Helpful or Destructive	31	99	130
12	The Human Body	62	98	160

Rank	Super Cluster Name	Basic N	Advanced N	Total N
4	Physical Location and Orientation	98	92	190
56	Disease and Health	24	92	116
16	Vehicles and Transportation	78	91	169
24	Arts and Entertainment	27	90	117
17	Money and Goods	43	86	129
46	Rocks, Metals, and Soil	23	86	109
7	Comparison and Contrast	35	85	120
15	Parts of Dwellings	61	84	145
14	Acquisition and Ownership	25	81	106
30	Shapes	50	67	117
42	Games, Sports, and Recreation	45	64	109
57	Popularity, Familiarity, and Likelihood	16	63	79
58	Light and Darkness	17	62	79
53	Physical Traits of People	23	49	72
49	Cleanliness	20	49	69
25	Seeing and Perceiving	15	48	63
35	Actions Involving Holding and Touching	28	46	74
47	Life, Death, and Survival	11	45	56
3	Cause and Effect	17	44	61
54	Language	15	44	59
18	Actions Involving Walking and Running	20	43	63
45	Events	11	39	50
59	Complexity and Conformity	11	39	50
36	Mathematical Operations and Quantities	16	37	53
48	Weather and Nature	20	35	55
8	Color	17	35	52
34	Combustion and Temperature	15	33	48
60	Chemicals and Matter	4	29	33
19	Attitudinals	12	28	40
51	Danger and Difficulty	10	24	34
27	Texture, Durability, and Consistency	10	22	32
40	Actions Involving the Face	18	20	38
38	Locations and Places Where People Live	17	18	35
2	Pronouns	48	15	63
31	Contractions	40	6	46
1	Auxiliary and Helping Verbs	29	6	35

FIGURE 7.4   Rank Order of Super Clusters Organized by Number of Advanced Terms

As shown in Figure 7.4, the super clusters have a very different organization when ordered by the number of advanced terms they contain. The first 10 super clusters contain 1,924 of the 5,162 advanced terms and the first 15 super clusters contain 2,554 of the 5,162 advanced terms. Thus, simply focusing on the first 15 super clusters might yield great benefits in terms of developing students' understanding of the content important to general literacy. Another approach would be to select super clusters that fit well with instructional topics. For example, assume that a teacher is planning a unit involving various aspects of the human body. The teacher might note that super cluster 12 is entitled The Human Body and contains 10 related clusters: 75, 76, 80, 115, 140, 157, 160, 191, 213, and 336. The teacher might then select specific advanced terms from this super cluster to augment his or her instruction.

When taking a whole-class approach to teaching advanced terms, the teacher would have students organize their notebooks by super clusters. For example, a teacher presenting a unit on the human body would ask students to entitle the first section in their vocabulary notebook, "The Human Body." Students would enter words as they were presented in class. The teacher might also provide students with a list of all the advanced terms from The Human Body super cluster, even though he or she did not intend to teach them all. Based on their own interests, students could select some of these extra advanced terms to enter into their notebooks, either as related terms or as separate entries.

The teacher would follow this same process for subsequent units of instruction. He or she would identify super clusters that relate to the context of the unit and select advanced words to teach to the whole class. A new section of students' vocabulary notebooks would be devoted to this new super cluster, and so on.

To facilitate the super cluster approach as a vehicle for teaching advanced terms, Appendix B contains 24 extra clusters that do not contain basic terms. These are labeled as cluster 421 through cluster 444. If the focus of instruction is advanced terms, these added clusters contain useful terms that could be introduced along with the advanced terms in clusters 1 through 420.

CONCLUSIONS

This book has provided a rationale for teaching basic terms to students who do not acquire these terms as a result of incidental learning within their environment. Many times, ELL students and students of poverty fall into this category. This book also provides a list of basic terms organized in a manner that does not require isolated instruction in each term. That organizational scheme is 420 semantic clusters that are then themselves organized into 60 super clusters. In addition to the basic terms, advanced terms are listed within each cluster. Perhaps for the first time, educators now have a well-defined corpus of basic and advanced terms that constitute the prerequisite knowledge for general literacy in the United States. The cluster/super cluster structure make for a cohesive and coordinated instructional approach to this knowledge—again, for the first time. It might also be true that for the first time K–12 education has little or no excuse for students lacking in this knowledge.

TEST WORDS FOR THE SNAPSHOT ASSESSMENT OF BASIC TERMS

This appendix contains the 840 test words that constitute the Snapshot Assessment of Basic Terms. Directions for using the assessments are found in Chapter 3.

Snapshot Assessment Test Words
Copyright 2009 Robert J. Marzano

1a – can	14a – good-bye	27a – without	40a – do
1b – will	14b – maybe	27b – instead	40b – use
2a – during	15a – more	28a – number	41a – own
2b – while	15b – very	28b – dozen	41b – belong
3a – do	16a – ready	29a – Tuesday	42a – we're
3b – have	16b – early	29b – February	42b – they're
4a – am	17a – left	30a – maybe	43a – sad
4b – is	17b – right	30b – allegedly	43b – sorry
5a – too	18a – almost	31a – please	44a – carry
5b – with	18b – enough	31b – hopefully	44b – mail
6a – they	19a – half	32a – turkey	45a – happy
6b – him	19b – less	32b – ostrich	45b – celebrate
7a – her	20a – far	33a – big	46a – choice
7b – its	20b – apart	33b – tiny	46b – appoint
8a – what	21a – forward	34a – any	47a – helmet
8b – when	21b – backward	34b – nobody	47b – glasses
9a – to	22a – outside	35a – tadpole	48a – breakfast
9b – at	22b – indoors	35b – kitten	48b – dessert
10a – to	23a – under	36a – tree	49a – point
10b – since	23b – underneath	36b – flower	49b – address
11a – that	24a – late	37a – corner	50a – moon
11b – which	24b – afterward	37b – edge	50b – planet
12a – how	25a – where	38a – catch	51a – drink
12b – why	25b – anywhere	38b – toss	51b – chew
13a – each	26a – top	39a – climb	52a – month
13b – either	26b – overhead	39b – lift	52b – decade

53a – lullaby	72b – mistake	92a – rope	111b – female
53b – rhyme	73a – foot	92b – glue	112a – paper
54a – ballet	73b – spoonful	93a – driveway	112b – chalkboard
54b – solo	74a – mix	93b – drawbridge	113a – chair
55a – care	74b – mustard	94a – aunt	113b – cradle
55b – enjoy	75a – finger	94b – grandparent	114a – lot
56a – person	75b – shoulders	95a – caterpillar	114b – place
56b – hero	76a – leg	95b – dragonfly	115a – face
57a – blue	76b – ankle	96a – cup	115b – forehead
57b – green	77a – show	96b – mug	116a – free
58a – best	77b – cartoon	97a – row	116b – expensive
58b – important	78a – cold	97b – glide	117a – fly
59a – fast	78b – hot	98a – pile	117b – soar
59b – hurry	79a – noon	98b – bunch	118a – oven
60a – kindergarten	79b – overnight	99a – deep	118b – furnace
60b – classroom	80a – tooth	99b – tall	119a – hammer
61a – say	80b – tongue	100a – greet	119b – shovel
61b – recite	81a – he's	100b – thank	120a – plane
62a – glove	81b – here's	101a – snow	120b – helicopter
62b – sandal	82a – turtle	101b – rainbow	121a – home
63a – run	82b – dinosaur	102a – lake	121b – tent
63b – hike	83a – today	102b – ocean	122a – buy
64a – dog	83b – ancient	103a – noise	122b – earn
64b – lion	84a – bell	103b – quiet	123a – floor
65a – horse	84b – siren	104a – money	123b – doorstep
65b – kangaroo	85a – I'll	104b – dime	124a – snack
66a – go	85b – she'll	105a – talk	124b – spaghetti
66b – travel	86a – butter	105b – discuss	125a – jeans
67a – idea	86b – cheese	106a – shelter	125b – nightgown
67b – forget	87a – island	106b – jail	126a – once
68a – student	87b – coast	107a – fix	126b – annual
68b – graduate	88a – nurse	107b – build	127a – sink
69a – empty	88b – doctor	108a – twig	127b – leak
69b – hollow	89a – win	108b – branch	128a – train
70a – fish	89b – champion	109a – bank	128b – motorcycle
70b – seal	90a – air	109b – purse	129a – fold
71a – read	90b – weather	110a – help	129b – wrinkle
71b – trace	91a – kitchen	110b – protect	130a – flake
72a – truth	91b – hallway	111a – lady	130b – slice

(Continued)

131a – hug	151a – grin	171a – keep	191a – blood
131b – cuddle	151b – frown	171b – hide	191b – sweat
132a – nap	152a – kiss	172a – city	192a – lawn
132b – dream	152b – lick	172b – downtown	192b – seaweed
133a – mud	153a – syrup	173a – mayor	193a – flat
133b – soil	153b – brownie	173b – candidate	193b – steep
134a – blanket	154a – coach	174a – banana	194a – pet
134b – pillowcase	154b – study	174b – strawberry	194b – fossil
135a – look	155a – beak	175a – meow	195a – scene
135b – focus	155b – fin	175b – purr	195b – image
136a – ham	156a – laugh	176a – milk	196a – blow
136b – bacon	156b – yawn	176b – coffee	196b – pant
137a – smart	157a – skin	177a – ask	197a – hit
137b – wise	157b – beard	177b – question	197b – knead
138a – story	158a – ball	178a – rag	198a – blame
138b – mystery	158b – softball	178b – cotton	198b – scold
139a – garden	159a – canoe	179a – circus	199a – roll
139b – playground	159b – submarine	179b – party	199b – spin
140a – ear	160a – body	180a – country	200a – family
140b – nostril	160b – lap	180b – continent	200b – democracy
141a – drop	161a – hurt	181a – stick	201a – prize
141b – tumble	161b – shoot	181b – log	201b – medal
142a – square	162a – grill	182a – pull	202a – soft
142b – cube	162b – fry	182b – yank	202b – hard
143a – doll	163a – scissors	183a – game	203a – boy
143b – toy	163b – axe	183b – race	203b – man
144a – calendar	164a – basket	184a – lose	204a – child
144b – watch	164b – tank	184b – trade	204b – teenager
145a – jacket	165a – ring	185a – clean	205a – friend
145b – cape	165b – creak	185b – sweep	205b – neighbor
146a – work	166a – add	186a – pretty	206a – villain
146b – hire	166b – multiply	186b – handsome	206b – pest
147a – start	167a – clown	187a – fat	207a – command
147b – try	167b – model	187b – skinny	207b – forbid
148a – steal	168a – hill	188a – mouse	208a – corn
148b – attract	168b – cliff	188b – squirrel	208b – tomato
149a – wave	169a – rest	189a – zoo	209a – swimming
149b – salute	169b – delay	189b – birdhouse	209b – football
150a – they've	170a – sit	190a – theater	210a – grocery
150b – we'll	170b – kneel	190b – stadium	210b – restaurant

211a – brave
211b – loyal
212a – button
212b – sleeve
213a – bone
213b – muscle
214a – price
214b – rent
215a – last
215b – finish
216a – rock
216b – slide
217a – gate
217b – fence
218a – line
218b – zigzag
219a – alphabet
219b – Braille
220a – burn
220b – ignite
221a – easy
221b – difficult
222a – sweet
222b – sour
223a – brush
223b – shampoo
224a – comb
224b – ribbon
225a – search
225b – investigate
226a – wind
226b – thunder
227a – cupid
227b – fairy
228a – gentle
228b – grateful
229a – runner
229b – batter
230a – sick

230b – disease
231a – pill
231b – crutch
232a – hunger
232b – thirsty
233a – time
233b – bedtime
234a – tire
234b – cockpit
235a – couldn't
235b – won't
236a – job
236b – chore
237a – jewel
237b – stone
238a – sentence
238b – noun
239a – art
239b – photograph
240a – safe
240b – risk
241a – sneeze
241b – snort
242a – cut
242b – carve
243a – evil
243b – worst
244a – piano
244b – banjo
245a – dead
245b – born
246a – food
246b – seafood
247a – meet
247b – connect
248a – dictionary
248b – diary
249a – solve
249b – compose

250a – break
250b – crash
251a – bar
251b – pipe
252a – copy
252b – example
253a – strong
253b – clumsy
254a – gun
254b – sword
255a – recommend
255b – convince
256a – postcard
256b – poster
257a – medicine
257b – religion
258a – band
258b – team
259a – steel
259b – metal
260a – fight
260b – war
261a – luck
261b – chance
262a – plain
262b – blank
263a – costume
263b – uniform
264a – choir
264b – singer
265a – firefighter
265b – policeman
266a – pastor
266b – bishop
267a – hole
267b – canyon
268a – mask
268b – flap
269a – rose

269b – daisy
270a – circle
270b – loop
271a – light
271b – bright
272a – candle
272b – lamp
273a – purpose
273b – cause
274a – I'd
274b – you'd
275a – battery
275b – engine
276a – keyboard
276b – robot
277a – plan
277b – goal
278a – proud
278b – confident
279a – map
279b – graph
280a – play
280b – motion
281a – shake
281b – vibrate
282a – bounce
282b – fidget
283a – magnify
283b – expand
284a – curtain
284b – banner
285a – seriously
285b – honestly
286a – language
286b – vocabulary
287a – itch
287b – fever
288a – trash
288b – litter

(Continued)

289a – popular	309a – shrimp	329a – grow	349a – opinion
289b – common	309b – lobster	329b – survive	349b – belief
290a – rare	310a – saddle	330a – giant	350a – shy
290b – weird	310b – leash	330b – dwarf	350b – bashful
291a – fear	311a – mean	331a – tractor	351a – naughty
291b – nervous	311b – violent	331b – wheelbarrow	351b – dishonest
292a – mad	312a – upset	332a – free	352a – hose
292b – dislike	312b – disappoint	332b – obedient	352b – faucet
293a – expect	313a – hope	333a – author	353a – cloud
293b – miss	313b – doubt	333b – speaker	353b – fog
294a – responsible	314a – oil	334a – janitor	354a – naked
294b – eager	314b – fuel	334b – garbageman	354b – informal
295a – crazy	315a – handle	335a – station	355a – barefoot
295b – wild	315b – knob	335b – airport	355b – owner
296a – pool	316a – ladder	336a – stomach	356a – babysitter
296b – dam	316b – pedal	336b – heart	356b – paperboy
297a – butcher	317a – guest	337a – sand	357a – astronaut
297b – baker	317b – stranger	337b – pebble	357b – scientist
298a – police	318a – sled	338a – stop	358a – guard
298b – navy	318b – snow plow	338b – avoid	358b – slave
299a – change	319a – title	339a – kick	359a – carpenter
299b – opposite	319b – nickname	339b – stamp	359b – plumber
300a – follow	320a – rule	340a – sum	360a – judge
300b – chase	320b – regulation	340b – total	360b – lawyer
301a – crumble	321a – church	341a – gorilla	361a – maid
301b – shorten	321b – shrine	341b – monkey	361b – butler
302a – split	322a – open	342a – become	362a – forest
302b – separate	322b – shut	342b – seem	362b – jungle
303a – shape	323a – strong	343a – pioneer	363a – prairie
303b – pattern	323b – delicate	343b – citizen	363b – field
304a – practice	324a – barn	344a – star	364a – tower
304b – stretch	324b – storeroom	344b – celebrity	364b – building
305a – blister	325a – thing	345a – tattle	365a – shop
305b – sunburn	325b – object	345b – admit	365b – office
306a – dark	326a – sharp	346a – record	366a – farm
306b – shadow	326b – dull	346b – video	366b – ranch
307a – avalanche	327a – angle	347a – attention	367a – tape
307b – earthquake	327b – radius	347b – interest	367b – pack
308a – hop	328a – secret	348a – recipe	368a – fail
308b – jump	328b – private	348b – routine	368b – succeed

369a – happily
369b – luckily
370a – magic
370b – trick
371a – blind
371b – deaf
372a – shine
372b – reflect
373a – measure
373b – weigh
374a – thermometer
374b – yardstick
375a – dry
375b – overcast
376a – smoke
376b – ash
377a – oxygen
377b – caffeine
378a – concern
378b – guilt
379a – grumpy
379b – rude
380a – surprise
380b – amaze
381a – skill
381b – talent

382a – expert
382b – beginner
383a – promise
383b – vow
384a – define
384b – represent
385a – lazy
385b – casual
386a – lucky
386b – successful
387a – strict
387b – stubborn
388a – holy
388b – heathen
389a – careful
389b – slack
390a – sideways
390b – diagonal
391a – afloat
391b – inland
392a – waiter
392b – chef
393a – mailman
393b – postmaster
394a – cowboy
394b – lumberjack

395a – customer
395b – merchant
396a – secretary
396b – clerk
397a – pilot
397b – skipper
398a – desert
398b – rural
399a – hospital
399b – clinic
400a – monument
400b – landmark
401a – audience
401b – council
402a – plant
402b – irrigate
403a – force
403b – pressure
404a – germ
404b – bacteria
405a – invisible
405b – dim
406a – cloud
406b – thunderhead
407a – neat
407b – tidy

408a – crawl
408b – sneak
409a – stand
409b – posture
410a – math
410b – algebra
411a – have to
411b – had better
412a – event
412b – attempt
413a – vote
413b – elect
414a – pipe
414b – cigar
415a – paint
415b – dye
416a – scare
416b – startle
417a – jealous
417b – grudge
418a – magnet
418b – electric
419a – machine
419b – appliance
420a – camera
420b – telescope

This appendix contains the 420 clusters, along with their basic and advanced terms, listed in order of how basic they are. Basic words are listed in bold; advanced words are not. Each word is accompanied by an index of basicness that ranges from 1 (most basic) to 5 (least basic). As described in Chapter 2, all words with an index of 3 or below are considered basic. However, teachers should also examine the terms with an index of 4 to determine whether they should be considered basic for specific students studying specific topics. Each word is also coded as to its part of speech. Finally, this appendix also contains 24 clusters (numbered 421–444) that do not contain any basic terms but that might be used when the instructional emphasis is on advanced terms.

1. Modals—related clusters: 3, 4, 342, 411

Word	Importance	Part of Speech	Word	Importance	Part of Speech
can	1	v	**shall**	1	v
cannot	1	v	**should**	1	v
could	1	v	**will**	1	v
may	1	v	**would**	1	v
might	1	v	ought	4	v
must	1	v	used to	4	v

2. Relationship Markers (Concurrent Action)—related clusters: 16, 24, 29, 52, 59, 79, 83, 126, 144, 233

Word	Importance	Part of Speech	Word	Importance	Part of Speech
as	1	conj	**while**	1	adv
at	1	prep	at the same time	4	adv
during	1	prep	at this point	4	adv
now	1	adv	meanwhile	4	n
of	1	prep	concurrently	5	adv
on	1	prep	in the meantime	5	adv
together	1	adv	nowadays	5	n
when	1	adv	simultaneously	5	adv

3. Primary Auxiliary Verbs—related clusters: 1, 4, 342, 411

Word	Importance	Part of Speech	Word	Importance	Part of Speech
did	1	v	done	1	v
do	1	v	had	1	v
docs	1	v	has	1	v
doing	1	v	have	1	v

4. Auxiliary Verbs—related clusters: 1, 3, 342, 411

Word	Importance	Part of Speech	Word	Importance	Part of Speech
am	1	v	is	1	v
are	1	v	was	1	v
be	1	v	were	1	v
been	1	v	being	2	v

5. Relationship Markers (Addition)—related clusters: 27, 252, 299

Word	Importance	Part of Speech	Word	Importance	Part of Speech
and	1	conj	further	4	adv
of	1	prep	in addition	4	adv
too	1	adv	moreover	4	adv
with	1	prep	namely	4	adv
as well	4	adv	likewise	5	adv
as well as	4	conj			

6. Pronouns/Reflexive Pronouns—related clusters: 7, 8, 11, 12, 34

Word	Importance	Part of Speech	Word	Importance	Part of Speech
he	1	pro	they	1	pro
him	1	pro	us	1	pro
I	1	pro	we	1	pro
it	1	pro	you	1	pro
me	1	pro	herself	2	pro
myself	1	pro	himself	2	pro
she	1	pro	yourself	3	pro
them	1	pro	itself	4	pro

(Continued)

Word	Importance	Part of Speech	Word	Importance	Part of Speech
oneself	4	pro	themselves	4	pro
ourselves	4	pro	thou	4	pro
thee	4	pro	thy	5	pro

7. Possessive Pronouns—related clusters: 6, 8, 11, 12, 34

Word	Importance	Part of Speech	Word	Importance	Part of Speech
her	1	pro	their	1	pro
hers	1	pro	your	1	pro
its	1	pro	yours	1	pro
mine	1	pro	his	2	pro
my	1	pro	ours	2	pro
our	1	pro	theirs	2	pro

8. Interrogative Pronouns—related clusters: 6, 7, 11, 12, 34

Word	Importance	Part of Speech	Word	Importance	Part of Speech
what	1	pro	which	1	pro
when	1	pro	whichever	4	Pro
where	1	pro			

9. Direction To and From—related clusters: 17, 20, 21, 22, 23, 25, 26, 37, 49, 390, 430

Word	Importance	Part of Speech	Word	Importance	Part of Speech
at	1	prep	bound for	4	v
from	1	prep	hither	5	adv
to	1	prep			

10. Cause/Effect (Relationship Markers)—related clusters: 273

Word	Importance	Part of Speech	Word	Importance	Part of Speech
because	1	conj	so	1	adv
by	1	prep	then	1	adv
for	1	prep	to	1	prep
from	1	prep	because of	2	prep
if	1	conj	if only	4	conj
since	1	prep	if…then	4	conj

Word	Importance	Part of Speech	Word	Importance	Part of Speech
in that case	4	conj	for all that	5	conj
now that	4	conj	for as much	5	conj
on account of	4	prep	for the fact that	5	conj
so that	4	adv	hence	5	adv
therefore	4	adv	hereby	5	adv
thus	4	adv	herein	5	adv
until...then	4	adv	hereupon	5	adv
when...then	4	conj	herewith	5	adv
where...there	4	conj	in that	5	conj
whereas	4	conj	lest	5	conj
accordingly	5	adv	thereby	5	adv
as a consequence	5	conj	whereby	5	conj
as a result	5	conj	wherefore	5	adv
consequently	5	adv	whereupon	5	conj
else	5	adj			

11. Relative Pronouns—related clusters: 6, 7, 8, 12, 34

Word	Importance	Part of Speech	Word	Importance	Part of Speech
that	1	pro	**who**	1	pro
which	1	pro	whom	4	pro

12. Indefinite/Interrogative Adverbs—related clusters: 6, 7, 8, 11, 34

Word	Importance	Part of Speech	Word	Importance	Part of Speech
how	1	pro	someway	4	pro
why	1	pro	whenever	4	pro
somehow	4	pro	wherever	4	pro

13. Specifiers—related clusters: 15, 18, 19, 28, 33, 73, 130, 327, 373, 374

Word	Importance	Part of Speech	Word	Importance	Part of Speech
a	1	art	**the**	1	art
an	1	art	**these**	1	pro
each	1	adj	**this**	1	pro
every	1	adj	**those**	1	pro
no	1	adj	**either**	2	pro
that	1	pro			

14. Exclamations (General)—related clusters: 61, 100, 105, 177, 198, 207, 255, 345, 346, 383

Word	Importance	Part of Speech	Word	Importance	Part of Speech
ah	1	int	okay	1	adj
aha	1	int	ooh	1	int
bye	1	int	yes	1	adv
gee	1	int	goodnight	2	int
good-bye	1	int	wow	2	int
ha	1	int	ay	4	int
hello	1	int	aye	4	int
hey	1	int	beware	4	v
hi	1	int	bravo	4	int
ho	1	int	farewell	4	int
maybe	1	adv	howdy	4	int
no	1	adv	hurrah	4	int
oh	1	int	ugh	4	int
ok	1	int	alas	5	int

15. Intensifiers—related clusters: 13, 18, 19, 28, 33, 73, 130, 327, 373, 374

Word	Importance	Part of Speech	Word	Importance	Part of Speech
more	1	adj	complete(ly)	4	adj
most	1	adj	deeply	4	adv
much	1	adj	highly	4	adv
so	1	adv	in all respects	4	adv
such	1	adj	intense	4	adj
sure	1	adj	perfectly	4	adv
too	1	adv	quite	4	adv
very	1	adv	totally	4	adv
well	1	adv	ultimately	4	adv
badly	3	adv	widely	4	adv
a great deal	4	adv	dynamic	5	adj
absolute(ly)	4	adj	extreme	5	adj
altogether	4	adv	utmost	5	adj
by far	4	adv			

16. Relationship Markers (Concurrent Action)—related clusters: 2, 24, 29, 52, 59, 79, 83, 126, 144, 233

Word	Importance	Part of Speech	Word	Importance	Part of Speech
already	1	adv	former	4	adj
early	1	adj	initial	4	adj
fresh	1	adj	modern	4	adj
new	1	adj	now that	4	conj
ready	1	adj	original	4	adj
since	1	adv	precede	4	v
young	2	adj	previous	4	adj
ago	3	adj	recent	4	adj
lately	3	adv	so far	4	adv
as yet	4	adv	source	4	n
at first	4	adv	until then	4	adv
before now	4	adv	beforehand	5	adv
before that	4	adv	heretofore	5	adv
current	4	adv	hitherto	5	adv
due	4	adj			

17. Directions—related clusters: 9, 20, 21, 22, 23, 25, 26, 37, 49, 390, 430

Word	Importance	Part of Speech	Word	Importance	Part of Speech
left	1	adj	northwest	4	n
right	1	adj	southeast	4	n
east	2	n	southeastern	4	adj
north	2	n	southern	4	adj
south	2	n	southland	4	n
west	2	n	southward	4	adj
midwest	4	n	southwest	4	n
northeast	4	n	starboard	4	n
northeastern	4	adj	western	4	adj
northern	4	adj	westward	4	adj
northward	4	adj			

18. Diminishers—related clusters: 13, 15, 19, 28, 33, 73, 130, 327, 373, 374

Word	Importance	Part of Speech	Word	Importance	Part of Speech
almost	1	adv	moderate	4	adj
enough	1	adj	more or less	4	adv
just	1	adj	overall	4	adj
only	1	adj	practically	4	adv
hardly	2	adv	precisely	4	adv
alone	3	adv	probable	4	adj
mostly	3	adv	purely	4	adv
nearly	3	adv	quite	4	adv
simply	3	adv	rather	4	adv
a bit	4	adv	scarcely	4	adv
a little	4	adv	slightly	4	adv
adequate	4	adj	somewhat	4	adv
as good as	4	adv	sort of	4	adv
at least	4	adv	specifically	4	adv
barely	4	adv	sufficient	4	adj
in part	4	adv	sufficiently	4	adv
in particular	4	adv	mere	5	adj
kind of	4	adv	particularly	5	adv
mainly	4	adv	to some extent	5	adv

19. Amounts—related clusters: 13, 15, 18, 28, 33, 73, 130, 327, 373, 374

Word	Importance	Part of Speech	Word	Importance	Part of Speech
all	1	adj	**other**	1	adj
another	1	adj	**pair**	1	n
both	1	pro	**two**	1	n
few	1	adj	**whole**	2	adj
half	1	n	**amount**	3	n
less	1	adj	**couple**	3	n
little	1	adj	**extra**	3	adj
lot	1	adj	**plenty**	3	n
many	1	adj	**several**	3	n
more	1	adj	**single**	3	n
most	1	adj	**twice**	3	adv
none	1	pro	additional	4	adj
only	1	adj	capacity	4	n

Word	Importance	Part of Speech	Word	Importance	Part of Speech
decrease	4	v	sole	4	adj
double	4	n	spare	4	adj
entire	4	adj	stub	4	n
exceed	4	v	surplus	4	n
excess	4	n	unit	4	n
increase	4	n	volume	4	n
lack	4	n	abundant	5	adj
least	4	adj	ample	5	adj
leftover	4	n	binary	5	adj
lone	4	adj	deduct	5	v
numerous	4	adj	lush	5	adj
outnumber	4	v	majority	5	n
partial	4	adj	mate	5	n
particular	4	adj	scarcity	5	n
plural	4	adj	sparse	5	adj
quantity	4	n	supplement	5	n
remainder	4	n	twain	5	n

20. Distances—related clusters: 9, 17, 21, 22, 23, 25, 26, 37, 49, 390, 430

Word	Importance	Part of Speech	Word	Importance	Part of Speech
along	1	prep	outer	3	adj
away	1	adv	abroad	4	adv
beside	1	prep	closeness	4	n
between	1	prep	contact	4	n
by	1	prep	distant	4	adj
close	1	adj	homeward	4	adv
far	1	adv	local	4	adj
near	1	prep	overseas	4	adv
past	1	prep	remote	4	adj
toward	1	prep	yonder	4	adv
apart	3	adv	abreast	5	adv
aside	3	adv	adjacent	5	adj
beyond	3	prep	nigh	5	adv
nearby	3	adj	outlying	5	adj
opposite	3	adj	vicinity	5	n

21. Front/Middle/Back—related clusters: 9, 17, 20, 22, 23, 25, 26, 37, 49, 390, 430

Word	Importance	Part of Speech	Word	Importance	Part of Speech
ahead	1	adv	**rear**	3	n
back	1	n	background	4	n
behind	1	prep	central	4	adj
end	1	n	core	4	n
forward	1	adj	forth	4	adv
front	1	n	hind	4	adj
middle	1	adj	intermediate	4	adj
center	2	n	medium	4	adj
last	2	adj	midst	4	n
ahead of	3	adv	midway	4	adv
among	3	prep	fore	5	adj
backward	3	adj	fro	5	adv
backwards	3	adv	obverse	5	adj

22. In/Out—related clusters: 9, 17, 20, 21, 23, 25, 26, 37, 49, 390, 430

Word	Importance	Part of Speech	Word	Importance	Part of Speech
across	1	prep	**within**	3	adv
in	1	prep	exterior	4	adj
inside	1	n	inland	4	adj
into	1	prep	inner	4	adj
out	1	adv	interior	4	adj
outside	1	n	inward	4	adj
through	1	prep	outward	4	adj
enter	2	v	overboard	4	adv
outdoors	2	n	embark	5	v
indoor	3	n	external	5	adj
indoors	3	n	internal	5	adj
throughout	3	prep			

23. Down/Under—related clusters: 9, 17, 20, 21, 22, 25, 26, 37, 49, 390, 430

Word	Importance	Part of Speech	Word	Importance	Part of Speech
below	1	prep	**low**	1	adj
bottom	1	n	**under**	1	prep
down	1	prep	**beneath**	2	prep

Word	Importance	Part of Speech	Word	Importance	Part of Speech
underneath	2	prep	downwind	4	adv
downhill	3	adv	underfoot	4	n
downstairs	3	n	underground	4	n
downward	3	adv	undergrowth	4	n

24. Relationship Markers (Subsequent Action)—related clusters: 2, 16, 29, 52, 59, 79, 83, 126, 144, 233

Word	Importance	Part of Speech	Word	Importance	Part of Speech
before	1	prep	later	3	adj
late	1	adj	latter	3	adj
next	1	adj	after that	4	adv
soon	1	adv	eventual	4	adj
then	1	adv	in the end	4	adv
until	1	prep	tardy	4	adj
afterward	3	adv	henceforth	5	adv
afterwards	3	adv	hereafter	5	adv

25. Locations (Nonspecific)—related clusters: 9, 17, 20, 21, 22, 23, 26, 37, 49, 390, 430

Word	Importance	Part of Speech	Word	Importance	Part of Speech
here	1	adv	anywhere	3	n
there	1	adv	someplace	3	adv
where	1	adv	all over	4	adv
nowhere	2	n	elsewhere	4	adv
somewhere	2	n			

26. Up/On—related clusters: 9, 17, 20, 21, 22, 23, 25, 37, 49, 390, 430

Word	Importance	Part of Speech	Word	Importance	Part of Speech
above	1	prep	up	1	prep
high	1	adj	onto	2	prep
off	1	prep	upon	2	prep
on	1	prep	aboard	3	adv
over	1	prep	overhead	3	adj
tip	1	n	upright	3	adj
top	1	n	upside-down	3	n

(Continued)

Word	Importance	Part of Speech	Word	Importance	Part of Speech
upstairs	3	n	summit	4	n
upward	3	adj	upland	4	adj
atop	4	prep	upper	4	adj
peak	4	n	pinnacle	5	n

27. Relationship Markers (Contrast)—related clusters: 5, 252, 299

Word	Importance	Part of Speech	Word	Importance	Part of Speech
but	1	conj	contrast	4	v
else	1	conj	however	4	adv
not	1	adv	in comparison	4	conj
or	1	conj	nevertheless	4	adv
still	1	conj	nor	4	conj
than	1	conj	otherwise	4	adv
without	1	prep	though	4	conj
yet	2	conj	whereas	4	conj
against	3	prep	alternatively	5	adv
compare	3	v	at any rate	5	conj
either	3	conj	despite	5	prep
except	3	prep	in any case	5	conj
instead	3	adv	in any event	5	conj
neither	3	conj	neither…nor	5	conj
unless	3	conj	nonetheless	5	conj
whether	3	conj	notwithstanding	5	prep
although	4	conj	on the other hand	5	conj
anyhow	4	adv	regardless of	5	conj
anyway	4	adv	versus	5	prep

28. Numbers—related clusters: 13, 15, 18, 19, 33, 73, 130, 327, 373, 374

Word	Importance	Part of Speech	Word	Importance	Part of Speech
eight	1	n	**seven**	1	n
five	1	n	**six**	1	n
four	1	n	**ten**	1	n
nine	1	n	**three**	1	n
one	1	n	**two**	1	n

Word	Importance	Part of Speech	Word	Importance	Part of Speech
zero	1	n	decimal	3	n
eighteen	2	n	dozen	3	n
eighty	2	n	million	3	n
eleven	2	n	ninth	3	adj
fifteen	2	n	seventh	3	adj
fifty	2	n	sixth	3	adj
first	2	n	tenth	3	adj
forty	2	n	third	3	adj
fourteen	2	n	data	4	n
hundred	2	n	digit	4	n
nineteen	2	n	fourscore	4	n
ninety	2	n	integer	4	n
number	2	n	nineteenth	4	adj
numeral	2	n	seventeenth	4	adj
second	2	n	sixteenth	4	adj
seventeen	2	n	sixtieth	4	adj
seventy	2	n	thirteenth	4	adj
sixteen	2	n	thousandth	4	adj
sixty	2	n	trillion	4	n
thirteen	2	n	triple	4	n
thirty	2	n	twelfth	4	adj
thousand	2	n	twentieth	4	adj
twelve	2	n	triad	5	n
twenty	2	n	trice	5	n
billion	3	n			

29. Days and Months—related clusters: 2, 16, 24, 52, 59, 79, 83, 126, 144, 233

Word	Importance	Part of Speech	Word	Importance	Part of Speech
April	2	n	Monday	2	n
August	2	n	November	2	n
December	2	n	October	2	n
February	2	n	Saturday	2	n
Friday	2	n	September	2	n
January	2	n	Sunday	2	n
July	2	n	Thursday	2	n
June	2	n	Tuesday	2	n
March	2	n	Wednesday	2	n
May	2	n			

30. Attitudinals (Lack of Truth/Doubt)—related clusters: 31, 285, 369, 431, 439, 440

Word	Importance	Part of Speech	Word	Importance	Part of Speech
maybe	1	adv	perhaps	4	adv
possibly	3	adv	supposedly	4	adv
allegedly	4	adv	seemingly	5	adv

31. Attitudinals (Other)—related clusters: 30, 285, 369, 431, 439, 440

Word	Importance	Part of Speech	Word	Importance	Part of Speech
please	1	adv	preferably	4	adv
hopefully	3	adv			

32. Birds—related clusters: 35, 64, 65, 70, 82, 95, 117, 155, 188, 189, 194, 309, 310, 341

Word	Importance	Part of Speech	Word	Importance	Part of Speech
bird	2	n	heron	4	n
chicken	2	n	hummingbird	4	n
crow	2	n	lark	4	n
duck	2	n	mockingbird	4	n
eagle	2	n	oriole	4	n
fowl	2	n	ostrich	4	n
goose	2	n	parakeet	4	n
hen	2	n	peacock	4	n
jay	2	n	pelican	4	n
owl	2	n	penguin	4	n
parrot	2	n	pheasant	4	n
robin	2	n	pigeon	4	n
rooster	2	n	quail	4	n
turkey	2	n	raven	4	n
bluebird	4	n	seagull	4	n
canary	4	n	sparrow	4	n
crane	4	n	swan	4	n
cuckoo	4	n	vulture	4	n
dodo	4	n	woodpecker	4	n
dove	4	n	wren	4	n
falcon	4	n	albatross	5	n
gull	4	n	cock	5	n
hawk	4	n	drake	5	n

Word	Importance	Part of Speech	Word	Importance	Part of Speech
finch	5	n	partridge	5	n
gander	5	n	starling	5	n
mallard	5	n			

33. Size and Weight—related clusters: 13, 15, 18, 19, 28, 73, 130, 327, 373, 374

Word	Importance	Part of Speech	Word	Importance	Part of Speech
big	1	adj	grand	4	adj
giant	2	adj	immense	4	adj
great	2	adj	mammoth	4	adj
huge	2	adj	massive	4	adj
large	2	adj	medium	4	adj
little	2	adj	miniature	4	adj
small	2	adj	monstrous	4	adj
tiny	2	adj	vast	4	adj
enormous	3	adj	compact	5	adj
gigantic	3	adj	petite	5	adj
jumbo	3	adj	wee	5	adj
bulk	4	adj			

34. Indefinite Pronouns—related clusters: 6, 7, 8, 11, 12

Word	Importance	Part of Speech	Word	Importance	Part of Speech
any	1	pro	**anyone**	3	pro
each	1	pro	**anything**	3	pro
enough	1	pro	**no one**	3	pro
nothing	1	pro	**somebody**	3	pro
some	1	pro	**someone**	3	pro
nobody	2	pro	**something**	3	pro
anybody	3	pro	whoever	4	pro

35. Baby Animals—related clusters: 32, 64, 65, 70, 82, 95, 117, 155, 188, 189, 194, 309, 310, 341

Word	Importance	Part of Speech	Word	Importance	Part of Speech
bunny	2	n	**kitten**	2	n
calf	2	n	**pup**	2	n
cub	2	n	**puppy**	2	n

(Continued)

Word	Importance	Part of Speech	Word	Importance	Part of Speech
tadpole	2	n	fawn	4	n
chick	4	n	yearling	4	n
colt	4	n			

36. Vegetation (General)—related clusters: 108, 192, 269, 421

Word	Importance	Part of Speech	Word	Importance	Part of Speech
bush	2	n	oasis	4	n
flower	2	n	shrub	4	n
plant	2	n	underbrush	4	n
tree	2	n	arbor	5	n
vegetation	2	n	flora	5	n
weed	2	n	photosynthesis	5	n

37. Boundaries—related clusters: 9, 17, 20, 21, 22, 23, 25, 26, 49, 390, 430

Word	Importance	Part of Speech	Word	Importance	Part of Speech
corner	2	n	perimeter	4	n
edge	2	n	ridge	4	n
limit	2	n	rim	4	n
margin	2	n	verge	4	n
side	2	n	bounds	5	n
border	4	n	brink	5	n
brim	4	n	flank	5	n
horizon	4	n			

38. Tossing and Catching—related clusters: 39, 40, 44, 66, 141, 147, 169, 170, 182, 199, 215, 216, 247, 280, 281, 282, 283, 300, 301, 302, 322, 338, 403

Word	Importance	Part of Speech	Word	Importance	Part of Speech
catch	2	v	fling	4	v
pass	2	v	flip	4	v
throw	2	v	heave	4	v
toss	2	v	pitch	4	v
cast	4	v	hurl	5	v
chuck	4	v	snag	5	v
flick	4	v	thrust	5	v

39. Ascending Motion—related clusters: 38, 40, 44, 66, 141, 147, 169, 170, 182, 199, 215, 216, 247, 280, 281, 282, 283, 300, 301, 302, 322, 338, 403

Word	Importance	Part of Speech	Word	Importance	Part of Speech
climb	2	v	hoist	4	v
lift	2	v	load	4	v
raise	2	v	mount	4	v
order	3	n	pry	4	v
rank	3	v	rate	4	v
rise	3	v	ascend	5	v
arise	4	v	elevate	5	v
blast-off	4	n			

40. The Act of Occurring—related clusters: 38, 39, 44, 66, 141, 147, 169, 170, 182, 199, 215, 216, 247, 280, 281, 282, 283, 300, 301, 302, 322, 338, 403

Word	Importance	Part of Speech	Word	Importance	Part of Speech
do	1	v	function	4	v
use	2	v	react	4	v
happen	3	v	reaction	4	n
occur	3	v	undergo	4	v
apply	4	v	commit	5	v

41. Ownership/Possession—related clusters: 89, 148, 171, 184, 426

Word	Importance	Part of Speech	Word	Importance	Part of Speech
have	1	v	occupy	4	v
belong	2	v	ownership	4	n
own	2	v	possession	4	n
possess	3	v	property	4	n
custody	4	n	heirloom	5	n
maintain	4	v	monopoly	5	n

42. Contractions (Are)—related clusters: 81, 85, 150, 235, 274

Word	Importance	Part of Speech	Word	Importance	Part of Speech
they're	2	cont	**you're**	2	cont
we're	2	cont			

43. Sadness—related clusters: 45, 55, 291, 292, 293, 311, 312, 313, 378, 379, 380, 381, 416, 417, 422, 427, 428

Word	Importance	Part of Speech	Word	Importance	Part of Speech
sad	2	adj	mourn	4	v
sorry	2	adj	pitiful	4	adj
unhappy	2	adj	pout	4	v
contrite	4	adj	sorrow	4	n
discomfort	4	n	suffer	4	v
forlorn	4	adj	sulk	4	v
gloom	4	n	dismay	5	n
grief	4	n	doldrums	5	n
heartache	4	n	misery	5	n
letdown	4	n	remorse	5	n
loneliness	4	n	repent	5	v
miserable	4	adj	woe	5	n

44. Giving and Taking—related clusters: 38, 39, 40, 66, 141, 147, 169, 170, 182, 199, 215, 216, 247, 280, 281, 282, 283, 300, 301, 302, 322, 338, 403

Word	Importance	Part of Speech	Word	Importance	Part of Speech
bring	2	v	export	4	v
carry	2	v	fetch	4	v
deliver	2	v	furnish	4	v
get	2	v	homecoming	4	n
give	2	v	import	4	v
mail	2	v	provide	4	v
move	2	v	relay	4	v
place	2	v	rid	4	v
present	2	v	ship	4	v
put	2	v	supply	4	v
return	2	v	transplant	4	v
send	2	v	bestow	5	v
set	2	v	dispatch	5	v
take	2	v	eliminate	5	v
bear	3	v	retrieve	5	v
remove	3	v	shuttle	5	v
airmail	4	n	transfer	5	v
deposit	4	v	trundle	5	v

45. Fun and Joy—related clusters: 43, 55, 291, 292, 293, 311, 312, 313, 378, 379, 380, 381, 416, 417, 422, 427, 428

Word	Importance	Part of Speech	Word	Importance	Part of Speech
fun	2	n	coddle	4	v
glad	2	adj	delight	4	v
happy	2	adj	entertain	4	v
joke	2	n	frolic	4	v
jolly	2	adj	gag	4	n
joy	2	n	glee	4	adj
merry	2	adj	jest	4	v
play	2	v	jubilant	4	adj
please	2	v	playful	4	adj
silly	2	adj	pleasure	4	n
celebrate	3	v	riddle	4	n
happiness	3	n	antic	5	n
humor	3	n	mirth	5	n
joyful	3	adj	pamper	5	v
amuse	4	v	wisecrack	5	n
cheerful	4	adj			

46. Choice—related clusters: 67, 132, 137, 154, 225, 249, 277, 347, 348, 349, 384

Word	Importance	Part of Speech	Word	Importance	Part of Speech
choice	2	n	assign	4	v
choose	2	v	decision	4	n
decide	2	v	dedicate	4	v
judge	2	v	judgment	4	n
pick	2	v	weed	4	v
select	2	v	discriminate	5	v
appoint	3	v	verdict	5	n
sort	3	v			

47. Things Worn on the Head—related clusters: 62, 125, 129, 145, 178, 212, 224, 263, 354, 435

Word	Importance	Part of Speech	Word	Importance	Part of Speech
cap	2	n	**helmet**	2	n
glasses	2	n	**hood**	2	n
hat	2	n	**mask**	2	n

(Continued)

Word	Importance	Part of Speech	Word	Importance	Part of Speech
sunglasses	2	n	turban	4	n
crown	3	n	veil	4	n
bonnet	4	n	visor	4	n
goggles	4	n	beret	5	n
headdress	4	n	tiara	5	n
spectacles	4	n			

48. Types of Meals—related clusters: 51, 74, 86, 124, 136, 153, 162, 174, 176, 208, 222, 232, 246

Word	Importance	Part of Speech	Word	Importance	Part of Speech
breakfast	2	n	**dessert**	3	n
dinner	2	n	banquet	4	n
lunch	2	n	buffet	4	n
meal	2	n	chow	4	n
picnic	2	n	feast	4	n
supper	2	n	refreshment	4	n
treat	2	n			

49. Location (General)—related clusters: 9, 17, 20, 21, 22, 23, 25, 26, 37, 390, 430

Word	Importance	Part of Speech	Word	Importance	Part of Speech
address	2	n	altitude	4	n
direction	2	n	axis	4	n
place	2	n	destination	4	n
point	2	n	distance	4	n
position	2	n	niche	4	n
spot	2	n	whereabouts	4	n
location	3	n			

50. Bodies in Space—related clusters: 114, 139, 168, 267, 362, 363, 398

Word	Importance	Part of Speech	Word	Importance	Part of Speech
moon	2	n	**sun**	2	n
sky	2	n	**universe**	2	n
star	2	n	**world**	2	n

Word	Importance	Part of Speech	Word	Importance	Part of Speech
meteor	3	n	Mars	4	n
planet	3	n	Mercury	4	n
space	3	n	Neptune	4	n
asteroid	4	n	Pluto	4	n
celestial	4	adj	satellite	4	n
comet	4	n	Saturn	4	n
constellation	4	n	solar	4	adj
eclipse	4	n	stratosphere	4	n
galaxy	4	n	Uranus	4	n
globe	4	n	Venus	4	n
Jupiter	4	n	cosmos	5	n
lunar	4	adj	stellar	5	adj

51. Eating and Drinking—related clusters: 48, 74, 86, 124, 136, 153, 162, 174, 176, 208, 222, 232, 246

Word	Importance	Part of Speech	Word	Importance	Part of Speech
bite	2	v	dine	4	v
drink	2	v	gargle	4	v
eat	2	v	gnaw	4	v
feed	2	v	gorge	4	v
sip	2	v	guzzle	4	v
swallow	2	v	munch	4	v
chew	3	v	nibble	4	v
devour	4	v	consume	5	v

52. Periods of Time—related clusters: 2, 16, 24, 29, 59, 79, 83, 126, 144, 233

Word	Importance	Part of Speech	Word	Importance	Part of Speech
age	2	n	**year**	2	n
fall	2	n	**century**	3	n
month	2	n	**decade**	3	n
season	2	n	**generation**	3	n
summer	2	n	**spring**	3	n
week	2	n	**weekday**	3	n
weekend	2	n	autumn	4	n
winter	2	n	cycle	4	n

(Continued)

Word	Importance	Part of Speech	Word	Importance	Part of Speech
millennium	4	n	duration	5	n
period	4	n	interval	5	n
semester	4	n	perennial	5	adj
term	4	n	yule	5	n

53. Poems and Songs—related clusters: 71, 112, 138, 248, 256, 279, 319, 320

Word	Importance	Part of Speech	Word	Importance	Part of Speech
lullaby	2	n	staff	4	n
music	2	n	stanza	4	n
poem	2	n	suite	4	n
rhyme	2	n	ditty	5	n
song	2	n	limerick	5	n
hymn	3	n	measure	5	n
anthem	4	n	meter	5	n
ballad	4	n	psalm	5	n
carol	4	n	refrain	5	n
lyric	4	n	serenade	5	n
score	4	n			

54. Music and Dance—related clusters: 77, 239, 244

Word	Importance	Part of Speech	Word	Importance	Part of Speech
dance	2	n	polka	4	n
music	2	n	rhythm	4	n
ballet	3	n	round	4	n
melody	3	n	scale	4	n
orchestra	3	n	treble	4	n
solo	3	n	tune	4	n
accent	4	n	waltz	4	n
concert	4	n	conduct	5	v
duet	4	n	interval	5	n
flat	4	n	jazz	5	n
jig	4	n	meter	5	n
minuet	4	n	octave	5	n
musical	4	n	pantomime	5	n
opera	4	n	presto	5	n

Word	Importance	Part of Speech	Word	Importance	Part of Speech
range	5	n	swing	5	n
register	5	n	symphony	5	n
rest	5	n	unison	5	n
stave	5	n			

55. Caring and Trusting—related clusters: 43, 45, 291, 292, 293, 311, 312, 313, 378, 379, 380, 381, 416, 417, 422, 427, 428

Word	Importance	Part of Speech	Word	Importance	Part of Speech
believe	2	v	fond	4	adj
care	2	n	gratitude	4	n
enjoy	2	v	pardon	4	v
like	2	v	prefer	4	v
love	2	v	privilege	4	n
forgive	3	v	regard	4	v
want	3	v	regret	4	v
admiration	4	n	rely	4	v
admire	4	v	respect	4	v
adore	4	v	support	4	v
affection	4	n	value	4	v
appreciate	4	v	entrust	5	v
approve	4	v	mania	5	n
depend	4	v	romance	5	n
favor	4	v	vouch	5	v

56. People (General Names)—related clusters: 94, 111, 203, 204, 205, 206, 227, 317, 330, 343, 344, 382, 432, 444

Word	Importance	Part of Speech	Word	Importance	Part of Speech
human	2	n	chap	4	n
individual	2	n	character	4	n
people	2	n	folk	4	n
person	2	n	heroine	4	n
hero	3	n	highness	4	n
self	3	n	majesty	4	n
being	4	n	mankind	4	n

57. Color—related clusters: 415

Word	Importance	Part of Speech	Word	Importance	Part of Speech
black	2	n	maroon	4	n
blue	2	n	pigment	4	n
brown	2	n	scarlet	4	n
color	2	n	tan	4	n
gold	2	n	tangerine	4	n
gray	2	n	taupe	4	n
green	2	n	vermilion	4	n
orange	2	n	violet	4	n
pink	2	n	amber	5	n
purple	2	n	azure	5	n
red	2	n	chromatic	5	adj
white	2	n	crimson	5	n
yellow	2	n	dapple	5	n
blonde	3	n	ecru	5	n
colorful	3	adj	indigo	5	n
silver	3	n	iridescent	5	adj
beige	4	n	livid	5	adj
brunette	4	n	magenta	5	n
buff	4	n	mauve	5	n
colorless	4	adj	russet	5	n
hazel	4	n	tawny	5	n
hue	4	n	towhead	5	n
lavender	4	n			

58. Importance and Value—related clusters: 72, 243, 368

Word	Importance	Part of Speech	Word	Importance	Part of Speech
best	2	adj	**useful**	3	adj
better	2	adj	absolute	4	adj
dear	2	adj	adequate	4	adj
fine	2	adj	base	4	n
good	2	adj	basic	4	adj
important	2	adj	dandy	4	adj
perfect	2	adj	desirable	4	adj
outstanding	3	adj	elementary	4	adj
super	3	adj	essence	4	n

Word	Importance	Part of Speech	Word	Importance	Part of Speech
essential	4	adj	superb	4	adj
excellent	4	adj	superior	4	adj
fabulous	4	adj	supreme	4	adj
fantastic	4	adj	terrific	4	adj
impressive	4	adj	tremendous	4	adj
magnificent	4	adj	urgent	4	adj
main	4	adj	usable	4	adj
major	4	adj	valuable	4	adj
marvelous	4	adj	value	4	n
memorable	4	adj	vital	4	adj
miraculous	4	adj	wonderful	4	adj
necessary	4	adj	worth	4	n
positive	4	adj	worthwhile	4	adj
practical	4	adj	acute	5	adj
precious	4	adj	crucial	5	adj
primary	4	adj	crux	5	n
prime	4	adj	delightful	5	adj
regal	4	adj	fundamental	5	adj
remarkable	4	adj	invaluable	5	adj
spectacular	4	adj	noteworthy	5	adj
splendid	4	adj	sublime	5	adj
sufficient	4	adj			

59. Speed—related clusters: 2, 16, 24, 29, 52, 79, 83, 126, 144, 233

Word	Importance	Part of Speech	Word	Importance	Part of Speech
fast	2	adj	automatic	4	adj
hurry	2	v	automatically	4	adv
quick	2	adj	brief	4	adj
race	2	n	brisk	4	adj
rush	2	v	bustle	4	v
slow	2	adj	charge	4	v
speed	2	n	decelerate	4	v
sudden	2	adj	fuss	4	n
dash	3	v	gradual	4	adj
slowdown	3	n	haste	4	n
abrupt	4	adj	immediate	4	adj

(Continued)

Word	Importance	Part of Speech	Word	Importance	Part of Speech
instant	4	adj	flurry	5	n
jiffy	4	n	frenzy	5	n
pace	4	n	headlong	5	adv
rapid	4	adj	helter-skelter	5	adv
scoot	4	v	hustle	5	v
speedy	4	adj	offhand	5	adv
spontaneous	4	adj	presto	5	adv
swift	4	adj	prompt	5	adj
tempo	4	n	scurry	5	v
accelerate	5	v	velocity	5	n
fleet	5	adj	whisk	5	v

60. Places Related to Learning/Experimentation—related clusters: 106, 121, 190, 210, 321, 324, 335, 364, 365, 366, 399, 400

Word	Importance	Part of Speech	Word	Importance	Part of Speech
kindergarten	2	n	lab	4	n
library	2	n	laboratory	4	n
museum	2	n	planetarium	4	n
school	2	n	schoolhouse	4	n
classroom	3	n	university	4	n
schoolroom	3	n	academy	5	n
campus	4	n	gallery	5	n
college	4	n	seminary	5	n

61. Communication (Presentation of Information)—related clusters: 14, 100, 105, 177, 198, 207, 255, 345, 346, 383

Word	Importance	Part of Speech	Word	Importance	Part of Speech
describe	2	v	**mention**	3	v
explain	2	v	**recite**	3	v
present	2	v	advertise	4	v
say	2	v	announce	4	v
state	2	v	boast	4	v
tell	2	v	claim	4	v
brag	3	v	declare	4	v
inform	3	v	demonstrate	4	v

Word	Importance	Part of Speech	Word	Importance	Part of Speech
detail	4	n	clarify	5	v
exclaim	4	v	convey	5	v
exhibit	4	v	indicate	5	v
express	4	v	specify	5	v
media	4	n	stress	5	v
notify	4	v	telecast	5	n
preach	4	v	telegraph	5	n
pronounce	4	v	testify	5	v
refer	4	v	transmit	5	v
acquaint	5	v	utter	5	v
allude	5	v	vouch	5	v
broadcast	5	v			

62. Things Worn on the Hands/Feet—related clusters: 47, 125, 129, 145, 178, 212, 224, 263, 354, 435

Word	Importance	Part of Speech	Word	Importance	Part of Speech
boot	2	n	stocking	2	n
glove	2	n	sandal	3	n
mittens	2	n	slipper	3	n
shoe	2	n	mitt	4	n
skate	2	n	moccasin	4	n
sock	2	n	garter	5	n

63. Walking/Running—related clusters: 308, 339, 408, 409

Word	Importance	Part of Speech	Word	Importance	Part of Speech
dance	2	v	tiptoe	3	v
march	2	v	trot	3	v
run	2	v	hobble	4	v
skip	2	v	jog	4	v
step	2	v	lope	4	v
trip	2	v	pace	4	v
walk	2	v	plod	4	v
hike	3	v	romp	4	v
limp	3	v	saunter	4	v
stumble	3	v	scamper	4	v

(Continued)

Word	Importance	Part of Speech	Word	Importance	Part of Speech
scramble	4	v	waddle	4	v
shuffle	4	v	amble	5	v
stagger	4	v	gait	5	n
stride	4	v	prance	5	v
stroll	4	v	promenade	5	v
strut	4	v	ramble	5	v
swagger	4	v	toddle	5	v
trudge	4	v	tread	5	v

64. Cats/Dogs—related clusters: 32, 35, 65, 70, 82, 95, 117, 155, 188, 189, 194, 309, 310, 341

Word	Importance	Part of Speech	Word	Importance	Part of Speech
cat	2	n	hound	4	n
dog	2	n	leopard	4	n
doggie	2	n	mutt	4	n
fox	2	n	panther	4	n
lion	2	n	poodle	4	n
tiger	2	n	pug	4	n
wolf	2	n	puma	4	n
bulldog	3	n	spaniel	4	n
collie	3	n	terrier	4	n
beagle	4	n	watchdog	4	n
bloodhound	4	n	wildcat	4	n
canine	4	n	bobcat	5	n
cougar	4	n	hyena	5	n
coyote	4	n	jackal	5	n
dingo	4	n	Labrador	5	n
greyhound	4	n	puss	5	n

65. Land Animals (General)—related clusters: 32, 35, 64, 70, 82, 95, 117, 155, 188, 189, 194, 309, 310, 341

Word	Importance	Part of Speech	Word	Importance	Part of Speech
bear	2	n	**elephant**	2	n
cow	2	n	**giraffe**	2	n
deer	2	n	**horse**	2	n
donkey	2	n	**lamb**	2	n

Word	Importance	Part of Speech	Word	Importance	Part of Speech
pig	2	n	hedgehog	4	n
pony	2	n	hippopotamus	4	n
rabbit	2	n	hog	4	n
sheep	2	n	jackass	4	n
bat	3	n	llama	4	n
bull	3	n	mare	4	n
kangaroo	3	n	mink	4	n
moose	3	n	mole	4	n
raccoon	3	n	mule	4	n
reindeer	3	n	mustang	4	n
skunk	3	n	opossum	4	n
zebra	3	n	ox	4	n
anteater	4	n	pinto	4	n
antelope	4	n	platypus	4	n
ass	4	n	rhinoceros	4	n
badger	4	n	sow	4	n
bronco	4	n	stag	4	n
buffalo	4	n	stallion	4	n
burro	4	n	steer	4	n
camel	4	n	stud	4	n
caribou	4	n	weasel	4	n
cattle	4	n	yak	4	n
cottontail	4	n	bison	5	n
doe	4	n	polecat	5	n
elk	4	n	ram	5	n
ferret	4	n	steed	5	n
gazelle	4	n	wombat	5	n
hare	4	n			

66. Coming/Going (General)—related clusters: 38, 39, 40, 44, 141, 147, 169, 170, 182, 199, 215, 216, 247, 280, 281, 282, 283, 300, 301, 302, 322, 338, 403

Word	Importance	Part of Speech	Word	Importance	Part of Speech
go	1	v	**wander**	2	v
come	2	v	**appear**	3	v
leave	2	v	**approach**	3	v
travel	2	v	**arrive**	3	v
visit	2	v	**depart**	3	v

(Continued)

Word	Importance	Part of Speech	Word	Importance	Part of Speech
disappear	3	v	migration	4	n
exit	3	v	oncoming	4	adj
journey	3	v	roam	4	v
proceed	3	v	sightseeing	4	n
access	4	v	stray	4	v
advance	4	v	tour	4	v
adventure	4	n	vanish	4	v
departure	4	n	voyage	4	n
dissolve	4	v	withdraw	4	v
expedition	4	n	headway	5	n
hitchhike	4	v	progress	5	n
migrate	4	v	retreat	5	v

67. Memory/Thought (General)—related clusters: 46, 132, 137, 154, 225, 249, 277, 347, 348, 349, 384

Word	Importance	Part of Speech	Word	Importance	Part of Speech
forget	2	v	memorize	4	v
idea	2	n	recall	4	v
remember	2	v	reflection	4	n
think	2	v	amnesia	5	n
thought	2	n	concept	5	n
wonder	2	v	conscience	5	n
imagine	3	v	contemplate	5	v
memory	3	n	ponder	5	v
concentrate	4	v	reckon	5	v
consider	4	v	recollect	5	v
imagination	4	n	visualize	5	v
meditate	4	v			

68. Students and Teachers—related clusters: 88, 146, 167, 173, 229, 236, 257, 264, 265, 266, 297, 333, 334, 355, 356, 357, 358, 359, 360, 361, 392, 393, 394, 395, 396, 397, 436

Word	Importance	Part of Speech	Word	Importance	Part of Speech
principal	2	n	**pupil**	3	n
student	2	n	**schoolteacher**	3	n
teacher	2	n	adviser	4	n
graduate	3	n	bookworm	4	n

Word	Importance	Part of Speech	Word	Importance	Part of Speech
counselor	4	n	tutor	4	n
freshman	4	n	dean	5	n
instructor	4	n	mentor	5	n
professor	4	n	sophomore	5	n

69. Emptiness and Fullness—related clusters: 99, 142, 193, 218, 270, 303, 326

Word	Importance	Part of Speech	Word	Importance	Part of Speech
empty	2	n	stuff	4	v
fill	2	v	swollen	4	adj
full	2	adj	vacant	4	adj
hollow	3	adj	void	4	adj
deflate	4	v	deplete	5	v
exhaust	4	v	fraught	5	adj
null	4	adj			

70. Sea Animals—related clusters: 32, 35, 64, 65, 82, 95, 117, 155, 188, 189, 194, 309, 310, 341

Word	Importance	Part of Speech	Word	Importance	Part of Speech
fish	2	n	guppy	4	n
seal	2	n	herring	4	n
whale	2	n	minnow	4	n
salmon	3	n	porpoise	4	n
shark	3	n	sardine	4	n
tuna	3	n	smelt	4	n
bass	4	n	snapper	4	n
carp	4	n	swordfish	4	n
catfish	4	n	trout	4	n
cod	4	n	walrus	4	n
dolphin	4	n	hammerhead	5	n
flounder	4	n			

71. Writing, Drawing, and Reading—related clusters: 53, 112, 138, 248, 256, 279, 319, 320

Word	Importance	Part of Speech	Word	Importance	Part of Speech
color	2	v	**paint**	2	v
copy	2	v	**print**	2	v
draw	2	v	**read**	2	v

(Continued)

Word	Importance	Part of Speech	Word	Importance	Part of Speech
scribble	2	v	indent	4	v
sign	2	v	penmanship	4	n
spell	2	v	proofread	4	v
write	2	v	punctuate	4	v
handwriting	3	n	rewrite	4	v
misspell	3	v	scan	4	v
publish	3	v	scrawl	4	v
skim	3	v	shorthand	4	n
trace	3	v	sketch	4	v
underline	3	v	watercolor	4	n
abbreviate	4	v	calligraphy	5	n
browse	4	v	etch	5	v
doodle	4	v	jot	5	v
draft	4	v	legible	5	adj
illustrate	4	v	stencil	5	v

72. Right and Wrong—related clusters: 58, 243, 368

Word	Importance	Part of Speech	Word	Importance	Part of Speech
correct	2	adj	candid	4	adj
just	2	adj	crime	4	n
real	2	adj	decent	4	adj
right	2	adj	flaw	4	n
true	2	adj	genuine	4	adj
truth	2	n	honesty	4	n
wrong	2	adj	honorable	4	adj
error	3	n	illegal	4	adj
fair	3	adj	incorrect	4	adj
false	3	adj	innocent	4	adj
fault	3	adj	justice	4	n
honest	3	adj	lapse	4	adj
mistake	3	n	legal	4	adj
acceptable	4	adj	precise	4	adj
accurate	4	adj	proper	4	adj
actual	4	adj	realistic	4	adj
appropriate	4	adj	relevant	4	adj
blunder	4	n	satisfactory	4	adj

Word	Importance	Part of Speech	Word	Importance	Part of Speech
suitable	4	adj	moral	5	adj
apt	5	adj	sin	5	n
authentic	5	adj	valid	5	adj
eligible	5	adj	wholesome	5	adj

73. Units of Measurement—related clusters: 13, 15, 18, 19, 28, 33, 130, 327, 373, 374

Word	Importance	Part of Speech	Word	Importance	Part of Speech
foot	2	n	gram	4	n
gallon	2	n	handful	4	n
grade	2	n	liter	4	n
inch	2	n	meter	4	n
mile	2	n	metric	4	adj
pound	2	n	ounce	4	n
quart	2	n	pinch	4	n
yard	2	n	pint	4	n
mouthful	3	n	teaspoonful	4	n
spoonful	3	n	ton	4	n
tablespoon	3	n	mil	5	n
bushel	4	n	volt	5	n
cupful	4	n	watt	5	n
degree	4	n			

74. Ingredients Used to Make Food—related clusters: 48, 51, 86, 124, 136, 153, 162, 174, 176, 208, 222, 232, 246

Word	Importance	Part of Speech	Word	Importance	Part of Speech
dough	2	n	**mustard**	3	n
flour	2	n	batter	4	n
gravy	2	n	cinnamon	4	n
mix	2	n	garlic	4	n
pepper	2	n	graham	4	n
salt	2	n	shortening	4	n
sauce	2	n	spice	4	n
sugar	2	n	starch	4	n
catsup (ketchup)	3	n	vinegar	4	n
mayonnaise	3	n	yeast	4	n

(Continued)

Word	Importance	Part of Speech	Word	Importance	Part of Speech
cloves	5	n	ingredient	5	n
ginger	5	n	nutmeg	5	n
herb	5	n	parsley	5	n

75. Limbs—related clusters: 76, 80, 115, 140, 157, 160, 191, 213, 336, 437

Word	Importance	Part of Speech	Word	Importance	Part of Speech
arm	2	n	armpit	4	n
elbow	2	n	forearm	4	n
finger	2	n	knuckle	4	n
hand	2	n	nails	4	n
thumb	2	n	palm	4	n
shoulders	3	n	biceps	5	n
wrist	3	n	cuticle	5	n

76. Legs and Feet—related clusters: 75, 80, 115, 140, 157, 160, 191, 213, 336, 437

Word	Importance	Part of Speech	Word	Importance	Part of Speech
feet	2	n	**heel**	3	n
foot	2	n	arch	4	n
knee	2	n	shin	4	n
leg	2	n	thigh	4	n
toe	2	n	crotch	5	n
ankle	3	n	shank	5	n

77. Movies and Plays—related clusters: 54, 239, 244

Word	Importance	Part of Speech	Word	Importance	Part of Speech
act	2	v	drama	4	n
cartoon	2	n	perform	4	v
film	2	n	plot	4	n
movie	2	n	preview	4	n
show	2	n	program	4	n
stage	2	n	rehearsal	4	n
comedy	3	n	scene	4	n
play	3	n	setting	4	n
background	4	n	skit	4	n

Word	Importance	Part of Speech	Word	Importance	Part of Speech
audition	5	n	matinee	5	n
cinema	5	n	scenery	5	n
climax	5	n	vaudeville	5	n

78. Temperature—related clusters: 220, 376, 414, 442

Word	Importance	Part of Speech	Word	Importance	Part of Speech
cold	2	adj	temperate	4	adj
heat	2	n	thermal	4	adj
hot	2	adj	warmth	4	n
temperature	2	n	Celsius	5	adj
warm	2	adj	Centigrade	5	adj
chill	3	n	Fahrenheit	5	adj
cool	3	adj	frigid	5	adj
arctic	4	adj	lukewarm	5	adj

79. Parts of a Day—related clusters: 2, 16, 24, 29, 52, 59, 83, 126, 144, 233

Word	Importance	Part of Speech	Word	Importance	Part of Speech
day	2	n	**sunrise**	3	n
evening	2	n	**sunset**	3	n
hour	2	n	dawn	4	n
minute	2	n	daybreak	4	n
morning	2	n	dusk	4	n
night	2	n	instant	4	adj
noon	2	n	midday	4	n
second	2	n	moment	4	n
tonight	2	adv	nightfall	4	n
afternoon	3	n	noonday	4	n
midnight	3	n	noontime	4	n
overnight	3	adv	workday	4	n
sundown	3	n	twilight	5	n

80. Throat and Mouth—related clusters: 75, 76, 115, 140, 157, 160, 191, 213, 336, 437

Word	Importance	Part of Speech	Word	Importance	Part of Speech
mouth	2	n	**tooth**	2	n
teeth	2	n	**voice**	2	n
throat	2	n	**gum**	3	n

(Continued)

Word	Importance	Part of Speech	Word	Importance	Part of Speech
jaw	3	n	windpipe	4	n
lip	3	n	bicuspid	5	n
tongue	3	n	molar	5	n
fang	4	n	oral	5	adj

81. Contractions (Is)—related clusters: 42, 85, 150, 235, 274

Word	Importance	Part of Speech	Word	Importance	Part of Speech
he's	2	cont	**there's**	2	cont
I'm	2	cont	**here's**	3	cont
it's	2	cont	**what's**	3	cont
she's	2	cont	**where's**	3	cont
that's	2	cont	how's	4	cont

82. Reptiles/Mythical Animals—related clusters: 32, 35, 64, 65, 70, 95, 117, 155, 188, 189, 194, 309, 310, 341

Word	Importance	Part of Speech	Word	Importance	Part of Speech
alligator	2	n	cobra	4	n
dragon	2	n	crocodile	4	n
frog	2	n	lizard	4	n
snake	2	n	rattlesnake	4	n
toad	2	n	reptile	4	n
turtle	2	n	tortoise	4	n
dinosaur	3	n	unicorn	4	n
mermaid	3	n	nymph	5	n
monster	3	n	serpent	5	n

83. Time (Relative)—related clusters: 2, 16, 24, 29, 52, 59, 79, 126, 144, 233

Word	Importance	Part of Speech	Word	Importance	Part of Speech
old	2	adj	**yesterday**	2	n
past	2	n	**ancient**	3	adj
present	2	n	**future**	3	n
today	2	n	**history**	3	n
tomorrow	2	n	**someday**	3	n

Word	Importance	Part of Speech	Word	Importance	Part of Speech
antique	4	adj	puberty	4	n
childhood	4	n	youth	4	n
eternity	4	n	heirloom	5	n
historic	4	adj	medieval	5	adj
primitive	4	adj	relic	5	n

84. Sound Producing Devices—related clusters: 103, 156, 165, 175

Word	Importance	Part of Speech	Word	Importance	Part of Speech
alarm	2	n	chime	4	n
bell	2	n	earphone	4	n
horn	2	n	gong	4	n
phone	2	n	loudspeaker	4	n
doorbell	3	n	sonar	4	n
siren	3	n	firebox	5	n
telephone	3	n			

85. Contractions (Will)—related clusters: 42, 81, 150, 235, 274

Word	Importance	Part of Speech	Word	Importance	Part of Speech
he'll	2	cont	**we'll**	3	cont
I'll	2	cont	**you'll**	3	cont
she'll	2	cont	there'll	4	cont
they'll	2	cont	what'll	4	cont

86. Dairy Products—related clusters: 48, 51, 74, 124, 136, 153, 162, 174, 176, 208, 222, 232, 246

Word	Importance	Part of Speech	Word	Importance	Part of Speech
butter	2	n	**cream**	3	n
cheese	2	n	**margarine**	3	n
egg	2	n	curd	5	n
yolk	2	n			

87. Locations Near Water—related clusters: 101, 102, 127, 296, 352, 353, 391, 424

Word	Importance	Part of Speech	Word	Importance	Part of Speech
beach	2	n	seashore	4	n
island	2	n	waterfront	4	n
coast	3	n	isthmus	5	n
shore	3	n	lakeside	5	n
mainland	4	n	riverside	5	n
peninsula	4	n	shoreline	5	n
pier	4	n	strand	5	n
riverbank	4	n			

88. Medical Occupations—related clusters: 68, 146, 167, 173, 229, 236, 257, 264, 265, 266, 297, 333, 334, 355, 356, 357, 358, 359, 360, 361, 392, 393, 394, 395, 396, 397, 436

Word	Importance	Part of Speech	Word	Importance	Part of Speech
dentist	2	n	physician	4	n
nurse	2	n	surgeon	4	n
doctor	3	n	intern	5	n
dentistry	4	n	therapist	5	n

89. Losing/Winning—related clusters: 41, 148, 171, 184, 426

Word	Importance	Part of Speech	Word	Importance	Part of Speech
loss	2	n	excel	4	v
winner	2	n	overcome	4	v
champion	3	n	overthrow	4	v
defeat	3	v	success	4	n
win	3	v	triumph	4	v
accomplishment	4	n	overrun	5	v
conquer	4	v	overtake	5	v
conquest	4	n	prevail	5	v
dominant	4	adj	subdue	5	v
dominate	4	v	triumphant	5	adj
downfall	4	n	victor	5	n

90. Nature and Weather (General)—related clusters: 226, 307, 375, 406

Word	Importance	Part of Speech	Word	Importance	Part of Speech
air	2	n	atmosphere	4	n
weather	2	n	climate	4	n
nature	3	n	environment	4	n

91. Rooms—related clusters: 113, 123, 134, 217, 284

Word	Importance	Part of Speech	Word	Importance	Part of Speech
basement	2	n	balcony	4	n
bathroom	2	n	ballroom	4	n
cellar	2	n	chamber	4	n
closet	2	n	cloakroom	4	n
garage	2	n	corridor	4	n
hall	2	n	den	4	n
kitchen	2	n	entrance	4	n
nursery	2	n	lobby	4	n
room	2	n	loft	4	n
bedroom	3	n	pantry	4	n
doorway	3	n	parlor	4	n
hallway	3	n	stateroom	4	n
playroom	3	n	veranda	4	n
porch	3	n	washroom	4	n
aisle	4	n	threshold	5	n
attic	4	n			

92. Fasteners—related clusters: 96, 118, 119, 163, 242, 254, 275, 276, 314, 315, 316, 419, 420

Word	Importance	Part of Speech	Word	Importance	Part of Speech
chain	2	n	**string**	2	n
glue	2	n	**cable**	3	n
key	2	n	**knot**	3	n
lock	2	n	**screw**	3	n
nail	2	n	**shoelace**	3	n
needle	2	n	**strap**	3	n
pin	2	n	bolt	4	n
rope	2	n	chord	4	n

(Continued)

Word	Importance	Part of Speech	Word	Importance	Part of Speech
clamp	4	n	slot	4	n
clothespin	4	n	spike	4	n
cord	4	n	staple	4	n
handcuff	4	n	tack	4	n
hinge	4	n	tether	4	n
keyhole	4	n	thong	4	n
lasso	4	n	thumbtack	4	n
latch	4	n	twine	4	n
padlock	4	n	lariat	5	n
peg	4	n	rivet	5	n
shoestring	4	n			

93. Things You Travel On—related clusters: 97, 120, 128, 159, 234, 318, 331

Word	Importance	Part of Speech	Word	Importance	Part of Speech
alley	2	n	drawbridge	4	n
bridge	2	n	intersection	4	n
driveway	2	n	lane	4	n
highway	2	n	pass	4	n
path	2	n	passage	4	n
railroad	2	n	passageway	4	n
road	2	n	pathway	4	n
sidewalk	2	n	rail	4	n
street	2	n	railway	4	n
track	2	n	runway	4	n
trail	2	n	waterway	4	n
avenue	3	n	way	4	n
freeway	3	n	airway	5	n
mall	3	n	blacktop	5	n
racetrack	3	n	boulevard	5	n
ramp	3	n	bypass	5	n
route	3	n	byway	5	n
tunnel	3	n	causeway	5	n
airfield	4	n	crossroad	5	n
airstrip	4	n	parkway	5	n
chute	4	n	seaway	5	n
course	4	n	span	5	n
detour	4	n			

94. Family Relationships—related clusters: 56, 111, 203, 204, 205, 206, 227, 317, 330, 343, 344, 382, 432, 444

Word	Importance	Part of Speech	Word	Importance	Part of Speech
aunt	2	n	mammy	3	n
brother	2	n	nephew	3	n
dad	2	n	niece	3	n
family	2	n	sibling	3	n
father	2	n	wife	3	n
granny	2	n	ancestor	4	n
ma	2	n	bride	4	n
mama	2	n	groom	4	n
mom	2	n	heir	4	n
mother	2	n	household	4	n
papa	2	n	offspring	4	n
parent	2	n	spouse	4	n
sister	2	n	domo	5	n
son	2	n	guardian	5	n
uncle	2	n	maternal	5	n
cousin	3	n	patriarch	5	n
daughter	3	n	pedigree	5	n
grandparent	3	n	ward	5	n
husband	3	n			

95. Insects—related clusters: 32, 35, 64, 65, 70, 82, 117, 155, 188, 189, 194, 309, 310, 341

Word	Importance	Part of Speech	Word	Importance	Part of Speech
ant	2	n	flea	3	n
bee	2	n	grasshopper	3	n
bug	2	n	mosquito	3	n
butterfly	2	n	moth	3	n
caterpillar	2	n	slug	3	n
fly	2	n	wasp	3	n
insect	2	n	beetle	4	n
ladybug	2	n	centipede	4	n
spider	2	n	cricket	4	n
worm	2	n	dragonfly	4	n
bumblebee	3	n	hornet	4	n
cockroach	3	n	housefly	4	n

(Continued)

Word	Importance	Part of Speech	Word	Importance	Part of Speech
larva	4	n	drone	5	n
millipede	4	n	firefly	5	n
mite	4	n	gnat	5	n
parasite	4	n	katydid	5	n
silkworm	4	n	leech	5	n
termite	4	n	lice	5	n
yellow jacket	4	n	mantis	5	n
arachnid	5	n	pupa	5	n

96. Cooking and Eating Utensils—related clusters: 92, 118, 119, 163, 242, 254, 275, 276, 314, 315, 316, 419, 420

Word	Importance	Part of Speech	Word	Importance	Part of Speech
bowl	2	n	crock	4	n
cup	2	n	kettle	4	n
dish	2	n	ladle	4	n
fork	2	n	platter	4	n
glass	2	n	saucer	4	n
knife	2	n	scoop	4	n
pan	2	n	sieve	4	n
plate	2	n	silverware	4	n
pot	2	n	skillet	4	n
spoon	2	n	spatula	4	n
chopsticks	3	n	teacup	4	n
mug	3	n	teapot	4	n
opener	3	n	tongs	4	n
tablespoon	3	n	chinaware	5	n
teaspoon	3	n	goblet	5	n
tray	3	n	stein	5	n
casserole	4	n			

97. Vehicles (Actions/Characteristics)—related clusters: 93, 120, 128, 159, 234, 318, 331

Word	Importance	Part of Speech	Word	Importance	Part of Speech
drive	2	v	**sail**	2	v
passenger	2	n	**cruise**	3	v
ride	2	v	**glide**	3	v
row	2	v	aviation	4	n

Word	Importance	Part of Speech	Word	Importance	Part of Speech
horsepower	4	n	navigate	4	v
launch	4	v	transport	4	v
marine	4	adj	aerial	5	adj
naval	4	adj	airborne	5	adj

98. General Names for Groups—related clusters: 200, 258, 298, 401

Word	Importance	Part of Speech	Word	Importance	Part of Speech
gather	2	v	directory	4	n
group	2	n	file	4	n
pile	2	n	heap	4	v
sequence	2	n	invoice	4	n
bunch	3	n	kit	4	n
classify	3	v	medley	4	n
collect	3	v	menu	4	n
list	3	v	mixture	4	n
organize	3	v	network	4	n
stack	3	v	roster	4	n
arrange	4	v	schedule	4	n
array	4	n	series	4	n
assemble	4	v	stock	4	n
assortment	4	n	summarize	4	v
bale	4	n	table	4	n
batch	4	n	wad	4	n
blend	4	v	web	4	n
bundle	4	n	aggregate	5	n
chronology	4	n	alloy	5	n
clump	4	n	hybrid	5	n
cluster	4	n	muster	5	n
collection	4	n	sheaf	5	n
compound	4	n	spectrum	5	n
curriculum	4	n	swath	5	n

99. Dimensionality—related clusters: 69, 142, 193, 218, 270, 303, 326

Word	Importance	Part of Speech	Word	Importance	Part of Speech
deep	2	adj	**length**	2	n
height	2	n	**long**	2	adj
high	2	adj	**short**	2	adj

(Continued)

Word	Importance	Part of Speech	Word	Importance	Part of Speech
size	2	n	dense	4	adj
tall	2	adj	dimension	4	n
thin	2	adj	extend	4	v
wide	2	adj	layer	4	n
depth	3	n	measurement	4	n
narrow	3	adj	scale	4	n
shallow	3	adj	thickness	4	n
thick	3	adj	trim	4	v
width	3	n	stature	5	n
broad	4	adj	tier	5	n
deepen	4	v			

100. Communication (Positive Information)—related clusters: 14, 61, 105, 177, 198, 207, 255, 345, 346, 383

Word	Importance	Part of Speech	Word	Importance	Part of Speech
agree	2	v	charm	4	v
bless	2	v	congratulate	4	v
greet	2	v	congratulations	4	n
pray	2	v	flatter	4	v
thank	2	v	inspire	4	v
welcome	2	v	participate	4	v
compliment	3	v	prayer	4	n
cooperate	3	v	soothe	4	v
encourage	3	v	teamwork	4	n
praise	3	v	tribute	4	n
apology	4	n	worship	4	v
assure	4	v	acknowledge	5	v
awe	4	n	credit	5	v
blessing	4	n			

101. Forms of Water/Liquid—related clusters: 87, 102, 127, 296, 352, 353, 391, 424

Word	Importance	Part of Speech	Word	Importance	Part of Speech
ice	2	n	**water**	2	n
rain	2	n	**hail**	3	n
snow	2	n	**icicle**	3	n

Word	Importance	Part of Speech	Word	Importance	Part of Speech
liquid	3	n	iceberg	4	n
rainbow	3	n	mist	4	n
raindrop	3	n	moisture	4	n
rainfall	3	n	precipitation	4	n
snowball	3	n	sleet	4	n
snowman	3	n	slush	4	n
steam	3	n	snowdrift	4	n
drizzle	4	n	snowfall	4	n
fluid	4	n	vapor	4	n
frost	4	n	aqua	5	n
glacier	4	n	floe	5	n

102. Bodies of Water—related clusters: 87, 101, 127, 296, 352, 353, 391, 424

Word	Importance	Part of Speech	Word	Importance	Part of Speech
lake	2	n	rapids	4	n
ocean	2	n	strait	4	n
puddle	2	n	surf	4	n
river	2	n	swamp	4	n
sea	2	n	tide	4	n
stream	2	n	tributary	4	n
bay	3	n	waterfall	4	n
creek	3	n	waterline	4	n
pond	3	n	bog	5	n
brook	4	n	eddy	5	n
cove	4	n	estuary	5	n
current	4	n	fjord	5	n
delta	4	n	geyser	5	n
gulf	4	n	headwaters	5	n
inlet	4	n	lagoon	5	n
marsh	4	n	marshland	5	n
outlet	4	n	reef	5	n

103. Noises (General)—related clusters: 84, 156, 165, 175

Word	Importance	Part of Speech	Word	Importance	Part of Speech
hear	2	v	hush	4	n
listen	2	v	pitch	4	n
loud	2	adj	racket	4	n
noise	2	n	serene	4	adj
quiet	2	adj	shrill	4	adj
sound	2	n	stillness	4	n
aloud	3	adv	tone	4	n
calm	3	adj	audio	5	n
echo	3	n	blare	5	n
silence	3	n	crescendo	5	n
silent	3	adj	eavesdrop	5	n
clamor	4	n	harken (hearken)	5	v
clatter	4	n	intensity	5	n
commotion	4	n	lull	5	n
earshot	4	n	peal	5	n
harsh	4	adj	tranquil	5	n
hoarse	4	adj	trill	5	n

104. Money and Goods—related clusters: 109, 116, 122, 201, 214

Word	Importance	Part of Speech	Word	Importance	Part of Speech
cent	2	n	fund	4	n
coin	2	n	payroll	4	n
dollar	2	n	postage	4	n
money	2	n	receipt	4	n
penny	2	n	shilling	4	n
quarter	2	n	souvenir	4	n
cash	3	n	stock	4	n
check	3	n	wealth	4	n
dime	3	n	currency	5	n
nickel	3	n	finance	5	n
pound	3	n	guinea	5	n
ticket	3	n	merchandise	5	n
capital	4	n	token	5	n
coupon	4	n			

105. Communication (General)—related clusters: 14, 61, 100, 177, 198, 207, 255, 345, 346, 383

Word	Importance	Part of Speech	Word	Importance	Part of Speech
speak	2	v	powwow	4	v
speech	2	n	proposal	4	n
talk	2	v	remark	4	v
chat	3	v	sermon	4	n
discuss	3	v	talkative	4	adj
statement	3	n	testimony	4	n
brainstorm	4	v	blab	5	v
comment	4	v	converse	5	v
communicate	4	v	drawl	5	v
declaration	4	n	eloquent	5	adj
dialogue	4	n	fluent	5	adj
discussion	4	n	negotiate	5	v
jabber	4	v	proclamation	5	n
lecture	4	n	verbal	5	adj
lisp	4	n	vocal	5	adj

106. Places Related to Protection/Incarceration—related clusters: 60, 121, 190, 210, 321, 324, 335, 364, 365, 366, 399, 400

Word	Importance	Part of Speech	Word	Importance	Part of Speech
cage	2	n	garrison	4	n
cave	2	n	haven	4	n
shelter	2	n	outpost	4	n
fort	3	n	prison	4	n
jail	3	n	pueblo	4	n
blockhouse	4	n	stockade	4	n
cell	4	n	acropolis	5	n
dugout	4	n	bunker	5	n
dungeon	4	n	quarantine	5	n
firehouse	4	n	stronghold	5	n
fortress	4	n			

107. Building and Repairing—related clusters: 164, 181, 251, 268, 325, 367

Word	Importance	Part of Speech	Word	Importance	Part of Speech
find	2	v	form	4	v
fix	2	v	generate	4	v
make	2	v	glaze	4	v
build	3	v	install	4	v
develop	3	v	manufacture	4	v
prepare	3	v	modify	4	v
produce	3	v	mold	4	v
repair	3	v	orient	4	v
shape	3	v	pave	4	v
adjust	4	v	preserve	4	v
constitute	4	v	process	4	v
construct	4	v	qualify	4	v
construction	4	n	rebuild	4	v
create	4	v	restore	4	v
establish	4	v	rehabilitate	5	v
forge	4	v			

108. Trees/Bushes (Parts)—related clusters: 36, 192, 269, 421

Word	Importance	Part of Speech	Word	Importance	Part of Speech
branch	2	n	rubber	4	n
leaf	2	n	sap	4	n
twig	2	n	stem	4	n
bark	3	n	sticker	4	n
limb	3	n	thorn	4	n
stump	3	n	treetop	4	n
bough	4	n	wicker	4	n
knothole	4	n	foliage	5	n
latex	4	n	pith	5	n
resin	4	n			

109. Places Where Money/Goods Are Kept—related clusters: 104, 116, 122, 201, 214

Word	Importance	Part of Speech	Word	Importance	Part of Speech
bank	2	n	**wallet**	3	n
safe	2	n	account	4	n
purse	3	n	billfold	4	n

Word	Importance	Part of Speech	Word	Importance	Part of Speech
commerce	4	n	vault	4	n
handbag	4	n	mint	5	n
pocketbook	4	n	strongbox	5	n

110. Actions Helpful to Humans—related clusters: 161, 250, 260

Word	Importance	Part of Speech	Word	Importance	Part of Speech
believe	2	v	promote	4	v
help	2	v	recover	4	v
save	2	v	recycle	4	v
heal	3	v	relieve	4	v
improve	3	v	rescue	4	v
protect	3	v	revive	4	v
advantage	4	n	sake	4	n
aid	4	v	accommodate	5	v
assist	4	v	avail	5	v
benefit	4	n	behalf	5	n
cure	4	v	contribute	5	v
defend	4	v	escort	5	v
enrich	4	v	fend	5	v
foster	4	v	refresh	5	v
guide	4	v	stead	5	n
nourish	4	v			

111. Women—related clusters: 56, 94, 203, 204, 205, 206, 227, 317, 330, 343, 344, 382, 432, 444

Word	Importance	Part of Speech	Word	Importance	Part of Speech
girl	2	n	mistress	4	n
lady	2	n	spinster	4	n
woman	2	n	squaw	4	n
female	3	n	tomboy	4	n
housewife	3	n	widow	4	n
schoolgirl	3	n	belle	5	n
dame	4	n	madam	5	n
hostess	4	n	mademoiselle	5	n
lass	4	n			

112. Things to Write On/With—related clusters: 53, 71, 138, 248, 256, 279, 319, 320

Word	Importance	Part of Speech	Word	Importance	Part of Speech
brush	2	n	**notebook**	3	n
card	2	n	**paintbrush**	3	n
crayon	2	n	ballpoint	4	n
ink	2	n	pastel	4	n
page	2	n	press	4	n
paper	2	n	scrapbook	4	n
pen	2	n	tablet	4	n
pencil	2	n	typewriter	4	n
blackboard	3	n	parchment	5	n
chalk	3	n	ream	5	n
chalkboard	3	n	scroll	5	n
loose-leaf	3	adj			

113. Furniture—related clusters: 91, 123, 134, 217, 284

Word	Importance	Part of Speech	Word	Importance	Part of Speech
bed	2	n	bleacher	4	n
bench	2	n	bunk	4	n
chair	2	n	cabinet	4	n
crib	2	n	cot	4	n
desk	2	n	furniture	4	n
drawer	2	n	hutch	4	n
seat	2	n	mat	4	n
table	2	n	mattress	4	n
bookcase	3	n	nook	4	n
couch	3	n	pulpit	4	n
counter	3	n	tabletop	4	n
cradle	3	n	throne	4	n
cupboard	3	n	wheelchair	4	n
playpen	3	n	bureau	5	n
sofa	3	n	decor	5	n
stool	3	n	hammock	5	n
altar	4	n	pew	5	n
armchair	4	n			

114. Areas of Land—related clusters: 50, 139, 168, 267, 362, 363, 398

Word	Importance	Part of Speech	Word	Importance	Part of Speech
land	2	n	frontier	4	n
lot	2	n	plot	4	n
place	2	n	site	4	n
region	2	n	surface	4	n
area	3	n	terrain	4	n
location	3	n	tropics	4	n
territory	3	n	domain	5	n
zone	3	n	mantle	5	n
acre	4	n	outback	5	n
clearing	4	n	premises	5	n

115. Head and Face—related clusters: 75, 76, 80, 140, 157, 160, 191, 213, 336, 437

Word	Importance	Part of Speech	Word	Importance	Part of Speech
cheek	2	n	forehead	3	n
chin	2	n	mind	3	n
face	2	n	skull	4	n
head	2	n	countenance	5	n
brain	3	n	ego	5	n

116. Money-Related Characteristics—related clusters: 104, 109, 122, 201, 214

Word	Importance	Part of Speech	Word	Importance	Part of Speech
free	2	n	costly	4	adj
poor	2	adj	humble	4	adj
poverty	2	n	luxury	4	n
rich	2	adj	needy	4	adj
broke	3	n	posh	4	adj
cheap	3	adj	royal	4	adj
expensive	3	adj	wasteful	4	adj

117. Actions Related to Animals—related clusters: 32, 35, 64, 65, 70, 82, 95, 155, 188, 189, 194, 309, 310, 341

Word	Importance	Part of Speech	Word	Importance	Part of Speech
fish	2	v	trap	2	v
fly	2	v	buck	3	v
hunt	2	v	gallop	3	v

(Continued)

Word	Importance	Part of Speech	Word	Importance	Part of Speech
soar	3	v	horseback	4	adv
sting	3	v	snare	4	v
bareback	4	adj	stampede	4	v
graze	4	v	swarm	4	v

118. Appliances—related clusters: 92, 96, 119, 163, 242, 254, 275, 276, 314, 315, 316, 419, 420

Word	Importance	Part of Speech	Word	Importance	Part of Speech
oven	2	n	microwave	4	n
radio	2	n	phonograph	4	n
stove	2	n	radiator	4	n
television	2	n	stereo	4	n
furnace	3	n	griddle	5	n
heater	3	n	kiln	5	n
refrigerator	3	n	wireless	5	adj
icebox	4	n			

119. Tools (General)—related clusters: 92, 96, 118, 163, 242, 254, 275, 276, 314, 315, 316, 419, 420

Word	Importance	Part of Speech	Word	Importance	Part of Speech
hammer	2	n	jack	4	n
saw	2	n	jigsaw	4	n
shovel	2	n	lever	4	n
tool	2	n	pitchfork	4	n
drill	3	n	pliers	4	n
rake	3	n	resource	4	n
screwdriver	3	n	sandpaper	4	n
tweezers	3	n	wedge	4	n
chisel	4	n	wrench	4	n
crowbar	4	n	shim	5	n
device	4	n	sledge	5	n
hoe	4	n	spade	5	n
implement	4	n	utensil	5	n
instrument	4	n			

120. Vehicles (Air Transportation)—related clusters: 93, 97, 128, 159, 234, 318, 331

Word	Importance	Part of Speech	Word	Importance	Part of Speech
balloon	2	n	**airline**	3	n
helicopter	2	n	**airplane**	3	n
kite	2	n	**spacecraft**	3	n
plane	2	n	airliner	4	n
rocket	2	n	blimp	5	n
aircraft	3	n	jetliner	5	n

121. Places to Live—related clusters: 60, 106, 190, 210, 321, 324, 335, 364, 365, 366, 399, 400

Word	Importance	Part of Speech	Word	Importance	Part of Speech
castle	2	n	lodge	4	n
home	2	n	manor	4	n
hotel	2	n	mansion	4	n
house	2	n	suite	4	n
hut	2	n	teepee	4	n
apartment	3	n	wigwam	4	n
motel	3	n	barracks	5	n
palace	3	n	bungalow	5	n
tent	3	n	chalet	5	n
cabin	4	n	dormitory	5	n
cottage	4	n	estate	5	n
habitat	4	n	hovel	5	n
homestead	4	n	shanty	5	n
igloo	4	n	villa	5	n
inn	4	n			

122. Actions Related to Money/Goods—related clusters: 104, 109, 116, 201, 214

Word	Importance	Part of Speech	Word	Importance	Part of Speech
buy	2	v	**earn**	3	v
pay	2	v	**owe**	3	v
sale	2	n	**purchase**	3	v
sell	2	v	afford	4	v
spend	2	v	bargain	4	n
bet	3	v	budget	4	n

(Continued)

Word	Importance	Part of Speech	Word	Importance	Part of Speech
deal	4	n	auction	5	n
discount	4	n	insure	5	v
donate	4	v	peddle	5	v
invest	4	v	ransom	5	v
lease	4	v	redeem	5	v
market	4	n	render	5	v
repay	4	v	retail	5	v
scrimp	4	v	splurge	5	v
subscribe	4	v	wholesale	5	adj

123. Parts of a Home—related clusters: 91, 113, 134, 217, 284

Word	Importance	Part of Speech	Word	Importance	Part of Speech
door	2	n	sill	4	n
floor	2	n	smokestack	4	n
roof	2	n	spire	4	n
stairs	2	n	steeple	4	n
wall	2	n	vent	4	n
window	2	n	awning	5	n
ceiling	3	n	baseboard	5	n
chimney	3	n	dormer	5	n
doorstep	3	n	eaves	5	n
stair	3	n	flue	5	n
staircase	3	n	hearth	5	n
stairway	3	n	lattice	5	n
banister	4	n	stile	5	n
mantel	4	n	stovepipe	5	n
pane	4	n	wicket	5	n

124. Foods that Are Prepared—related clusters: 48, 51, 74, 86, 136, 153, 162, 174, 176, 208, 222, 232, 246

Word	Importance	Part of Speech	Word	Importance	Part of Speech
bread	2	n	**crust**	2	n
bun	2	n	**hamburger**	2	n
cereal	2	n	**hotdog**	2	n
chips	2	n	**jelly**	2	n
cracker	2	n	**pancake**	2	n

Word	Importance	Part of Speech	Word	Importance	Part of Speech
pizza	2	n	**omelet**	3	n
salad	2	n	**pretzel**	3	n
sandwich	2	n	**spaghetti**	3	n
snack	2	n	**taco**	3	n
toast	2	n	**tortilla**	3	n
biscuit	3	n	**waffle**	3	n
coleslaw	3	n	mush	4	n
loaf	3	n	porridge	4	n
macaroni	3	n	flapjack	5	n
muffin	3	n	gruel	5	n
noodle	3	n	lasagna	5	n
oatmeal	3	n	watercress	5	n

125. Pants, Shirts, and Skirts—related clusters: 47, 62, 129, 145, 178, 212, 224, 263, 354, 435

Word	Importance	Part of Speech	Word	Importance	Part of Speech
belt	2	n	**tights**	3	n
diaper	2	n	blouse	4	n
dress	2	n	gown	4	n
jeans	2	n	jersey	4	n
pajamas	2	n	overalls	4	n
pants	2	n	petticoat	4	n
pocket	2	n	pinafore	4	n
shirt	2	n	pullover	4	n
skirt	2	n	slacks	4	n
apron	3	n	trousers	4	n
bathrobe	3	n	vest	4	n
nightgown	3	n	cardigan	5	n
robe	3	n	dungarees	5	n
shorts	3	n	kimono	5	n
sweater	3	n			

126. Frequency and Duration—related clusters: 2, 16, 24, 29, 52, 59, 79, 83, 144, 233

Word	Importance	Part of Speech	Word	Importance	Part of Speech
long	1	adj	**once**	1	adv
never	1	adv	**sometimes**	2	adv
often	1	adv	**always**	3	adv

(Continued)

Word	Importance	Part of Speech	Word	Importance	Part of Speech
anymore	3	adv	continuous	4	adj
awhile	3	adv	customary	4	adj
daily	3	adv	general	4	adj
ever	3	adv	habitual	4	adj
forever	3	adv	infrequent	4	adj
frequent	3	adj	irregular	4	adj
hourly	3	adv	longtime	4	adj
rare	3	adj	momentary	4	adj
regular	3	adj	nightly	4	adv
repeat	3	adj	occasional	4	adj
seldom	3	adv	permanent	4	adj
twice	3	adv	rehearse	4	v
usual	3	adj	temporary	4	adj
weekly	3	adv	consecutive	5	adj
annual	4	adj	eternal	5	adj
common	4	adj	persist	5	v
constant	4	adj	sporadic	5	adj
continue	4	v			

127. Water/Liquid (Related Actions)—related clusters: 87, 101, 102, 296, 352, 353, 391, 424

Word	Importance	Part of Speech	Word	Importance	Part of Speech
boil	2	v	**flush**	3	v
dive	2	v	**freeze**	3	v
drain	2	v	**leak**	3	v
drip	2	v	**slick**	3	adj
float	2	v	**slippery**	3	adj
melt	2	v	**soak**	3	v
pour	2	v	**spray**	3	v
sink	2	v	**sprinkle**	3	v
spill	2	v	**squirt**	3	v
splash	2	v	**trickle**	3	v
stir	2	v	absorb	4	v
swim	2	v	damp	4	adj
wet	2	adj	defrost	4	v
bubble	3	v	dissolve	4	v
dribble	3	v	drench	4	v

Word	Importance	Part of Speech	Word	Importance	Part of Speech
drift	4	v	soggy	4	adj
drown	4	v	spatter	4	v
evaporate	4	v	splatter	4	v
flow	4	v	spurt	4	v
gush	4	v	submerge	4	v
humid	4	adj	thaw	4	v
moist	4	adj	wade	4	v
moisten	4	v	waterproof	4	adj
ooze	4	v	cascade	5	v
overflow	4	v	dilute	5	v
penetrate	4	v	douse	5	v
ripple	4	v	ebb	5	v
secrete	4	v	ford	5	v
seep	4	v	souse	5	v
slosh	4	v	surge	5	v
snorkel	4	v	waterlog	5	v

128. Transportation (Types)—related clusters: 93, 97, 120, 159, 234, 318, 331

Word	Importance	Part of Speech	Word	Importance	Part of Speech
bicycle	2	n	taxi	3	n
bike	2	n	taxicab	3	n
bus	2	n	trailer	3	n
car	2	n	auto	4	n
train	2	n	buggy	4	n
tricycle	2	n	caboose	4	n
truck	2	n	carriage	4	n
van	2	n	cart	4	n
wagon	2	n	chariot	4	n
ambulance	3	n	jeep	4	n
automobile	3	n	pickup	4	n
cab	3	n	streetcar	4	n
locomotive	3	n	unicycle	4	n
motorcycle	3	n	vehicle	4	n
scooter	3	n	jalopy	5	n
stagecoach	3	n	sedan	5	n
subway	3	n	trolley	5	n

129. Clothing-Related Actions—related clusters: 47, 62, 125, 145, 178, 212, 224, 263, 354, 435

Word	Importance	Part of Speech	Word	Importance	Part of Speech
fit	2	v	furl	4	v
fold	2	v	knit	4	v
sew	2	v	mend	4	v
tear	2	v	pucker	4	v
wear	2	v	stitch	4	v
braid	3	v	tatter	4	v
patch	3	v	weave	4	v
rip	3	v	alter	5	v
wrinkle	3	v	baste	5	v
zip	3	v	crochet	5	v
clad	4	v	don	5	v
clothe	4	v	ravel	5	v
crease	4	v	rumple	5	v
embroider	4	v			

130. Parts—related clusters: 13, 15, 18, 19, 28, 33, 73, 327, 373, 374

Word	Importance	Part of Speech	Word	Importance	Part of Speech
bit	2	n	element	4	n
dot	2	n	factor	4	n
flake	2	n	fragment	4	n
part	2	n	gob	4	n
piece	2	n	item	4	n
crumb	3	n	module	4	n
member	3	n	sample	4	n
portion	3	n	scrap	4	n
section	3	n	segment	4	n
slice	3	n	slab	4	n
sliver	3	n	species	4	n
splinter	3	n	speck	4	n
type	3	n	jot	5	n
category	4	n	morsel	5	n
chunk	4	n	particle	5	n
department	4	n	version	5	n

131. Grabbing and Holding—related clusters: 149, 197

Word	Importance	Part of Speech	Word	Importance	Part of Speech
catch	2	v	embrace	4	v
hold	2	v	grasp	4	v
hug	2	v	grip	4	v
pick	2	v	nab	4	v
clasp	3	v	nuzzle	4	v
cuddle	3	v	secure	4	v
grab	3	v	strum	4	v
pinch	3	v	wrap	4	v
snuggle	3	v	wring	4	v
squeeze	3	v	clinch	5	v
clench	4	v	nip	5	v
cling	4	v	pluck	5	v
clutch	4	v	vise	5	n

132. Consciousness/Unconsciousness—related clusters: 46, 67, 137, 154, 225, 249, 277, 347, 348, 349, 384

Word	Importance	Part of Speech	Word	Importance	Part of Speech
asleep	2	n	hallucination	4	n
awake	2	n	hibernate	4	v
nap	2	n	nightmare	4	n
sleep	2	v	slumber	4	v
daydream	3	v	snooze	4	v
dream	3	v	unconscious	4	adj
pretend	3	v	waken	4	v
wake	3	v	weary	4	adj
conscious	4	adj	conceive	5	v
daze	4	v	hypnosis	5	n
doze	4	v	rouse	5	v
drowsy	4	adj	stupor	5	n
fantasy	4	n	trance	5	n

133. Soil—related clusters: 237, 259, 337, 402, 438

Word	Importance	Part of Speech	Word	Importance	Part of Speech
ground	2	n	**soil**	2	n
land	2	n	**clay**	3	n
mud	2	n	**dirt**	3	n

(Continued)

Word	Importance	Part of Speech	Word	Importance	Part of Speech
dust	3	n	turf	4	n
earth	3	n	clod	5	n
humus	4	n	dung	5	n
manure	4	n	peat	5	n
sod	4	n			

134. Linens—related clusters: 91, 113, 123, 217, 284

Word	Importance	Part of Speech	Word	Importance	Part of Speech
blanket	2	n	**pillowcase**	3	n
cover	2	n	**sheet**	3	n
pillow	2	n	**tablecloth**	3	n
towel	2	n	drape	4	n
bedspread	3	n	pad	4	n
cushion	3	n	quilt	4	n
napkin	3	n	doily	5	n

135. Looking and Perceiving—related clusters: 195

Word	Importance	Part of Speech	Word	Importance	Part of Speech
look	2	v	gaze	4	v
see	2	v	glance	4	v
stare	2	v	glare	4	v
watch	2	v	glimpse	4	v
blink	3	v	identify	4	v
peek	3	v	ignore	4	v
spy	3	v	loom	4	v
wink	3	v	monitor	4	v
aim	4	v	notice	4	v
attend	4	v	observe	4	v
behold	4	v	peer	4	v
detect	4	v	perceive	4	v
distinguish	4	v	recognize	4	v
focus	4	v	scout	4	v
gape	4	v	sense	4	v

Word	Importance	Part of Speech	Word	Importance	Part of Speech
shun	4	v	verify	4	v
snoop	4	v	glower	5	v
snub	4	v	vigil	5	n
squint	4	v			

136. Meats—related clusters: 48, 51, 74, 86, 124, 153, 162, 174, 176, 208, 222, 232, 246

Word	Importance	Part of Speech	Word	Importance	Part of Speech
bacon	2	n	**pork**	3	n
beef	2	n	**steak**	3	n
ham	2	n	poultry	4	n
hotdog	2	n	lard	5	n
sausage	2	n	mutton	5	n
bologna	3	n	pemmican	5	n

137. Intelligence—related clusters: 46, 67, 132, 154, 225, 249, 277, 347, 348, 349, 384

Word	Importance	Part of Speech	Word	Importance	Part of Speech
able	2	adj	logical	4	adj
smart	2	adj	practical	4	adj
stupid	2	adj	proficient	4	adj
alert	3	adj	skillful	4	adj
brilliant	3	adj	wisdom	4	n
wise	3	adj	wit	4	n
aware	4	adj	adept	5	adj
capable	4	adj	crude	5	adj
clever	4	adj	deft	5	adj
competent	4	adj	imaginative	5	adj
creative	4	adj	naïve	5	adj
curious	4	adj	rational	5	adj
ignorant	4	adj	versatile	5	adj
intelligence	4	n	vulgar	5	adj
intelligent	4	adj			

138. Literature (Types)—related clusters: 53, 71, 112, 248, 256, 279, 319, 320

Word	Importance	Part of Speech	Word	Importance	Part of Speech
myth	2	n	**writing**	3	n
story	2	n	comedy	4	n
fiction	3	n	fable	4	n
legend	3	n	parable	4	n
literature	3	n	proverb	4	n
mystery	3	n	suspense	4	n
poetry	3	n	verse	4	n
riddle	3	n	prose	5	n
tale	3	n			

139. Parks and Yards—related clusters: 50, 114, 168, 267, 362, 363, 398

Word	Importance	Part of Speech	Word	Importance	Part of Speech
garden	2	n	**schoolyard**	3	n
park	2	n	barnyard	4	n
yard	2	n	cemetery	4	n
patio	3	n	courtyard	4	n
playground	3	n	plaza	4	n

140. Ears, Eyes, and Nose—related clusters: 75, 76, 80, 115, 157, 160, 191, 213, 336, 437

Word	Importance	Part of Speech	Word	Importance	Part of Speech
ear	2	n	**nostril**	3	n
eye	2	n	brow	4	n
nose	2	n	eardrum	4	n
eyebrow	3	n	lobe	4	n
eyelash	3	n	retina	4	n

141. Descending Motion (General)—related clusters: 38, 39, 40, 44, 66, 147, 169, 170, 182, 199, 215, 216, 247, 280, 281, 282, 283, 300, 301, 302, 322, 338, 403

Word	Importance	Part of Speech	Word	Importance	Part of Speech
drop	2	v	**dump**	3	v
fall	2	v	**slump**	3	v
lay	2	v	**tumble**	3	v

Word	Importance	Part of Speech	Word	Importance	Part of Speech
collapse	4	v	sag	4	v
descend	4	v	swoop	4	v
dip	4	v	tilt	4	v
droop	4	v	dunk	5	v
landslide	4	n	slouch	5	v
plunge	4	v	topple	5	v

142. Rectangular/Square Shapes—related clusters: 69, 99, 193, 218, 270, 303, 326

Word	Importance	Part of Speech	Word	Importance	Part of Speech
block	2	n	hexagon	4	n
rectangle	2	n	octagon	4	n
square	2	n	parallelogram	4	n
triangle	2	n	pentagon	4	n
cube	3	n	polygon	4	n
pyramid	3	n	prism	4	n
triangular	3	adj	quadrilateral	4	n
cubic	4	adj	trapezoid	4	n
equilateral	4	adj	foursquare	5	n

143. Board/Other Games—related clusters: 158, 183, 209, 304, 370

Word	Importance	Part of Speech	Word	Importance	Part of Speech
doll	2	n	crossword	4	n
toy	2	n	dice	4	n
toys	2	n	hopscotch	4	n
puppet	3	n	lottery	4	n
puzzle	3	n	pinball	4	n
cards	4	n	poker	4	n
checkers	4	n	tiddlywinks	4	n
checkmate	4	n	marionette	5	n
chess	4	n	raffle	5	n

144. Time Measurement Devices—related clusters: 2, 16, 24, 29, 52, 59, 79, 83, 126, 233

Word	Importance	Part of Speech	Word	Importance	Part of Speech
calendar	2	n	hourglass	4	n
clock	2	n	stopwatch	4	n
watch	2	n	sundial	4	n
date	3	n	wristwatch	4	n
o'clock	3	adv			

145. Coats—related clusters: 47, 62, 125, 129, 178, 212, 224, 263, 354, 435

Word	Importance	Part of Speech	Word	Importance	Part of Speech
coat	2	n	overcoat	4	n
jacket	2	n	parka	4	n
cape	3	n	poncho	4	n
raincoat	3	n	shawl	4	n
cloak	4	n	topcoat	5	n
mantle	4	n			

146. Actions Related to Work—related clusters: 68, 88, 167, 173, 229, 236, 257, 264, 265, 266, 297, 333, 334, 355, 356, 357, 358, 359, 360, 361, 392, 393, 394, 395, 396, 397, 436

Word	Importance	Part of Speech	Word	Importance	Part of Speech
quit	2	v	retire	4	v
work	2	v	toil	4	v
hire	3	v	drudge	5	v
labor	3	v	engage	5	v
effort	4	n	strive	5	v
employ	4	v	travail	5	v

147. Beginning Motion—related clusters: 38, 39, 40, 44, 66, 141, 169, 170, 182, 199, 215, 216, 247, 280, 281, 282, 283, 300, 301, 302, 322, 338, 403

Word	Importance	Part of Speech	Word	Importance	Part of Speech
begin	2	v	beginning	3	n
start	2	v	origin	3	n
try	2	v	introduce	4	v

Word	Importance	Part of Speech	Word	Importance	Part of Speech
introduction	4	n	genesis	5	n
source	4	n	preface	5	v
embark	5	v			

148. Receiving/Taking Actions—related clusters: 11, 89, 171, 184, 426

Word	Importance	Part of Speech	Word	Importance	Part of Speech
get	2	v	plunder	4	v
steal	2	v	reach	4	v
accept	3	v	reap	4	v
attract	3	v	receive	4	v
capture	3	v	regain	4	v
achieve	4	v	rob	4	v
acquire	4	v	seize	4	v
adopt	4	v	theft	4	n
arrest	4	v	trespass	4	v
attain	4	v	abduct	5	v
deprive	4	v	extract	5	v
kidnap	4	v	hijack	5	v
loot	4	n	inherit	5	v
obtain	4	v	ransack	5	v

149. Specific Actions Done with the Hands—related clusters: 131, 197

Word	Importance	Part of Speech	Word	Importance	Part of Speech
point	2	v	shrug	4	v
wave	2	v	fumble	5	v
clap	3	v	handiwork	5	n
handshake	3	n	wield	5	v
salute	3	v			

150. Contractions (Have)—related clusters: 42, 81, 85, 235, 274

Word	Importance	Part of Speech	Word	Importance	Part of Speech
I've	2	cont	**we've**	3	cont
they've	2	cont	**you've**	3	cont

151. Facial Expressions—related clusters: 152, 196, 241

Word	Importance	Part of Speech	Word	Importance	Part of Speech
grin	2	n	blush	4	n
smile	2	n	scowl	4	n
frown	3	n	smirk	4	n
nod	3	n	sneer	4	n

152. Actions Associated with the Mouth—related clusters: 151, 196, 241

Word	Importance	Part of Speech	Word	Importance	Part of Speech
kiss	2	v	**spit**	3	v
suck	2	v	spew	5	v
lick	3	v			

153. Candy and Sweets—related clusters: 48, 51, 74, 86, 124, 136, 162, 174, 176, 208, 222, 232, 246

Word	Importance	Part of Speech	Word	Importance	Part of Speech
cake	2	n	**marshmallow**	3	n
candy	2	n	**sherbet**	3	n
cookie	2	n	**sundae**	3	n
cupcake	2	n	**vanilla**	3	n
doughnut	2	n	lozenge	4	n
gum	2	n	marmalade	4	n
honey	2	n	molasses	4	n
jam	2	n	pastry	4	n
pie	2	n	patty	4	n
pudding	2	n	peppermint	4	n
syrup	2	n	popover	4	n
brownie	3	n	spearmint	4	n
butterscotch	3	n	taffy	4	n
caramel	3	n	tart	4	n
chocolate	3	n	toffee	4	n
cocoa	3	n	bonbon	5	n
fudge	3	n	shortcake	5	n
licorice	3	n	wafer	5	n
lollipop	3	n			

154. Learning and Teaching—related clusters: 46, 67, 132, 137, 225, 249, 277, 347, 348, 349, 384

Word	Importance	Part of Speech	Word	Importance	Part of Speech
coach	2	v	trick	3	v
direction	2	n	complicate	4	v
know	2	v	decoy	4	n
learn	2	v	educate	4	v
teach	2	v	fake	4	v
understand	2	v	input	4	v
advice	3	n	realize	4	v
comprehend	3	v	suggestion	4	n
confuse	3	v	breakthrough	5	n
discover	3	v	confound	5	v
information	3	n	glean	5	v
instruct	3	v	lore	5	n
outsmart	3	v	mystify	5	v
study	3	v	outwit	5	v
suggest	3	v			

155. Parts of Animals—related clusters: 32, 35, 64, 65, 70, 82, 95, 117, 188, 189, 194, 309, 310, 341

Word	Importance	Part of Speech	Word	Importance	Part of Speech
feather	2	n	antler	4	n
fur	2	n	bristle	4	n
hide	2	n	gill	4	n
paw	2	n	pelt	4	n
tail	2	n	plume	4	n
whisker	2	n	pouch	4	n
beak	3	n	quill	4	n
bill	3	n	cud	5	n
claw	3	n	fleece	5	n
fin	3	n	ivory	5	n
flipper	3	n	mane	5	n
hoof	3	n	rawhide	5	n
snout	3	n	talon	5	n
antenna	4	n	tusk	5	n

156. Noises that People Make—related clusters: 84, 103, 165, 175

Word	Importance	Part of Speech	Word	Importance	Part of Speech
cheer	2	v	moan	4	v
cry	2	v	mumble	4	v
laugh	2	v	murmur	4	v
roar	2	v	mutter	4	v
shout	2	v	ruckus	4	n
sing	2	v	rumpus	4	n
whisper	2	v	screech	4	v
yell	2	v	shriek	4	v
applause	3	n	sigh	4	v
chuckle	3	v	snicker	4	v
cough	3	v	sob	4	v
giggle	3	v	squeal	4	v
holler	3	v	stammer	4	v
laughter	3	n	stutter	4	v
scream	3	v	uproar	4	n
snore	3	v	wail	4	v
whistle	3	v	weep	4	v
yawn	3	v	wheeze	4	v
applaud	4	v	whimper	4	v
babble	4	v	whine	4	v
bawl	4	v	whoop	4	v
belch	4	v	yodel	4	v
burp	4	v	bellow	5	v
burr	4	v	blurt	5	v
chant	4	v	fracas	5	n
gasp	4	v	ovation	5	n
groan	4	v	rant	5	v
gulp	4	v	rave	5	v
hiccup	4	v	titter	5	v
hum	4	v			

157. Body Coverings and Marks—related clusters: 75, 76, 80, 115, 140, 160, 191, 213, 336, 437

Word	Importance	Part of Speech	Word	Importance	Part of Speech
bump	2	n	mustache	4	n
hair	2	n	pimple	4	n
rash	2	n	pore	4	n
skin	2	n	ruddy	4	adj
bald	3	adj	scalp	4	n
beard	3	n	sideburns	4	n
bruise	3	n	suntan	4	n
freckle	3	n	tissue	4	n
pigtail	3	n	tumor	4	n
scar	3	n	wart	4	n
birthmark	4	n	wig	4	n
blubber	4	n	blackhead	5	n
complexion	4	n	blemish	5	n
dandruff	4	n	cowlick	5	n
flesh	4	n	dermis	5	n
hairline	4	n	membrane	5	n
hump	4	n	pock	5	n
lump	4	n	tuft	5	n

158. Recreation/Sports Equipment—related clusters: 143, 183, 209, 304, 370

Word	Importance	Part of Speech	Word	Importance	Part of Speech
ball	2	n	dumbbell	4	n
bat	2	n	inning	4	n
glove	2	n	knockout	4	n
swing	2	v	maypole	4	n
base	3	n	offense	4	n
goal	3	n	out	4	n
net	3	n	puck	4	n
softball	3	n	putter	4	v
touchdown	3	n	racket	4	n
arcade	4	n	ski	4	v
carousel	4	n	tackle	4	v
defense	4	n	target	4	n

(Continued)

Word	Importance	Part of Speech	Word	Importance	Part of Speech
tee	4	n	homer	5	n
trampoline	4	n	hurdle	5	n
trapeze	4	n	javelin	5	n
volley	4	n	reel	5	n
bunt	5	v			

159. Vehicles (Sea Transportation)—related clusters: 93, 97, 120, 128, 234, 318, 331

Word	Importance	Part of Speech	Word	Importance	Part of Speech
boat	2	n	lifeboat	4	n
canoe	2	n	liner	4	n
ship	2	n	motorboat	4	n
raft	3	n	shipwreck	4	n
submarine	3	n	tug	4	n
tugboat	3	n	vessel	4	n
yacht	3	n	barge	5	n
ark	4	n	cutter	5	n
battleship	4	n	dinghy	5	n
carrier	4	n	flagship	5	n
ferry	4	n	schooner	5	n
kayak	4	n			

160. The Body (General)—related clusters: 75, 76, 80, 115, 140, 157, 191, 213, 336, 437

Word	Importance	Part of Speech	Word	Importance	Part of Speech
body	2	n	physical	4	adj
lap	2	n	rump	4	n
neck	2	n	trunk	4	n
belly	3	n	udder	4	n
chest	3	n	vertebrate	4	n
hip	3	n	bosom	5	n
waist	3	n	nape	5	n
breast	4	n	organ	5	n
limbs	4	n	scruff	5	n
mental	4	adj	thorax	5	n

161. Actions Harmful to Humans—related clusters: 110, 250, 260

Word	Importance	Part of Speech	Word	Importance	Part of Speech
hurt	2	v	slay	4	v
kill	2	v	stun	4	v
punish	2	v	suicide	4	n
harm	3	v	toxic	4	adj
injure	3	v	vengeance	4	n
murder	3	v	afflict	5	v
shoot	3	v	assault	5	n
abuse	4	v	beset	5	v
ambush	4	v	cripple	5	v
attack	4	v	execute	5	v
deadly	4	adv	massacre	5	v
discipline	4	v	molest	5	v
fatal	4	adj	persecute	5	v
offend	4	v	prosecute	5	v
overwhelm	4	v	rape	5	v
painful	4	adj	scourge	5	v
paralyze	4	v	torment	5	v
penalty	4	n	torture	5	v
poisonous	4	adj	violate	5	v
slaughter	4	v			

162. Food-Related Actions—related clusters: 48, 51, 74, 86, 124, 136, 153, 174, 176, 208, 222, 232, 246

Word	Importance	Part of Speech	Word	Importance	Part of Speech
bake	2	v	cookout	4	n
boil	2	v	decay	4	v
cook	2	v	knead	4	v
barbecue	3	v	poach	4	v
broil	3	v	rot	4	v
fry	3	v	sift	4	v
grill	3	v	spoil	4	v
roast	3	v	deteriorate	5	v
serve	3	v	scald	5	v
brew	4	v	simmer	5	v
churn	4	v	taint	5	v

163. Cutting Tools—related clusters: 92, 96, 118, 119, 242, 254, 275, 276, 314, 315, 316, 419, 420

Word	Importance	Part of Speech	Word	Importance	Part of Speech
ax	2	n	hatchet	4	n
axe	2	n	jackknife	4	n
knife	2	n	razor	4	n
scissors	2	n	straightedge	4	n
blade	3	n	barb	5	n
lawnmower	3	n	scythe	5	n
pocketknife	3	n	sickle	5	n
clipper	4	n			

164. Containers—related clusters: 107, 181, 251, 268, 325, 367

Word	Importance	Part of Speech	Word	Importance	Part of Speech
bag	2	n	canteen	4	n
basket	2	n	capsule	4	n
bath	2	n	cargo	4	n
bathtub	2	n	carton	4	n
bottle	2	n	cartridge	4	n
box	2	n	case	4	n
bucket	2	n	cask	4	n
jar	2	n	coffin	4	n
barrel	3	n	compartment	4	n
coffeepot	3	n	cubbyhole	4	n
container	3	n	envelope	4	n
crate	3	n	flask	4	n
folder	3	n	freight	4	n
hamper	3	n	holder	4	n
jug	3	n	hopper	4	n
package	3	n	keg	4	n
pail	3	n	luggage	4	n
pitcher	3	n	packet	4	n
sack	3	n	parcel	4	n
suitcase	3	n	shipment	4	n
tub	3	n	tank	4	n
baggage	4	n	tinderbox	4	n
basin	4	n	trough	4	n

Word	Importance	Part of Speech	Word	Importance	Part of Speech
vat	4	n	knapsack	5	n
water bottle	4	n	rack	5	n
bin	5	n	socket	5	n
cistern	5	n	valise	5	n
gourd	5	n	washtub	5	n

165. Noises that Objects Make—related clusters: 84, 103, 156, 175

Word	Importance	Part of Speech	Word	Importance	Part of Speech
bang	2	n	crunch	4	n
beep	2	n	fizz	4	n
boom	2	n	gurgle	4	n
ring	2	n	jingle	4	n
tick	2	n	ping	4	n
click	3	n	plunk	4	n
creak	3	n	rustle	4	n
plop	3	n	swish	4	n
rattle	3	n	thud	4	n
slam	3	n	thump	4	n
squeak	3	n	ting	4	n
toot	3	n	tinkle	4	n
zoom	3	n	twang	4	n
chug	4	n	wail	4	n
clang	4	n	whir	4	n
clank	4	n	whoosh	4	n
clink	4	n	jangle	5	n
clop	4	n			

166. Mathematical Operations—related clusters: 340, 410, 423

Word	Importance	Part of Speech	Word	Importance	Part of Speech
add	2	v	**addition**	3	n
count	2	v	**cube**	3	v
minus	2	prep	**divide**	3	v
plus	2	prep	**division**	3	n
subtract	2	v	**multiplication**	3	n

(Continued)

Word	Importance	Part of Speech	Word	Importance	Part of Speech
multiply	3	v	per	4	prep
subtraction	3	n	times	4	n
divisible	4	n	tally	5	v

167. Performers and Entertainers—related clusters: 68, 88, 146, 173, 229, 236, 257, 264, 265, 266, 297, 333, 334, 355, 356, 357, 358, 359, 360, 361, 392, 393, 394, 395, 396, 397, 436

Word	Importance	Part of Speech	Word	Importance	Part of Speech
clown	2	n	**model**	3	n
dancer	2	n	comic	4	n
actor	3	n	performer	4	n
actress	3	n	ventriloquist	4	n
magician	3	n			

168. Hills and Mountains—related clusters: 50, 114, 139, 267, 362, 363, 398

Word	Importance	Part of Speech	Word	Importance	Part of Speech
hill	2	n	mountaintop	4	n
mountain	2	n	plateau	4	n
cliff	3	n	range	4	n
hillside	3	n	ridge	4	n
mound	3	n	slope	4	n
bluff	4	n	volcano	4	n
butte	4	n	crest	5	n
crag	4	n	embankment	5	n
dune	4	n	knoll	5	n
foothill	4	n	mesa	5	n
hilltop	4	n	sierra	5	n
mountainside	4	n	watershed	5	n

169. Lack of Motion—related clusters: 38, 39, 40, 44, 66, 141, 147, 170, 182, 199, 215, 216, 247, 280, 281, 282, 283, 300, 301, 302, 322, 338, 403

Word	Importance	Part of Speech	Word	Importance	Part of Speech
rest	2	v	**pause**	3	v
stay	2	v	**relax**	3	v
delay	3	v	**remain**	3	v

Word	Importance	Part of Speech	Word	Importance	Part of Speech
wait	3	v	putter	4	v
await	4	v	settle	4	v
dangle	4	v	standstill	4	n
deadlock	4	n	static	4	adj
hang	4	v	suspension	4	n
hesitate	4	v	detain	5	v
interrupt	4	v	falter	5	v
intervene	4	v	hinder	5	v
lag	4	v	hover	5	v
linger	4	v	inert	5	adj
lounge	4	v	probation	5	n
motionless	4	adj	stationary	5	adj
postpone	4	v	suspend	5	v
procrastinate	4	v	waylay	5	v

170. Descending Motion—related clusters: 38, 39, 40, 44, 66, 141, 147, 169, 182, 199, 215, 216, 247, 280, 281, 282, 283, 300, 301, 302, 322, 338, 403

Word	Importance	Part of Speech	Word	Importance	Part of Speech
lie	2	v	**squat**	3	v
sit	2	v	flop	4	v
crouch	3	v	sprawl	4	v
kneel	3	v	stoop	4	v

171. Finding/Keeping—related clusters: 41, 89, 148, 184, 426

Word	Importance	Part of Speech	Word	Importance	Part of Speech
find	2	v	masquerade	4	v
keep	2	v	reserve	4	v
bury	3	v	tuck	4	v
hide	3	v	withhold	4	v
spot	3	v	camouflage	5	n
conceal	4	v	hoard	5	v
conserve	4	v	pinpoint	5	v
disguise	4	v	restrict	5	v
distinguish	4	v	retain	5	v
locate	4	v			

172. Locations Where People Might Live—related clusters: 180

Word	Importance	Part of Speech	Word	Importance	Part of Speech
city	2	n	colony	4	n
neighborhood	2	n	empire	4	n
state	2	n	hell	4	n
town	2	n	homeland	4	n
village	2	n	kingdom	4	n
camp	3	n	outskirts	4	n
county	3	n	province	4	n
downtown	3	n	resort	4	n
ghetto	3	n	spa	4	n
heaven	3	n	underworld	4	n
slum	3	n	district	5	n
suburb	3	n	metropolis	5	n
birthplace	4	n	paradise	5	n
capital	4	n	wonderland	5	n

173. Royalty and Statesmen—related clusters: 68, 88, 146, 167, 229, 236, 257, 264, 265, 266, 297, 333, 334, 355, 356, 357, 358, 359, 360, 361, 392, 393, 394, 395, 396, 397, 436

Word	Importance	Part of Speech	Word	Importance	Part of Speech
king	2	n	senator	4	n
mayor	2	n	sire	4	n
president	2	n	sultan	4	n
candidate	3	n	vice president	4	n
knight	3	n	baron	5	n
official	3	n	congressman	5	n
prince	3	n	congresswoman	5	n
princess	3	n	councilman	5	n
queen	3	n	councilwoman	5	n
ambassador	4	n	czar	5	n
chief	4	n	delegate	5	n
dictator	4	n	diplomat	5	n
duchess	4	n	figurehead	5	n
duke	4	n	nobleman	5	n
earl	4	n	prefect	5	n
lord	4	n	squire	5	n
monarch	4	n	statesman	5	n
politician	4	n	tribune	5	n

174. Fruits—related clusters: 48, 51, 74, 86, 124, 136, 153, 162, 176, 208, 222, 232, 246

Word	Importance	Part of Speech	Word	Importance	Part of Speech
apple	2	n	lemon	3	n
banana	2	n	melon	3	n
cherry	2	n	pineapple	3	n
grape	2	n	plum	3	n
orange	2	n	prune	3	n
peach	2	n	raisin	3	n
pear	2	n	raspberry	3	n
strawberry	2	n	applesauce	4	n
avocado	3	n	apricot	4	n
berry	3	n	fig	4	n
blueberry	3	n	honeydew	4	n
coconut	3	n	lime	4	n
cranberry	3	n	tangerine	4	n
grapefruit	3	n	watermelon	4	n

175. Noises that Animals Make—related clusters: 84, 103, 156, 165

Word	Importance	Part of Speech	Word	Importance	Part of Speech
bark	2	n	grunt	4	n
buzz	2	n	hiss	4	n
meow	2	n	honk	4	n
moo	2	n	hoot	4	n
baa	3	n	howl	4	n
cluck	3	n	snarl	4	n
gobble	3	n	snort	4	n
growl	3	n	squawk	4	n
peep	3	n	whinny	4	n
purr	3	n	yap	4	n
quack	3	n	yelp	4	n
bleat	4	n	yip	4	n
cackle	4	n	yowl	4	n
caw	4	n	bray	5	n
cheep	4	n	neigh	5	n
chirp	4	n	warble	5	n
croak	4	n			

176. Drinks—related clusters: 48, 51, 74, 86, 124, 136, 153, 162, 174, 208, 222, 232, 246

Word	Importance	Part of Speech	Word	Importance	Part of Speech
juice	2	n	alcohol	4	n
milk	2	n	broth	4	n
pop	2	n	chowder	4	n
soup	2	n	cider	4	n
beer	3	n	nectar	4	n
chili	3	n	beverage	5	n
coffee	3	n	champagne	5	n
soda	3	n	gin	5	n
stew	3	n	liquor	5	n
tea	3	n	moonshine	5	n
wine	3	n	whiskey	5	n

177. Questioning—related clusters: 14, 61, 100, 105, 198, 207, 255, 345, 346, 383

Word	Importance	Part of Speech	Word	Importance	Part of Speech
answer	2	v	consult	4	v
ask	2	v	inquire	4	v
call	2	v	interview	4	v
offer	3	v	invite	4	v
question	3	v	poll	4	v
reply	3	v	quiz	4	v
request	3	v	beckon	5	v
respond	3	v	confer	5	v
test	3	v	propose	5	v
bid	4	v			

178. Fabrics—related clusters: 47, 62, 125, 129, 145, 212, 224, 263, 354, 435

Word	Importance	Part of Speech	Word	Importance	Part of Speech
cloth	2	n	nylon	3	n
rag	2	n	silk	3	n
thread	2	n	wool	3	n
cotton	3	n	calico	4	n
lace	3	n	denim	4	n
leather	3	n	fabric	4	n

Word	Importance	Part of Speech	Word	Importance	Part of Speech
fiber	4	n	velvet	4	n
flannel	4	n	yarn	4	n
linen	4	n	buckskin	5	n
satin	4	n	dry goods	5	n
suede	4	n	felt	5	n
terry	4	n	gauze	5	n
textile	4	n	homespun	5	n
texture	4	n	khaki	5	n
tint	4	n			

179. Recreational Events and Festivals—related clusters: 412, 413

Word	Importance	Part of Speech	Word	Importance	Part of Speech
birthday	2	n	ceremony	4	n
party	2	n	festival	4	n
recess	2	n	honeymoon	4	n
circus	3	n	masquerade	4	n
date	3	n	pageant	4	n
fair	3	n	pastime	4	n
holiday	3	n	procession	4	n
parade	3	n	prom	4	n
vacation	3	n	rodeo	4	n
amusement	4	n	bazaar	5	n
anniversary	4	n	debut	5	n
caravan	4	n	leisure	5	n
carnival	4	n			

180. Countries and Continents—related clusters: 172

Word	Importance	Part of Speech	Word	Importance	Part of Speech
country	2	n	**hemisphere**	3	n
nation	2	n	nationwide	4	adj
continent	3	n	sovereign	4	n
equator	3	n			

181. Wooden Building Materials—related clusters: 107, 164, 251, 268, 325, 367

Word	Importance	Part of Speech	Word	Importance	Part of Speech
stick	2	n	pillar	4	n
wood	2	n	plywood	4	n
board	3	n	shingle	4	n
log	3	n	slat	4	n
post	3	n	basswood	5	n
timber	3	n	palette	5	n
lumber	4	n	veneer	5	n
panel	4	n			

182. Pulling and Pushing—related clusters: 38, 39, 40, 44, 66, 141, 147, 169, 170, 199, 215, 216, 247, 280, 281, 282, 283, 300, 301, 302, 322, 338, 403

Word	Importance	Part of Speech	Word	Importance	Part of Speech
pull	2	v	gravity	4	n
push	2	v	insert	4	v
drag	3	v	propel	4	v
haul	3	v	tow	4	v
shove	3	v	inject	5	v
yank	3	v	lug	5	v

183. Recreation and Sports—related clusters: 143, 158, 209, 304, 370

Word	Importance	Part of Speech	Word	Importance	Part of Speech
game	2	n	competition	4	n
recess	2	n	hobby	4	n
contest	3	n	match	4	n
race	3	n	derby	5	n
recreation	3	n	marathon	5	n
sport	3	n	tournament	5	n
compete	4	v			

184. Giving Up/Losing—related clusters: 41, 89, 148, 171, 426

Word	Importance	Part of Speech	Word	Importance	Part of Speech
show	2	v	exchange	4	v
trade	2	v	lease	4	v
borrow	3	v	lend	4	v
lose	3	v	loan	4	v
loser	3	n	swap	4	v
share	3	v	alternate	5	v
abandon	4	v	barter	5	v
dismiss	4	v	discard	5	v
displace	4	v	eject	5	v
dispose	4	v			

185. Cleanliness/Hygiene—related clusters: 223, 288

Word	Importance	Part of Speech	Word	Importance	Part of Speech
clean	2	v	polish	4	v
wipe	2	v	sterile	4	adj
rinse	3	v	strain	4	v
scrub	3	v	turnout	4	v
sweep	3	v	wax	4	v
wash	3	v	hygiene	5	n
bathe	4	v	immaculate	5	adj
buff	4	v	preen	5	v
cleanliness	4	n	purge	5	v
filter	4	v	purify	5	v
haircut	4	n	scour	5	v
manicure	4	n	swab	5	v
pasteurize	4	v			

186. Attractiveness—related clusters: 187, 253, 407

Word	Importance	Part of Speech	Word	Importance	Part of Speech
pretty	2	adj	**handsome**	3	adj
ugly	2	adj	**lovely**	3	adj
beautiful	3	adj	adorable	4	adj
cute	3	adj	attractive	4	adj

(Continued)

Word	Importance	Part of Speech	Word	Importance	Part of Speech
breathtaking	4	adj	bonny	5	adj
elegant	4	adj	classic	5	adj
formal	4	adj	exquisite	5	adj
homely	4	adj	gorgeous	5	adj
sightly	4	adj	hideous	5	adj
unattractive	4	adj	sleek	5	adj

187. Physical Trait (Size)—related clusters: 186, 253, 407

Word	Importance	Part of Speech	Word	Importance	Part of Speech
fat	2	adj	plump	4	adj
heavy	2	adj	pudgy	4	adj
chubby	3	adj	slender	4	adj
lean	3	adj	slight	4	adj
skinny	3	adj	burly	5	adj
slim	3	adj	dainty	5	adj
husky	4	adj	scrag	5	n
obese	4	adj	stout	5	adj

188. Rodents—related clusters: 32, 35, 64, 65, 70, 82, 95, 117, 155, 189, 194, 309, 310, 341

Word	Importance	Part of Speech	Word	Importance	Part of Speech
mouse	2	n	chipmunk	4	n
squirrel	2	n	muskrat	4	n
beaver	3	n	otter	4	n
groundhog	3	n	porcupine	4	n
hamster	3	n	woodchuck	4	n
rat	3	n	rodent	5	n

189. Dwellings for Animals—related clusters: 32, 35, 64, 65, 70, 82, 95, 117, 155, 188, 194, 309, 310, 341

Word	Importance	Part of Speech	Word	Importance	Part of Speech
nest	2	n	birdhouse	3	n
zoo	2	n	cocoon	3	n
aquarium	3	n	hive	3	n
beehive	3	n	coop	4	n

Word	Importance	Part of Speech	Word	Importance	Part of Speech
corral	4	n	stall	4	n
kennel	4	n	honeycomb	5	n
roost	4	n	lair	5	n
stable	4	n	perch	5	n

190. Places Related to Sports/Entertainment—related clusters: 60, 106, 121, 210, 321, 324, 335, 364, 365, 366, 399, 400

Word	Importance	Part of Speech	Word	Importance	Part of Speech
theater	2	n	coliseum	4	n
court	3	n	grandstand	4	n
gym	3	n	opera	4	n
stadium	3	n	playhouse	4	n
arena	4	n	rink	4	n
auditorium	4	n			

191. Body Fluids—related clusters: 75, 76, 80, 115, 140, 157, 160, 213, 336, 437

Word	Importance	Part of Speech	Word	Importance	Part of Speech
blood	2	n	vein	4	n
bleed	3	v	vessel	4	n
sweat	3	v	capillary	5	n
artery	4	n	circulate	5	v
clot	4	n	hemoglobin	5	n
pus	4	n	mucus	5	n
saliva	4	n	perspiration	5	n
sperm	4	n	ventricle	5	n

192. Vegetation (Other)—related clusters: 36, 108, 269, 421

Word	Importance	Part of Speech	Word	Importance	Part of Speech
grass	2	n	cob	4	n
lawn	3	n	fern	4	n
root	3	n	fungus	4	n
vine	3	n	hay	4	n
bamboo	4	n	husk	4	n
clover	4	n	kelp	4	n

(Continued)

Word	Importance	Part of Speech	Word	Importance	Part of Speech
mildew	4	n	straw	4	n
moss	4	n	thatch	4	n
mushroom	4	n	toadstool	4	n
ragweed	4	n	alfalfa	5	n
reed	4	n	algae	5	n
rind	4	n	cattail	5	n
seaweed	4	n	lichen	5	n
stalk	4	n			

193. Inclination—related clusters: 69, 99, 142, 218, 270, 303, 326

Word	Importance	Part of Speech	Word	Importance	Part of Speech
flat	2	adj	incline	4	n
even	3	adj	plumb	4	adj
lean	3	adv	slant	4	adv
level	3	adj	tilt	4	adv
steep	3	adj	erect	5	adj

194. Animals (General)—related clusters: 32, 35, 64, 65, 70, 82, 95, 117, 155, 188, 189, 309, 310, 341

Word	Importance	Part of Speech	Word	Importance	Part of Speech
animal	2	n	fossil	4	n
pet	3	n	mammal	4	n
wildlife	3	n	mascot	4	n
beast	4	n	amphibian	5	n
carnivorous	4	adj	prey	5	n
creature	4	n			

195. Visual Perceptions and Images—related clusters: 135

Word	Importance	Part of Speech	Word	Importance	Part of Speech
appearance	3	n	**sight**	3	n
badge	3	n	**view**	3	n
flag	3	n	demonstration	4	n
image	3	n	display	4	n
scene	3	n	emblem	4	n

Word	Importance	Part of Speech	Word	Importance	Part of Speech
identify	4	v	visual	4	n
observer	4	n	witness	4	v
panorama	4	n	distract	5	v
reflect	4	v	flaunt	5	v
reflection	4	n	phenomenon	5	n
represent	4	v	portray	5	v
reveal	4	v	prospect	5	n
visible	4	adj	scope	5	n
vision	4	n			

196. Breathing—related clusters: 151, 152, 241

Word	Importance	Part of Speech	Word	Importance	Part of Speech
blow	2	v	puff	4	v
breath	3	n	strangle	4	v
choke	3	v	whiff	4	n
exhale	3	v	respire	5	v
pant	4	v			

197. Feeling and Striking—related clusters: 131, 149

Word	Importance	Part of Speech	Word	Importance	Part of Speech
hit	2	v	grope	4	v
slap	2	v	jab	4	v
spank	2	v	knead	4	v
touch	2	v	lash	4	v
beat	3	v	lob	4	v
feel	3	v	nudge	4	v
knock	3	v	poke	4	v
pat	3	v	pulse	4	n
pound	3	v	rap	4	v
punch	3	v	smack	4	v
smash	3	v	spur	4	v
tap	3	v	strike	4	v
tickle	3	v	stroke	4	v
butt	4	v	thrash	4	v
dab	4	v	whack	4	v

(Continued)

Word	Importance	Part of Speech	Word	Importance	Part of Speech
wham	4	v	massage	5	v
whop	4	v	prod	5	v
buffet	5	v	putt	5	v
caress	5	v	wallop	5	v
fondle	5	v			

198. Communication (Confrontation/Negative Information)—related clusters: 14, 61, 100, 105, 177, 207, 255, 345, 346, 383

Word	Importance	Part of Speech	Word	Importance	Part of Speech
blame	2	v	detract	4	v
cheat	2	v	disgrace	4	v
lie	2	v	dispute	4	v
accuse	3	v	embarrass	4	v
argue	3	v	exaggerate	4	v
complain	3	v	fib	4	v
dare	3	v	insult	4	v
disagree	3	v	mock	4	v
disobey	3	v	nag	4	v
quarrel	3	n	object	4	v
scold	3	v	objection	4	n
tease	3	v	protest	4	v
warn	3	v	rebel	4	v
annoy	4	v	revolt	4	v
betray	4	v	ridicule	4	v
caution	4	v	rumor	4	v
challenge	4	v	scoff	4	v
complaint	4	n	swear	4	v
confront	4	v	taunt	4	v
controversy	4	n	threat	4	n
criticism	4	n	threaten	4	v
criticize	4	v	trial	4	n
curse	4	v	warning	4	n
deceit	4	n	cant	5	n
deceive	4	v	con	5	v
decline	4	v	condemn	5	v
delude	4	v	damn	5	v

Word	Importance	Part of Speech	Word	Importance	Part of Speech
debate	5	v	prophecy	5	n
defy	5	v	reject	5	v
denounce	5	v	retort	5	v
distort	5	v	slur	5	v
gripe	5	v	spat	5	n
hyperbole	5	n	squabble	5	v
jeer	5	v	sue	5	v
menace	5	v			

199. Angular and Circular Motions—related clusters: 38, 39, 40, 44, 66, 141, 147, 169, 170, 182, 215, 216, 247, 280, 281, 282, 283, 300, 301, 302, 322, 338, 403

Word	Importance	Part of Speech	Word	Importance	Part of Speech
around	2	prep	invert	4	v
roll	2	v	orbit	4	n
turn	2	v	pinwheel	4	n
clockwise	3	adv	recoil	4	v
counterclockwise	3	adv	reverse	4	v
rotate	3	v	swirl	4	v
spin	3	v	whirl	4	v
surround	3	v	reciprocal	5	adj
swing	3	v	revolve	5	v
twirl	3	v	swerve	5	v
twist	3	v	swivel	5	v
circulation	4	n			

200. Social and Political Groups—related clusters: 98, 258, 298, 401

Word	Importance	Part of Speech	Word	Importance	Part of Speech
country	2	n	civilization	4	n
family	2	n	clan	4	n
community	3	n	congress	4	n
democracy	3	n	culture	4	n
nation	3	n	federal	4	adj
race	3	n	international	4	adj
society	3	n	jury	4	n
tribe	3	n	minority	4	n

(Continued)

Word	Importance	Part of Speech	Word	Importance	Part of Speech
national	4	adj	caste	5	n
parliament	4	n	civic	5	n
republic	4	n	cult	5	n
senate	4	n	regime	5	n
cabinet	5	n	sect	5	n

201. Money/Goods (Received)—related clusters: 104, 109, 116, 122, 214

Word	Importance	Part of Speech	Word	Importance	Part of Speech
gift	2	n	insurance	4	n
prize	2	n	premium	4	n
award	3	n	profit	4	n
medal	3	n	salary	4	n
reward	3	n	scholarship	4	n
savings	3	n	trophy	4	n
treasure	3	n	wage	4	n
allowance	4	n	bounty	5	n
bonus	4	n	grant	5	n
contribution	4	n	legacy	5	n
credit	4	n	patent	5	n
fortune	4	n	refund	5	n
gain	4	n	windfall	5	n
income	4	n			

202. Texture—related clusters: 323, 441

Word	Importance	Part of Speech	Word	Importance	Part of Speech
hard	2	adj	crisp	4	adj
soft	2	adj	rigid	4	adj
bumpy	3	adj	solid	4	adj
firm	3	adj	stiff	4	adj
rough	3	adj	texture	4	n
smooth	3	adj	tough	4	adj
tight	3	adj	tangible	5	adj
coarse	4	adj	taut	5	adj

203. Men—related clusters: 56, 94, 111, 204, 205, 206, 227, 317, 330, 343, 344, 382, 432, 444

Word	Importance	Part of Speech	Word	Importance	Part of Speech
boy	2	n	host	4	n
man	2	n	junior	4	n
guy	3	n	lad	4	n
hero	3	n	masculine	4	n
male	3	n	master	4	n
schoolboy	3	n	mister	4	n
sir	3	n	bachelor	5	n
dude	4	n	señor	5	n
fellow	4	n	urchin	5	n
heroine	4	n			

204. Names that Indicate Age—related clusters: 56, 94, 111, 203, 205, 206, 227, 317, 330, 343, 344, 382, 432, 444

Word	Importance	Part of Speech	Word	Importance	Part of Speech
baby	2	n	juvenile	4	n
child	2	n	minor	4	n
adult	3	n	newborn	4	n
grown-up	3	n	orphan	4	n
kid	3	n	papoose	4	n
teenager	3	n	senior	4	n
toddler	3	n	tot	4	n
babe	4	n	youngster	4	n
elder	4	n	embryo	5	n
infant	4	n			

205. Names that Indicate Camaraderie/Friendship—related clusters: 56, 94, 111, 203, 204, 206, 227, 317, 330, 343, 344, 382, 432, 444

Word	Importance	Part of Speech	Word	Importance	Part of Speech
friend	2	n	**playmate**	3	n
neighbor	2	n	acquaintance	4	n
boyfriend	3	n	buddy	4	n
classmate	3	n	chum	4	n
pal	3	n	companion	4	n
partner	3	n	darling	4	n

(Continued)

Word	Importance	Part of Speech	Word	Importance	Part of Speech
lover	4	n	teammate	4	n
mate	4	n	ally	5	n
peer	4	n	fiancé (fiancée)	5	n
schoolmate	4	n	suitor	5	n
sweetheart	4	n			

206. Names that Indicate Negative Characteristics About People—related clusters: 56, 94, 111, 203, 204, 205, 227, 317, 330, 343, 344, 382, 432, 444

Word	Importance	Part of Speech	Word	Importance	Part of Speech
bandit	2	n	outlaw	4	n
villain	2	n	pest	4	n
bully	3	n	prey	4	n
criminal	3	n	rascal	4	n
enemy	3	n	rival	4	n
killer	3	n	rustler	4	n
liar	3	n	scamp	4	n
pirate	3	n	slowpoke	4	n
thief	3	n	snob	4	n
blockhead	4	n	storyteller	4	n
brute	4	n	suspect	4	n
burglar	4	n	telltale	4	n
cad	4	n	vandal	4	n
cannibal	4	n	victim	4	n
convict	4	n	wallflower	4	n
coward	4	n	captive	5	n
crook	4	n	delinquent	5	n
culprit	4	n	dolt	5	n
dope	4	n	hostage	5	n
dunce	4	n	moron	5	n
foe	4	n	nuisance	5	n
fool	4	n	pickpocket	5	n
gossip	4	n	ruffian	5	n
jailbird	4	n	scoundrel	5	n
opponent	4	n	tyrant	5	n

207. Communication (Supervision/Commands)—related clusters: 14, 61, 100, 105, 177, 198, 255, 345, 346, 383

Word	Importance	Part of Speech	Word	Importance	Part of Speech
correct	2	v	insist	4	v
let	2	v	instruction	4	n
obey	2	v	leadership	4	n
advice	3	n	license	4	n
allow	3	v	manage	4	v
command	3	v	reign	4	v
control	3	v	revoke	4	v
demand	3	v	suggestion	4	n
direct	3	v	taboo	4	n
direction	3	n	veto	4	v
excuse	3	v	yield	4	v
forbid	3	v	commission	5	v
force	3	v	conform	5	v
permit	3	v	decree	5	v
refuse	3	v	demote	5	v
remind	3	v	enforce	5	v
require	3	v	manipulate	5	v
administer	4	v	preside	5	v
authority	4	n	regulate	5	v
ban	4	v	reinstate	5	v
compel	4	v	repeal	5	v
compromise	4	v	reprimand	5	v
consent	4	v	submit	5	v
counsel	4	v	summon	5	v
deny	4	v	supervise	5	v
govern	4	v	suppress	5	v
input	4	n			

208. Vegetables, Grains, and Nuts—related clusters: 48, 51, 74, 86, 124, 136, 153, 162, 174, 176, 222, 232, 246

Word	Importance	Part of Speech	Word	Importance	Part of Speech
carrot	2	n	**peanut**	2	n
corn	2	n	**popcorn**	2	n
nut	2	n	**seed**	2	n

(Continued)

Word	Importance	Part of Speech	Word	Importance	Part of Speech
almond	3	n	beet	4	n
bean	3	n	cabbage	4	n
cashew	3	n	cauliflower	4	n
celery	3	n	chestnut	4	n
cucumber	3	n	grain	4	n
lettuce	3	n	kernel	4	n
olive	3	n	maize	4	n
onion	3	n	malt	4	n
peas	3	n	oats	4	n
pickle	3	n	pecan	4	n
potato	3	n	radish	4	n
pumpkin	3	n	soybean	4	n
rice	3	n	turnip	4	n
spinach	3	n	barley	5	n
squash	3	n	bran	5	n
tomato	3	n	eggplant	5	n
walnut	3	n	gourd	5	n
wheat	3	n	rye	5	n
acorn	4	n	yam	5	n
asparagus	4	n			

209. Sports (Specific Types)—related clusters: 143, 158, 183, 304, 370

Word	Importance	Part of Speech	Word	Importance	Part of Speech
baseball	2	n	**ski**	3	v
soccer	2	n	**skiing**	3	n
softball	2	n	**tennis**	3	n
swim	2	v	**volleyball**	3	n
swimming	2	n	**wrestling**	3	n
basketball	3	n	archery	4	n
bicycle	3	n	badminton	4	n
bowling	3	n	handball	4	n
boxing	3	n	lacrosse	4	n
football	3	n	polo	4	n
golf	3	n	backhand	5	n
hockey	3	n	croquet	5	n
racing	3	n	fencing	5	n
skate	3	v	steeplechase	5	n
skating	3	n			

210. Places Where Goods Can Be Bought/Sold—related clusters: 60, 106, 121, 190, 321, 324, 335, 364, 365, 366, 399, 400

Word	Importance	Part of Speech	Word	Importance	Part of Speech
grocery	2	n	café	4	n
store	2	n	casino	4	n
bakery	3	n	market	4	n
bookstore	3	n	pharmacy	4	n
cafeteria	3	n	salon	4	n
drugstore	3	n	saloon	4	n
lunchroom	3	n	supermarket	4	n
restaurant	3	n	tavern	5	n
booth	4	n			

211. Courage and Loyalty—related clusters: 228, 278, 294, 295, 332, 350, 351, 385, 386, 387, 388, 389, 429, 433, 434

Word	Importance	Part of Speech	Word	Importance	Part of Speech
brave	2	adj	bravery	4	n
courage	3	n	chivalry	4	n
heroic	3	adj	courageous	4	adj
honest	3	adj	devotion	4	n
loyal	3	adj	gallant	4	adj
adventurous	4	adj	obedience	4	n
allegiance	4	n	grit	5	n
bold	4	adj	valor	5	n

212. Clothing Parts—related clusters: 47, 62, 125, 129, 145, 178, 224, 263, 354, 435

Word	Importance	Part of Speech	Word	Importance	Part of Speech
button	2	n	bib	4	n
collar	3	n	cuff	4	n
sleeve	3	n	frill	4	n
zipper	3	n	fringe	4	n

(Continued)

Word	Importance	Part of Speech	Word	Importance	Part of Speech
hem	4	n	ruffle	4	n
pompom	4	n	seam	4	n
ruff	4	n	tassel	4	n

213. Muscles, Bones, and Nerves—related clusters: 75, 76, 80, 115, 140, 157, 160, 191, 336, 437

Word	Importance	Part of Speech	Word	Importance	Part of Speech
bone	2	n	spine	4	n
joint	3	n	cartilage	5	n
muscle	3	n	ligament	5	n
skeleton	3	n	nerve	5	n
backbone	4	n	sinew	5	n
rib	4	n	tendon	5	n

214. Money/Goods (Paid Out)—related clusters: 104, 109, 116, 122, 201

Word	Importance	Part of Speech	Word	Importance	Part of Speech
price	2	n	tab	4	n
cost	3	n	tax	4	n
payment	3	n	taxation	4	n
rent	3	n	toll	4	n
bail	4	n	tuition	4	n
debt	4	n	interest	5	n
fare	4	n	levy	5	n
fee	4	n	mortgage	5	n
loss	4	n	tariff	5	n
product	4	n			

215. Completion—related clusters: 38, 39, 40, 44, 66, 141, 147, 169, 170, 182, 199, 216, 247, 280, 281, 282, 283, 300, 301, 302, 322, 338, 403

Word	Importance	Part of Speech	Word	Importance	Part of Speech
end	2	v	**last**	3	adj
complete	3	v	accomplish	4	v
finish	3	v	completion	4	n

Word	Importance	Part of Speech	Word	Importance	Part of Speech
deadline	4	n	graduate	4	v
deed	4	n	fulfill	5	v
final	4	adj			

216. Shifting Motion—related clusters: 38, 39, 40, 44, 66, 141, 147, 169, 170, 182, 199, 215, 247, 280, 281, 282, 283, 300, 301, 302, 322, 338, 403

Word	Importance	Part of Speech	Word	Importance	Part of Speech
slip	2	v	**slide**	3	v
rock	3	v	shift	4	v
skid	3	v	sway	4	v

217. Fences and Ledges—related clusters: 91, 113, 123, 134, 284

Word	Importance	Part of Speech	Word	Importance	Part of Speech
gate	2	n	gutter	4	n
fence	3	n	hedge	4	n
mailbox	3	n	ledge	4	n
shelf	3	n	screen	4	n
curb	4	n	trellis	5	n

218. Crookedness/Straightness—related clusters: 69, 99, 142, 193, 270, 303, 326

Word	Importance	Part of Speech	Word	Importance	Part of Speech
line	2	n	**stripe**	3	n
bent	3	adj	strip	4	n
crooked	3	adj	zigzag	4	n
cross	3	n	beeline	5	n
straight	3	adj	crisscross	5	n

219. Alphabet and Letters—related clusters: 238, 286

Word	Importance	Part of Speech	Word	Importance	Part of Speech
alphabet	2	n	**symbol**	3	n
consonant	3	n	**vowel**	3	n
letter	3	n	alphabetically	4	adv

(Continued)

Word	Importance	Part of Speech	Word	Importance	Part of Speech
Braille	4	n	beta	5	n
code	4	n	cuneiform	5	n
alpha	5	n	italic	5	adj

220. Fire—related clusters: 78, 376, 414, 442

Word	Importance	Part of Speech	Word	Importance	Part of Speech
fire	2	n	stoke	4	v
burn	3	v	torch	4	n
campfire	3	n	wildfire	4	n
flame	3	n	arson	5	n
spark	3	n	backfire	5	n
blaze	4	n	combustion	5	n
bonfire	4	n	inferno	5	n
ignite	4	v	kindle	5	v
scorch	4	v	sizzle	5	v
singe	4	v	smolder	5	v

221. Ease and Difficulty—related clusters: 240

Word	Importance	Part of Speech	Word	Importance	Part of Speech
easy	2	adj	simplify	4	v
difficult	3	adj	tiresome	4	adj
impossible	3	adj	troublesome	4	adj
problem	3	n	unbearable	4	adj
cinch	4	n	uneasy	4	adj
comfortable	4	adj	fluent	5	adj
convenient	4	adj	grueling	5	adj
difficulty	4	n	hardship	5	adj
ease	4	n	predicament	5	n

222. Tastes Related to Food—related clusters: 48, 51, 74, 86, 124, 136, 153, 162, 174, 176, 208, 232, 246

Word	Importance	Part of Speech	Word	Importance	Part of Speech
taste	2	n	**ripe**	3	adj
flavor	3	n	**sour**	3	adj
juicy	3	adj	**sweet**	3	adj

Word	Importance	Part of Speech	Word	Importance	Part of Speech
tasty	3	adj	stale	4	adj
bitter	4	adj	savor	5	v
delicious	4	adj	succulent	5	adj
edible	4	adj	tangy	5	adj

223. Cleaning Tools—related clusters: 185, 288

Word	Importance	Part of Speech	Word	Importance	Part of Speech
brush	2	n	broom	4	n
soap	2	n	cleaner	4	n
broomstick	3	n	detergent	4	n
floss	3	n	lather	4	n
mop	3	n	lotion	4	n
shampoo	3	n	toothpick	4	n
sponge	3	n	vacuum	4	n
suds	3	n	bleach	5	n
toothbrush	3	n	lye	5	n
toothpaste	3	n			

224. Clothing and Grooming Accessories—related clusters: 47, 62, 125, 129, 145, 178, 212, 263, 354, 435

Word	Importance	Part of Speech	Word	Importance	Part of Speech
brush	2	n	**umbrella**	3	n
comb	2	n	bead	4	n
handkerchief	2	n	bracelet	4	n
buckle	3	n	cane	4	n
fan	3	n	cologne	4	n
jewelry	3	n	garland	4	n
kerchief	3	n	lipstick	4	n
necklace	3	n	locket	4	n
perfume	3	n	makeup	4	n
pin	3	n	muffler	4	n
ribbon	3	n	necktie	4	n
ring	3	n	parasol	4	n
scarf	3	n	razor	4	n
tie	3	n	sash	4	n

(Continued)

Word	Importance	Part of Speech	Word	Importance	Part of Speech
suspender	4	n	cosmetics	5	n
trinket	4	n	pendant	5	n
bandanna	5	n	scepter	5	n
corsage	5	n	sequin	5	n

225. Mental Exploration—related clusters: 46, 67, 132, 137, 154, 249, 277, 347, 348, 349, 384

Word	Importance	Part of Speech	Word	Importance	Part of Speech
news	2	n	inspect	4	v
search	2	v	inspection	4	n
analyze	3	v	probe	4	v
examine	3	v	research	4	n
experiment	3	n	review	4	v
explore	3	v	survey	4	n
homework	3	n	hypothesis	5	n
investigate	3	v	imprint	5	v
lesson	3	n	rummage	5	v
schoolwork	3	n			

226. Wind and Storms—related clusters: 90, 307, 375, 406

Word	Importance	Part of Speech	Word	Importance	Part of Speech
storm	2	n	gust	4	n
thunder	2	n	monsoon	4	n
blizzard	3	n	rainstorm	4	n
downpour	3	n	snowstorm	4	n
draft	3	n	squall	4	n
hurricane	3	n	tempest	4	n
lightning	3	n	thunderbolt	4	n
thunderstorm	3	n	twister	4	n
tornado	3	n	windstorm	4	n
wind	3	n	Chinook	5	n
breeze	4	n	torrent	5	n
cyclone	4	n	typhoon	5	n
gale	4	n			

227. Names for Spiritual/Mythological Characters—related clusters: 56, 94, 111, 203, 204, 205, 206, 317, 330, 343, 344, 382, 432, 444

Word	Importance	Part of Speech	Word	Importance	Part of Speech
angel	2	n	genie	4	n
god	2	n	goblin	4	n
cupid	3	n	imp	4	n
devil	3	n	phantom	4	n
elf	3	n	pixie	4	n
fairy	3	n	saint	4	n
ghost	3	n	spook	4	n
monster	3	n	vampire	4	n
witch	3	n	werewolf	4	n
wizard	3	n	ghoul	5	n
deity	4	n	hag	5	n
demon	4	n	soul	5	n

228. Goodness and Kindness—related clusters: 211, 278, 294, 295, 332, 350, 351, 385, 386, 387, 388, 389, 429, 433, 434

Word	Importance	Part of Speech	Word	Importance	Part of Speech
thankful	2	adj	kindness	4	n
considerate	3	adj	mercy	4	n
courteous	3	adj	noble	4	adj
gentle	3	adj	pleasant	4	adj
grateful	3	adj	sensitive	4	adj
kind	3	adj	social	4	adj
nice	3	adj	tender	4	adj
polite	3	adj	thoughtful	4	adj
respectful	3	adj	unselfish	4	adj
affectionate	4	adj	willing	4	adj
charity	4	n	amiable	5	adj
civil	4	adj	hospitality	5	n
consideration	4	n	liberal	5	adj
generous	4	adj	sympathetic	5	adj
grace	4	n	tactful	5	adj

229. Names of People in Sports—related clusters: 68, 88, 146, 167, 173, 236, 257, 264, 265, 266, 297, 333, 334, 355, 356, 357, 358, 359, 360, 361, 392, 393, 394, 395, 396, 397, 436

Word	Importance	Part of Speech	Word	Importance	Part of Speech
athlete	2	n	swimmer	4	n
batter	3	n	trainer	4	n
boxer	3	n	umpire	4	n
catcher	3	n	underdog	4	n
coach	3	n	wrestler	4	n
loser	3	n	daredevil	5	n
runner	3	n	fullback	5	n
winner	3	n	halfback	5	n
acrobat	4	n	horseman	5	n
ballplayer	4	n	horsewoman	5	n
lifeguard	4	n	jockey	5	n
player	4	n	marksman	5	n
quarterback	4	n	referee	5	n
shortstop	4	n	timekeeper	5	n
skier	4	n			

230. Disease—related clusters: 231, 287, 305, 371, 404

Word	Importance	Part of Speech	Word	Importance	Part of Speech
sick	2	adj	famine	4	n
disease	3	n	infection	4	n
health	3	n	plague	4	n
ill	3	adj	sickness	4	n
injury	3	n	symptom	4	n
well	3	adj	hale	5	adj
ailment	4	n	robust	5	adj
condition	4	n	sane	5	adj
contagious	4	adj	wholesome	5	adj
epidemic	4	n			

231. Medicine—related clusters: 230, 287, 305, 371, 404

Word	Importance	Part of Speech	Word	Importance	Part of Speech
pill	2	n	surgery	4	n
aspirin	3	n	transplant	4	v
bandage	3	n	treatment	4	n
crutch	3	n	vaccination	4	n
medicine	3	n	vaccine	4	n
vitamin	3	n	antidote	5	n
antibiotics	4	n	dissect	5	v
Band-Aid	4	n	dose	5	n
cast	4	n	inoculate	5	v
diagnose	4	v	iodine	5	n
drug	4	n	narcotic	5	n
ointment	4	n	remedy	5	n
operate	4	v	serum	5	n
operation	4	n	splint	5	n
penicillin	4	n	therapy	5	n
potion	4	n	tonic	5	n
sling	4	n	transfusion	5	n

232. Hunger and Thirst—related clusters: 48, 51, 74, 86, 124, 136, 153, 162, 174, 176, 208, 222, 246

Word	Importance	Part of Speech	Word	Importance	Part of Speech
hungry	2	adj	**thirst**	3	n
hunger	3	n	**thirsty**	3	adj
starve	3	v	appetite	4	n

233. Time (General)—related clusters: 2, 16, 24, 29, 52, 59, 79, 83, 126, 144

Word	Importance	Part of Speech	Word	Importance	Part of Speech
time	2	n	mealtime	4	n
bedtime	3	n	springtime	4	n
daytime	3	n	summertime	4	n
dinnertime	3	n	suppertime	4	n
lunchtime	3	n	wartime	4	n
lifetime	4	n	wintertime	4	n

234. Parts of Vehicles—related clusters: 93, 97, 120, 128, 159, 318, 331

Word	Importance	Part of Speech	Word	Importance	Part of Speech
paddle	2	n	deck	4	n
wheel	2	n	gangplank	4	n
anchor	3	n	mast	4	n
fender	3	n	propeller	4	n
mirror	3	n	rudder	4	n
oar	3	n	windshield	4	n
parachute	3	n	buoy	5	n
seatbelt	3	n	dashboard	5	n
tail	3	n	helm	5	n
tire	3	n	hub	5	n
trunk	3	n	mainstay	5	n
wing	3	n	outboard	5	n
axle	4	n	prow	5	n
cockpit	4	n	rotor	5	n

235. Contractions (Not)—related clusters: 42, 81, 85, 150, 274

Word	Importance	Part of Speech	Word	Importance	Part of Speech
don't	2	cont	**haven't**	3	cont
isn't	2	cont	**shouldn't**	3	cont
ain't	3	cont	**weren't**	3	cont
aren't	3	cont	**won't**	3	cont
can't	3	cont	**wouldn't**	3	cont
couldn't	3	cont	hadn't	4	cont
doesn't	3	cont	mustn't	4	cont
hasn't	3	cont	wasn't	4	cont

236. Occupations (General)—related clusters: 68, 88, 146, 167, 173, 229, 257, 264, 265, 266, 297, 333, 334, 355, 356, 357, 358, 359, 360, 361, 392, 393, 394, 395, 396, 397, 436

Word	Importance	Part of Speech	Word	Importance	Part of Speech
job	2	n	**task**	3	n
career	3	n	**worker**	3	n
chore	3	n	craft	4	n
housework	3	n	errand	4	n
profession	3	n	homemaker	4	n

Word	Importance	Part of Speech	Word	Importance	Part of Speech
livelihood	4	n	workman	4	n
occupation	4	n	breadwinner	5	n
production	4	n	sideline	5	n
profession	4	n	vocation	5	n
role	4	n			

237. Rocks and Jewels—related clusters: 133, 259, 337, 402, 438

Word	Importance	Part of Speech	Word	Importance	Part of Speech
rock	2	n	limestone	4	n
boulder	3	n	nugget	4	n
diamond	3	n	opal	4	n
jewel	3	n	pearl	4	n
marble	3	n	rubble	4	n
stone	3	n	ruby	4	n
bedrock	4	n	shale	4	n
charcoal	4	n	slate	4	n
coal	4	n	turquoise	4	n
cobblestone	4	n	aggregate	5	n
coke	4	n	amethyst	5	n
crystal	4	n	anthracite	5	n
emerald	4	n	asphalt	5	n
gem	4	n	conglomerate	5	n
granite	4	n	jade	5	n
gravel	4	n	topaz	5	n

238. Words, Phrases, and Sentences—related clusters: 219, 286

Word	Importance	Part of Speech	Word	Importance	Part of Speech
word	2	n	clause	4	n
adjective	3	n	conjunction	4	n
adverb	3	n	object	4	n
noun	3	n	participle	4	n
sentence	3	n	phrase	4	n
verb	3	n	predicate	4	n
affix	4	n	prefix	4	n
antonym	4	n	preposition	4	n

(Continued)

Word	Importance	Part of Speech	Word	Importance	Part of Speech
pronoun	4	n	syllable	4	n
pun	4	n	synonym	4	n
subject	4	n	homograph	5	n
suffix	4	n	homonym	5	n
superlative	4	n	homophone	5	n

239. Art—related clusters: 54, 77, 244

Word	Importance	Part of Speech	Word	Importance	Part of Speech
art	2	n	mural	4	n
painting	3	n	portfolio	4	n
photo	3	n	portrait	4	n
photograph	3	n	snapshot	4	n
picture	3	n	space	4	n
statue	3	n	tattoo	4	n
album	4	n	mosaic	5	n

240. Safety and Danger—related clusters: 221

Word	Importance	Part of Speech	Word	Importance	Part of Speech
safe	2	adj	hazard	4	n
danger	3	n	immune	4	adj
dangerous	3	adj	protective	4	adj
risk	3	n	secure	4	adj
trouble	3	n	jeopardy	5	n
unsafe	3	adj	peril	5	n
harmful	4	adj	pitfall	5	n
harmless	4	adj	treacherous	5	adj

241. Actions Associated with the Nose—related clusters: 151, 152, 196

Word	Importance	Part of Speech	Word	Importance	Part of Speech
smell	2	v	**stink**	3	n
sneeze	3	v	aroma	4	n
sniff	3	v	fragrant	4	adj
snore	3	v	fume	4	n
snort	3	v	incense	4	n

Word	Importance	Part of Speech	Word	Importance	Part of Speech
inhale	4	v	scent	4	n
odor	4	n	reek	5	v
perfume	4	n	stench	5	n

242. Abrasive/Cutting Actions—related clusters: 92, 96, 118, 119, 163, 254, 275, 276, 314, 315, 316, 419, 420

Word	Importance	Part of Speech	Word	Importance	Part of Speech
cut	2	v	grate	4	v
rub	2	v	grind	4	v
carve	3	v	peck	4	v
chop	3	v	pierce	4	v
clip	3	v	prick	4	v
dig	3	v	scrape	4	v
mow	3	v	shear	4	v
peel	3	v	shred	4	v
scoop	3	v	slash	4	v
scratch	3	v	slit	4	v
shave	3	v	whittle	4	v
slice	3	v	dredge	5	v
snip	3	v	excavate	5	v
stab	3	v	gnash	5	v
bulldoze	4	v	hack	5	v
burrow	4	v	mince	5	v
chafe	4	v	pare	5	v
crop	4	v			

243. Lack of Value—related clusters: 58, 72, 368

Word	Importance	Part of Speech	Word	Importance	Part of Speech
bad	2	adj	absurd	4	adj
awful	3	adj	corrupt	4	adj
evil	3	adj	foul	4	adj
terrible	3	adj	grim	4	adj
wicked	3	adj	horrible	4	adj
worse	3	adj	inferior	4	adj
worst	3	adj	negative	4	adj

(Continued)

Word	Importance	Part of Speech	Word	Importance	Part of Speech
ridiculous	4	adj	ghastly	5	adj
unimportant	4	adj	petty	5	adj
useless	4	adj	shabby	5	adj
worthless	4	adj	shoddy	5	adj
dire	5	adj	sinister	5	adj

244. Musical Instruments—related clusters: 54, 77, 239

Word	Importance	Part of Speech	Word	Importance	Part of Speech
instrument	2	n	piccolo	4	n
banjo	3	n	recorder	4	n
drum	3	n	saxophone	4	n
guitar	3	n	tambourine	4	n
piano	3	n	trombone	4	n
triangle	3	n	trumpet	4	n
violin	3	n	tuba	4	n
accordion	4	n	xylophone	4	n
alto	4	n	cymbal	5	n
bagpipe	4	n	fife	5	n
bass	4	n	glockenspiel	5	n
bugle	4	n	harpsichord	5	n
cello	4	n	lute	5	n
clarinet	4	n	lyre	5	n
cornet	4	n	mandolin	5	n
fiddle	4	n	oboe	5	n
flute	4	n	spinet	5	n
harmonica	4	n	tom-tom	5	n
harp	4	n	ukulele	5	n
keyboard	4	n	viola	5	n
organ	4	n	woodwind	5	n
percussion	4	n			

245. Birth, Life, and Death—related clusters: 329

Word	Importance	Part of Speech	Word	Importance	Part of Speech
dead	2	adj	**die**	3	v
alive	3	adj	**egg**	3	n
born	3	v	**hatch**	3	v

Word	Importance	Part of Speech	Word	Importance	Part of Speech
life	3	n	subsist	4	v
live	3	v	animate	5	v
wake	3	v	carcass	5	n
birth	4	n	conceive	5	v
breed	4	v	corpse	5	n
burial	4	n	dwell	5	v
death	4	n	entity	5	n
exist	4	v	funeral	5	n
extinct	4	adj	gene	5	n
fertile	4	adj	genetic	5	adj
inhabit	4	v	germinate	5	v
mortal	4	adj	incubate	5	v
mummy	4	n	natal	5	adj
perish	4	v	populate	5	v
pregnant	4	adj	reside	5	v
reproduction	4	n	spawn	5	v
sex	4	n	suffocate	5	v
sperm	4	n			

246. Types of Food—related clusters: 48, 51, 74, 86, 124, 136, 153, 162, 174, 176, 208, 222, 232

Word	Importance	Part of Speech	Word	Importance	Part of Speech
food	2	n	relish	4	n
crop	3	n	supplies	4	n
fruit	3	n	cellulose	5	n
meat	3	n	garnish	5	n
seafood	3	n	glucose	5	n
sweets	3	n	hash	5	n
vegetables	3	n	legume	5	n
calorie	4	n	nourishment	5	n
carbohydrate	4	n	nutrient	5	n
diet	4	n	provisions	5	n
nutrition	4	n	pulp	5	n
protein	4	n			

247. Joining—related clusters: 38, 39, 40, 44, 66, 141, 147, 169, 170, 182, 199, 215, 216, 280, 281, 282, 283, 300, 301, 302, 322, 338, 403

Word	Importance	Part of Speech	Word	Importance	Part of Speech
meet	2	v	link	4	v
attach	3	v	matrimony	4	n
combine	3	v	seam	4	n
connect	3	v	splice	4	v
fasten	3	v	synthesis	4	n
include	3	v	tether	4	v
join	3	v	union	4	n
marriage	3	n	unite	4	v
marry	3	v	wed	4	v
stick	3	v	affix	5	v
wedding	3	n	associate	5	v
accompany	4	v	bond	5	v
connection	4	n	collide	5	v
consist	4	v	comprise	5	v
constitute	4	v	engage	5	v
contain	4	v	fuse	5	v
hitch	4	v	graft	5	v
intersect	4	v	merge	5	v
involve	4	v	shackle	5	v
junction	4	n			

248. Publication Types—related clusters: 53, 71, 112, 138, 256, 279, 319, 320

Word	Importance	Part of Speech	Word	Importance	Part of Speech
book	2	n	**novel**	3	n
bible	3	n	**outline**	3	n
booklet	3	n	**storybook**	3	n
chapter	3	n	**summary**	3	n
cookbook	3	n	**text**	3	n
diary	3	n	**textbook**	3	n
dictionary	3	n	album	4	n
essay	3	n	almanac	4	n
journal	3	n	appendix	4	n
magazine	3	n	article	4	n
newspaper	3	n	atlas	4	n

Word	Importance	Part of Speech	Word	Importance	Part of Speech
autobiography	4	n	passage	4	n
bibliography	4	n	preface	4	n
biography	4	n	primer	4	n
catalogue	4	n	publication	4	n
column	4	n	report	4	n
document	4	n	schoolbook	4	n
encyclopedia	4	n	script	4	n
episode	4	n	scripture	4	n
foreword	4	n	testament	4	n
glossary	4	n	thesaurus	4	n
headline	4	n	thesis	4	n
index	4	n	volume	4	n
issue	4	n	excerpt	5	n
manual	4	n	format	5	n
pamphlet	4	n	log	5	n
paperback	4	n	manuscript	5	n
paragraph	4	n	media	5	n

249. Conclusions—related clusters: 46, 67, 132, 137, 154, 225, 277, 347, 348, 349, 384

Word	Importance	Part of Speech	Word	Importance	Part of Speech
guess	2	v	suppose	3	v
calculate	3	v	assume	4	v
clue	3	n	calculation	4	n
compose	3	v	compute	4	v
conclude	3	v	confirm	4	v
create	3	v	determine	4	v
design	3	v	discovery	4	n
estimate	3	v	evaluate	4	v
fact	3	n	evidence	4	n
information	3	n	forecast	4	v
invent	3	v	hunch	4	n
invention	3	n	infer	4	v
mystery	3	n	prediction	4	n
predict	3	v	principle	4	n
prove	3	v	proof	4	n
solve	3	v	revise	4	v

(Continued)

Word	Importance	Part of Speech	Word	Importance	Part of Speech
solution	4	n	enigma	5	n
suspect	4	v	foresee	5	v
theory	4	n	improvise	5	v
abstract	5	n	resolve	5	v
basis	5	n	speculate	5	v
criteria	5	n	suspicion	5	n
devise	5	v			

250. Destructive Actions—related clusters: 110, 161, 260

Word	Importance	Part of Speech	Word	Importance	Part of Speech
accident	3	n	extinguish	4	v
break	3	v	mar	4	v
crash	3	v	mash	4	v
crush	3	v	puncture	4	v
damage	3	v	shatter	4	v
dent	3	v	squelch	4	v
destroy	3	v	wreckage	4	n
mark	3	v	devastate	5	v
ruin	3	v	erode	5	v
scratch	3	v	fracture	5	v
waste	3	v	mangle	5	v
wreck	3	v	mishap	5	n
chip	4	v	nick	5	v
demolish	4	v	rupture	5	v
destruction	4	n	snuff	5	v
erase	4	v			

251. Building Materials (General)—related clusters: 107, 164, 181, 268, 325, 367

Word	Importance	Part of Speech	Word	Importance	Part of Speech
bar	3	n	**sewer**	3	n
brick	3	n	**tube**	3	n
cardboard	3	n	**wire**	3	n
paste	3	n	adobe	4	n
pipe	3	n	asbestos	4	n
plastic	3	n	brace	4	n

Word	Importance	Part of Speech	Word	Importance	Part of Speech
cement	4	n	stilt	4	n
ceramic	4	n	support	4	n
concrete	4	n	tar	4	n
culvert	4	n	tile	4	n
drainpipe	4	n	tin	4	n
duct	4	n	adhesive	5	n
hoop	4	n	bracket	5	n
pavement	4	n	clapboard	5	n
plaster	4	n	cornerstone	5	n
pole	4	n	fixture	5	n
porcelain	4	n	grout	5	n
prop	4	n	mainstay	5	n
putty	4	n	mortar	5	n
rod	4	n	pedestal	5	n
rung	4	n	stucco	5	n

252. Similarity—related clusters: 5, 27, 299

Word	Importance	Part of Speech	Word	Importance	Part of Speech
alike	3	adj	imitate	4	v
copy	3	n	imitation	4	n
equal	3	adj	likeness	4	n
even	3	adj	match	4	n
example	3	n	mimic	4	v
like	3	adj	parallel	4	adj
same	3	adj	related	4	adj
similar	3	adj	resemblance	4	n
twin	3	n	resemble	4	v
agreement	4	n	similarity	4	n
approximate	4	adj	unanimous	4	adj
artificial	4	adj	accord	5	n
comparison	4	n	alternate	5	adj
consistent	4	adj	analogy	5	n
counterfeit	4	adj	compatible	5	adj
echo	4	v	conform	5	v
exact	4	adj	congruent	5	adj
harmony	4	n	ditto	5	n

(Continued)

Word	Importance	Part of Speech	Word	Importance	Part of Speech
duplicate	5	n	monotony	5	n
identical	5	adj	simile	5	n
metaphor	5	n	substitute	5	n
mimeograph	5	n	synthetic	5	adj

253. Physical Characteristics—related clusters: 186, 187, 407

Word	Importance	Part of Speech	Word	Importance	Part of Speech
athletic	3	adj	nimble	4	adj
beauty	3	n	powerful	4	adj
clumsy	3	adj	puny	4	adj
health	3	n	rickety	4	adj
might	3	n	rugged	4	adj
power	3	n	scrawny	4	adj
strength	3	n	vigor	4	n
strong	3	adj	agility	5	n
weak	3	adj	brawn	5	n
weakness	3	n	dexterity	5	n
agile	4	adj	feeble	5	adj
awkward	4	adj	gaunt	5	adj
frail	4	adj	gawky	5	adj
handicap	4	n	potent	5	adj
muscular	4	adj	spry	5	adj

254. Weapons—related clusters: 92, 96, 118, 119, 163, 242, 275, 276, 314, 315, 316, 419, 420

Word	Importance	Part of Speech	Word	Importance	Part of Speech
arrow	3	n	arms	4	n
bomb	3	n	boomerang	4	n
bullet	3	n	bow	4	n
firecracker	3	n	cannon	4	n
fireworks	3	n	dagger	4	n
gun	3	n	dart	4	n
sword	3	n	dynamite	4	n
ammunition	4	n	firearms	4	n

Word	Importance	Part of Speech	Word	Importance	Part of Speech
grenade	4	n	spear	4	n
harpoon	4	n	tomahawk	4	n
holster	4	n	torpedo	4	n
missile	4	n	weapon	4	n
pellet	4	n	whip	4	n
pistol	4	n	cutlass	5	n
revolver	4	n	guillotine	5	n
rifle	4	n	javelin	5	n
shotgun	4	n	lance	5	n
sling	4	n	musket	5	n
slingshot	4	n	noose	5	n

255. Persuasion/Advice—related clusters: 14, 61, 100, 105, 177, 198, 207, 345, 346, 383

Word	Importance	Part of Speech	Word	Importance	Part of Speech
advise	3	v	plead	4	v
appeal	3	v	sway	4	v
beg	3	v	tempt	4	v
convince	3	v	urge	4	v
cue	3	v	bait	5	v
persuade	3	v	bias	5	n
recommend	3	v	bribe	5	v
suggest	3	v	canvass	5	n
coax	4	v	corrupt	5	v
hint	4	v	induce	5	v
influence	4	v	lure	5	v
petition	4	v	petition	5	v

256. Messages—related clusters: 53, 71, 112, 138, 248, 279, 319, 320

Word	Importance	Part of Speech	Word	Importance	Part of Speech
letter	3	n	**signal**	3	n
message	3	n	**valentine**	3	n
note	3	n	advertisement	4	n
postcard	3	n	bulletin	4	n
poster	3	n	commercial	4	n

(Continued)

Word	Importance	Part of Speech	Word	Importance	Part of Speech
motto	4	n	billboard	5	n
signpost	4	n	memo	5	n
slogan	4	n	tidings	5	n
telegram	4	n			

257. Domains of Work—related clusters: 68, 88, 146, 167, 173, 229, 236, 264, 265, 266, 297, 333, 334, 355, 356, 357, 358, 359, 360, 361, 392, 393, 394, 395, 396, 397, 436

Word	Importance	Part of Speech	Word	Importance	Part of Speech
business	3	n	**science**	3	n
law	3	n	**technology**	3	n
medicine	3	n	agriculture	4	n
military	3	n	industry	4	n
religion	3	n	politics	4	n

258. Groups of Animals/People—related clusters: 98, 200, 298, 401

Word	Importance	Part of Speech	Word	Importance	Part of Speech
band	3	n	quartet	4	n
class	3	n	species	4	n
club	3	n	throng	4	n
crowd	3	n	trio	4	n
herd	3	n	bevy	5	n
team	3	n	brood	5	n
cast	4	n	covey	5	n
chorus	4	n	denomination	5	n
crew	4	n	ensemble	5	n
flock	4	n	fraternity	5	n
gang	4	n	gaggle	5	n
horde	4	n	mass	5	n
huddle	4	n	phylum	5	n
mob	4	n	pod	5	n
multitude	4	n	quintet	5	n
posse	4	n			

259. Metals—related clusters: 133, 237, 337, 402, 438

Word	Importance	Part of Speech	Word	Importance	Part of Speech
gold	3	n	beryllium	5	n
iron	3	n	cobalt	5	n
magnet	3	n	feldspar	5	n
metal	3	n	gneiss	5	n
silver	3	n	graphite	5	n
steel	3	n	lodestone	5	n
aluminum	4	n	magma	5	n
brass	4	n	magnesium	5	n
bronze	4	n	manganese	5	n
calcium	4	n	mica	5	n
carbon	4	n	obsidian	5	n
chrome	4	n	phosphorus	5	n
copper	4	n	potassium	5	n
flint	4	n	pumice	5	n
lava	4	n	quartz	5	n
lead	4	n	radium	5	n
ore	4	n	silicon	5	n
uranium	4	n	solder	5	n
zinc	4	n	talc	5	n
alloy	5	n	tungsten	5	n
bauxite	5	n			

260. War and Fighting—related clusters: 110, 161, 250

Word	Importance	Part of Speech	Word	Importance	Part of Speech
battle	3	n	combat	4	v
fight	3	v	conflict	4	n
peace	3	n	duel	4	v
revolution	3	n	friction	4	n
war	3	n	invade	4	v
wrestle	3	v	invasion	4	n
brawl	4	n	raid	4	n
challenge	4	v	repel	4	v
clash	4	v	revolution	4	n

(Continued)

Word	Importance	Part of Speech	Word	Importance	Part of Speech
riot	4	n	struggle	4	v
rumble	4	v	fray	5	n
scuffle	4	n	onslaught	5	n
showdown	4	n	siege	5	n
skirmish	4	n	warfare	5	n
strife	4	n			

261. Likelihood and Certainty—related clusters: 289, 328

Word	Importance	Part of Speech	Word	Importance	Part of Speech
bet	3	n	gamble	4	v
certain	3	adj	hazard	4	n
chance	3	n	lottery	4	n
likely	3	adj	mysterious	4	adj
luck	3	n	opportunity	4	n
miracle	3	n	probable	4	adj
possible	3	adj	stake	4	n
absolute	4	adj	uncertain	4	adj
accidental	4	adj	ambiguous	5	adj
bid	4	n	boon	5	n
casual	4	adj	contingent	5	adj
definite	4	adj	haphazard	5	adj
destiny	4	n	jinx	5	n
doom	4	n	liable	5	adj
doubtful	4	adj	potential	5	adj
fate	4	n	random	5	adj
fluke	4	n	venture	5	n

262. Order and Complexity—related clusters: 290

Word	Importance	Part of Speech	Word	Importance	Part of Speech
balance	3	n	**order**	3	n
blank	3	adj	**plain**	3	adj
fancy	3	adj	**simple**	3	adj

Word	Importance	Part of Speech	Word	Importance	Part of Speech
bare	4	adj	uniform	4	adj
bleak	4	adj	void	4	n
complex	4	adj	bedlam	5	n
confusion	4	n	cosmos	5	n
neutral	4	adj	elaborate	5	adj
offset	4	adj	equilibrium	5	n
ornate	4	adj	intricate	5	adj
pure	4	adj	maze	5	n
steady	4	adj	muddle	5	v
symmetry	4	n	turmoil	5	n
tangle	4	n	wrought	5	v
technical	4	adj			

263. Clothing (General)—related clusters: 47, 62, 125, 129, 145, 178, 212, 224, 354, 435

Word	Importance	Part of Speech	Word	Importance	Part of Speech
clothes	3	n	fashion	4	n
clothing	3	n	outfit	4	n
costume	3	n	style	4	n
suit	3	n	wardrobe	4	n
uniform	3	n	apparel	5	n
array	4	n	garb	5	n
attire	4	n	garment	5	n
design	4	n	lingerie	5	n
fad	4	n			

264. Artists and Performers—related clusters: 68, 88, 146, 167, 173, 229, 236, 257, 265, 266, 297, 333, 334, 355, 356, 357, 358, 359, 360, 361, 392, 393, 394, 395, 396, 397, 436

Word	Importance	Part of Speech	Word	Importance	Part of Speech
artist	3	n	**painter**	3	n
choir	3	n	**singer**	3	n
drummer	3	n	conductor	4	n

(Continued)

Word	Importance	Part of Speech	Word	Importance	Part of Speech
designer	4	n	soprano	4	n
musician	4	n	violinist	4	n
photographer	4	n			

265. Public Officials—related clusters: 68, 88, 146, 167, 173, 229, 236, 257, 264, 266, 297, 333, 334, 355, 356, 357, 358, 359, 360, 361, 392, 393, 394, 395, 396, 397, 436

Word	Importance	Part of Speech	Word	Importance	Part of Speech
firefighter	3	n	marshal	4	n
officer	3	n	policewoman	4	n
policeman	3	n	redcoat	4	n
sheriff	3	n	trooper	4	n
soldier	3	n	colonel	5	n
admiral	4	n	constable	5	n
airman	4	n	corporal	5	n
captain	4	n	lieutenant	5	n
deputy	4	n	sergeant	5	n
detective	4	n			

266. Religious and Clergy—related clusters: 68, 88, 146, 167, 173, 229, 236, 257, 264, 265, 297, 333, 334, 355, 356, 357, 358, 359, 360, 361, 392, 393, 394, 395, 396, 397, 436

Word	Importance	Part of Speech	Word	Importance	Part of Speech
minister	3	n	rabbi	4	n
nun	3	n	abbot	5	n
pastor	3	n	apostle	5	n
pope	3	n	cardinal	5	n
priest	3	n	clergyman	5	n
bishop	4	n	deacon	5	n
missionary	4	n	hermit	5	n
monk	4	n	parson	5	n
prophet	4	n			

267. Craters and Valleys—related clusters: 50, 114, 139, 168, 362, 363, 398

Word	Importance	Part of Speech	Word	Importance	Part of Speech
hole	2	n	ravine	4	n
canyon	3	n	shaft	4	n
crack	3	n	trench	4	n
ditch	3	n	cavity	5	n
manhole	3	n	chasm	5	n
pit	3	n	cleft	5	n
valley	3	n	crevice	5	n
cavern	4	n	dale	5	n
cove	4	n	furrow	5	n
crater	4	n	glen	5	n
gap	4	n	gulch	5	n
groove	4	n	rift	5	n
gully	4	n	rut	5	n
notch	4	n	silo	5	n

268. Objects/Materials Used to Cover Things—related clusters: 107, 164, 181, 251, 325, 367

Word	Importance	Part of Speech	Word	Importance	Part of Speech
cork	3	n	foil	4	n
cover	3	n	plug	4	n
flap	3	n	thimble	4	n
lid	3	n	tinfoil	4	n
mask	3	n	wrapper	4	n
canvas	4	n	camouflage	5	n
cellophane	4	n			

269. Plants and Flowers—related clusters: 36, 108, 192, 421

Word	Importance	Part of Speech	Word	Importance	Part of Speech
berry	3	n	bud	4	n
blossom	3	n	bulb	4	n
dandelion	3	n	buttercup	4	n
rose	3	n	cactus	4	n
seed	3	n	carnation	4	n
bouquet	4	n	daffodil	4	n

(Continued)

Word	Importance	Part of Speech	Word	Importance	Part of Speech
daisy	4	n	bluebell	5	n
holly	4	n	briar	5	n
huckleberry	4	n	chrysanthemum	5	n
ivy	4	n	cowslip	5	n
lilac	4	n	flax	5	n
lily	4	n	gardenia	5	n
mistletoe	4	n	geranium	5	n
petal	4	n	goldenrod	5	n
pod	4	n	hemp	5	n
pollen	4	n	honeysuckle	5	n
poppy	4	n	jute	5	n
sprout	4	n	larkspur	5	n
stamen	4	n	linseed	5	n
sunflower	4	n	marigold	5	n
thistle	4	n	petunia	5	n
tulip	4	n	pistil	5	n
wildflower	4	n	snapdragon	5	n
anemone	5	n	spore	5	n

270. Curved and Circular Shapes—related clusters: 69, 99, 142, 193, 218, 303, 326

Word	Importance	Part of Speech	Word	Importance	Part of Speech
circle	2	n	convex	4	adj
bend	3	n	disk	4	n
curl	3	n	flex	4	v
curve	3	n	halo	4	n
cylinder	3	n	sphere	4	n
loop	3	n	spiral	4	n
oval	3	n	warp	4	v
round	3	adj	arc	5	n
twist	3	n	concave	5	adj
circuit	4	n	crescent	5	n
circular	4	adj	kink	5	n
coil	4	n	parabola	5	n
cone	4	n			

271. Light—related clusters: 272, 306, 372, 405

Word	Importance	Part of Speech	Word	Importance	Part of Speech
bright	3	adj	moonlight	4	n
clear	3	adj	radiant	4	adj
light	3	adj	starlight	4	n
shiny	3	adj	sunlight	4	n
sunshine	3	n	vivid	4	adj
brightness	4	n	glimmer	5	n
brilliant	4	adj	glint	5	n
candlelight	4	n	gloss	5	n
daylight	4	n	luminous	5	adj
gleam	4	n	luster	5	n
lamplight	4	n	sheen	5	n

272. Light Producers—related clusters: 271, 306, 372, 405

Word	Importance	Part of Speech	Word	Importance	Part of Speech
candle	3	n	lantern	4	n
candlestick	3	n	laser	4	n
lamp	3	n	moonbeam	4	n
light	3	n	ray	4	n
lightbulb	3	n	searchlight	4	n
beacon	4	n	sunbeam	4	n
beam	4	n	torch	4	n
bonfire	4	n	filament	5	n
chandelier	4	n	fluorescent	5	n
flare	4	n	sunspot	5	n

273. Cause/Effect—related clusters: 10

Word	Importance	Part of Speech	Word	Importance	Part of Speech
cause	3	n	**result**	3	n
change	3	v	affect	4	v
effect	3	n	agent	4	n
outcome	3	n	consequence	4	n
purpose	3	n	impress	4	v
reason	3	n	incentive	4	n

(Continued)

Word	Importance	Part of Speech	Word	Importance	Part of Speech
influence	4	v	vary	4	v
intent	4	n	impact	5	n
motive	4	n	induce	5	v
stimulate	4	v	initiate	5	v

274. Contractions (Would)—related clusters: 42, 81, 85, 150, 235

Word	Importance	Part of Speech	Word	Importance	Part of Speech
he'd	3	cont	**they'd**	3	cont
I'd	3	cont	**you'd**	3	cont
she'd	3	cont			

275. Engines—related clusters: 92, 96, 118, 119, 163, 242, 254, 276, 314, 315, 316, 419, 420

Word	Importance	Part of Speech	Word	Importance	Part of Speech
battery	3	n	headset	4	n
brake	3	n	crankshaft	5	n
engine	3	n	piston	5	n
jet	3	n	starter	5	n
motor	3	n	throttle	5	n
gear	4	n	turbine	5	n

276. Electronics—related clusters: 92, 96, 118, 119, 163, 242, 254, 275, 314, 315, 316, 419, 420

Word	Importance	Part of Speech	Word	Importance	Part of Speech
computer	3	n	transistor	4	n
keyboard	3	n	bit	5	n
monitor	3	n	chip	5	n
mouse	3	n	format	5	v
robot	3	n	network	5	n
memory	4	n	register	5	n
projector	4	n	thermostat	5	n
terminal	4	n			

277. Topics and Subjects—related clusters: 46, 67, 132, 137, 154, 225, 249, 347, 348, 349, 384

Word	Importance	Part of Speech	Word	Importance	Part of Speech
goal	3	n	scheme	4	n
plan	3	n	strategy	4	n
subject	3	n	theme	4	n
topic	3	n	viewpoint	4	n
core	4	n	keynote	5	n
essence	4	n	scope	5	n
objective	4	n	thesis	5	n

278. Pride and Confidence—related clusters: 211, 228, 294, 295, 332, 350, 351, 385, 386, 387, 388, 389, 429, 433, 434

Word	Importance	Part of Speech	Word	Importance	Part of Speech
certain	3	adj	pride	4	n
confident	3	adj	smug	4	adj
hopeful	3	adj	vain	4	adj
proud	3	adj	conceit	5	n
sure	3	adj	frank	5	adj
confidence	4	n	haughty	5	adj

279. Illustrations and Drawings—related clusters: 53, 71, 112, 138, 248, 256, 319, 320

Word	Importance	Part of Speech	Word	Importance	Part of Speech
diagram	3	n	**map**	3	n
drawing	3	n	chart	4	n
graph	3	n			

280. Motion (General)—related clusters: 38, 39, 40, 44, 66, 141, 147, 169, 170, 182, 199, 215, 216, 247, 281, 282, 283, 300, 301, 302, 322, 338, 403

Word	Importance	Part of Speech	Word	Importance	Part of Speech
action	3	n	portable	4	adj
activity	3	n	traffic	4	n
motion	3	n	kinetic	5	adj
play	3	n	mobile	5	adj
movable	4	adj	osmosis	5	n

281. Vibration—related clusters: 38, 39, 40, 44, 66, 141, 147, 169, 170, 182, 199, 215, 216, 247, 280, 282, 283, 300, 301, 302, 322, 338, 403

Word	Importance	Part of Speech	Word	Importance	Part of Speech
juggle	3	v	sputter	4	v
shake	3	v	squirm	4	v
shiver	3	v	throb	4	v
vibrate	3	v	tremble	4	v
wiggle	3	v	vibration	4	n
flutter	4	v	wobble	4	v
jitter	4	v	wriggle	4	v
quake	4	v	jumble	5	v
quiver	4	v	teeter	5	v
scramble	4	v	totter	5	v
shudder	4	v	waver	5	n

282. Jerking Motion—related clusters: 38, 39, 40, 44, 66, 141, 147, 169, 170, 182, 199, 215, 216, 247, 280, 281, 283, 300, 301, 302, 322, 338, 403

Word	Importance	Part of Speech	Word	Importance	Part of Speech
bounce	3	v	jolt	4	v
fidget	3	v	lurch	4	v
snap	3	v	twitch	4	v
wag	3	v	deflect	5	v
bob	4	v	flounce	5	v
budge	4	v	jounce	5	v
jerk	4	v			

283. Expanding Motion—related clusters: 38, 39, 40, 44, 66, 141, 147, 169, 170, 182, 199, 215, 216, 247, 280, 281, 282, 300, 301, 302, 322, 338, 403

Word	Importance	Part of Speech	Word	Importance	Part of Speech
blast	3	v	erupt	4	v
expand	3	v	extend	4	v
explode	3	v	protrude	4	v
magnify	3	v	scatter	4	v
spread	3	v	swell	4	v
burst	4	v	discharge	5	v
enlarge	4	v	jut	5	v

284. Furnishing and Decorations—related clusters: 91, 113, 123, 134, 217

Word	Importance	Part of Speech	Word	Importance	Part of Speech
banner	3	n	ornament	4	n
carpet	3	n	pennant	4	n
curtain	3	n	tinsel	4	n
rug	3	n	upholster	4	n
vase	3	n	varnish	4	n
accessory	4	n	wallpaper	4	n
canopy	4	n	wreath	4	n
confetti	4	n	cornucopia	5	n
domestic	4	n	spangle	5	n
furnish	4	n	tapestry	5	n
homemade	4	adj	trifle	5	n
linoleum	4	n	urn	5	n
knickknack	4	n			

285. Attitudinals (Truth)—related clusters: 30, 31, 369, 431, 439, 440

Word	Importance	Part of Speech	Word	Importance	Part of Speech
certainly	3	adv	definitely	4	adv
honestly	3	adv	ideally	4	adv
really	3	adv	indeed	4	adv
seriously	3	adv	obviously	4	adv
simply	3	adv	plainly	4	adv
truly	3	adv	strictly	4	adv
apparently	4	adv	surely	4	adv
basically	4	adv	undoubtedly	5	adv
clearly	4	adv	unquestionably	5	adv

286. Language Conventions—related clusters: 219, 238

Word	Importance	Part of Speech	Word	Importance	Part of Speech
comma	3	n	apostrophe	4	n
language	3	n	colon	4	n
period	3	n	dialect	4	n
vocabulary	3	n	diction	4	n
accent	4	n	emphasis	4	n

(Continued)

Word	Importance	Part of Speech	Word	Importance	Part of Speech
grammar	4	n	syntax	4	n
hyphen	4	n	tense	4	n
parenthesis	4	n	voice	4	n
pronunciation	4	n	dash	5	n
punctuation	4	n	idiom	5	n
slang	4	n			

287. Symptoms—related clusters: 230, 231, 305, 371, 404

Word	Importance	Part of Speech	Word	Importance	Part of Speech
dizzy	3	adj	sore	4	n
fever	3	n	toothache	4	n
itch	3	n	coma	5	n
pain	3	n	delirious	5	adj
ache	4	n	impair	5	v
fatigue	4	n	nausea	5	n
groggy	4	adj	pang	5	n
headache	4	n	twinge	5	n
numb	4	adj	vomit	5	v
raw	4	adj	weariness	5	n

288. Uncleanliness and Filth—related clusters: 185, 223

Word	Importance	Part of Speech	Word	Importance	Part of Speech
garbage	3	n	pollute	4	v
junk	3	n	rubbish	4	n
litter	3	n	sewage	4	n
trash	3	n	slop	4	n
bleak	4	adj	smear	4	v
clutter	4	n	smudge	4	n
dismal	4	adj	streak	4	n
dreary	4	adj	contaminate	5	v
filth	4	n	debris	5	n
foul	4	adj	dingy	5	adj
grime	4	n	eyesore	5	n
infect	4	v	taint	5	v
nasty	4	adj			

289. Familiarity and Popularity—related clusters: 261, 328

Word	Importance	Part of Speech	Word	Importance	Part of Speech
common	3	adj	obvious	4	adj
familiar	3	adj	patent	4	adj
normal	3	adj	public	4	adj
ordinary	3	adj	recognition	4	n
popular	3	adj	scandal	4	n
regular	3	adj	traditional	4	adj
usual	3	adj	typical	4	adj
appeal	4	n	universal	4	adj
attraction	4	n	widespread	4	adj
commonplace	4	adj	apparent	5	adj
customary	4	adj	conspicuous	5	adj
dignity	4	n	evident	5	adj
fame	4	n	limelight	5	n
glory	4	n	par	5	n
hip	4	adj	pedestrian	5	adj
honor	4	n	prominent	5	adj
legendary	4	adj	repute	5	n
norm	4	n	standard	5	n

290. Conformity to a Norm—related clusters: 262

Word	Importance	Part of Speech	Word	Importance	Part of Speech
odd	3	adj	scarce	4	adj
rare	3	adj	uncommon	4	adj
special	3	adj	unfinished	4	adj
strange	3	adj	unique	4	adj
weird	3	adj	bizarre	5	adj
distinct	4	adj	defect	5	n
foreign	4	adj	eccentric	5	adj
original	4	adj	grotesque	5	adj
peculiar	4	adj	outlandish	5	adj
quaint	4	adj	uncanny	5	adj
queer	4	adj			

291. Fear—related clusters: 43, 45, 55, 292, 293, 311, 312, 313, 378, 379, 380, 381, 416, 417, 422, 427, 428

Word	Importance	Part of Speech	Word	Importance	Part of Speech
afraid	3	adj	frantic	4	adj
alarm	3	n	horror	4	n
fear	3	n	panic	4	n
nervous	3	adj	shock	4	n
dread	4	n	terror	4	n
eerie	4	adj	fright	5	n

292. Anger—related clusters: 43, 45, 55, 291, 293, 311, 312, 313, 378, 379, 380, 381, 416, 417, 422, 427, 428

Word	Importance	Part of Speech	Word	Importance	Part of Speech
anger	3	n	tantrum	4	n
angry	3	adj	temper	4	n
dislike	3	v	vengeance	4	n
hate	3	v	contempt	5	n
mad	3	adj	despise	5	v
fury	4	n	disgust	5	n
hatred	4	n	huff	5	n
hostile	4	adj	outrage	5	n
incense	4	v	revenge	5	n
irritate	4	v	scorn	5	n
offend	4	v	vehement	5	adj
rage	4	n	wrath	5	n
resent	4	v			

293. Desire—related clusters: 43, 45, 55, 291, 292, 311, 312, 313, 378, 379, 380, 381, 416, 417, 422, 427, 428

Word	Importance	Part of Speech	Word	Importance	Part of Speech
expect	3	v	crave	4	v
miss	3	v	desire	4	v
need	3	v	lust	4	n
selfish	3	adj	seek	4	v
want	3	v	greed	5	n
wish	3	v	hanker	5	v
anticipate	4	v	yearn	5	v

294. Dependability and Eagerness—related clusters: 211, 228, 278, 295, 332, 350, 351, 385, 386, 387, 388, 389, 429, 433, 434

Word	Importance	Part of Speech	Word	Importance	Part of Speech
active	3	adj	pep	4	n
busy	3	adj	productive	4	adj
eager	3	adj	reliable	4	adj
responsible	3	adj	rely	4	v
ambition	4	n	responsibility	4	n
ambitious	4	adj	service	4	n
burden	4	n	sincere	4	adj
credible	4	adj	spirit	4	n
depend	4	v	thorough	4	adj
dependable	4	adj	trustworthy	4	adj
determination	4	n	diligent	5	adj
duty	4	n	industrious	5	adj
earnest	4	adj	vigor	5	n
efficient	4	adj	vigorous	5	adj
enthusiasm	4	n	zest	5	n
lively	4	adv			

295. Instability—related clusters: 211, 228, 278, 294, 332, 350, 351, 385, 386, 387, 388, 389, 429, 433, 434

Word	Importance	Part of Speech	Word	Importance	Part of Speech
crazy	3	adj	unstable	4	adj
mad	3	adj	amuck	5	adj
wild	3	adj	fanatic	5	n
frantic	4	adj	fickle	5	adj
hectic	4	adj	giddy	5	adj
uncontrolled	4	adj			

296. Locations For/Near Water (Manmade)—related clusters: 87, 101, 102, 127, 352, 353, 391, 424

Word	Importance	Part of Speech	Word	Importance	Part of Speech
aquarium	3	n	**dock**	3	n
canal	3	n	**pool**	3	n
dam	3	n	aqueduct	4	n

(Continued)

Word	Importance	Part of Speech	Word	Importance	Part of Speech
channel	4	n	seaport	4	n
dike	4	n	wharf	4	n
harbor	4	n	berth	5	n
lighthouse	4	n	breakwater	5	n
port	4	n	moat	5	n
reservoir	4	n	sluice	5	n

297. Small Businesses—related clusters: 68, 88, 146, 167, 173, 229, 236, 257, 264, 265, 266, 333, 334, 355, 356, 357, 358, 359, 360, 361, 392, 393, 394, 395, 396, 397, 436

Word	Importance	Part of Speech	Word	Importance	Part of Speech
baker	3	n	smith	4	n
barber	3	n	tailor	4	n
butcher	3	n	florist	5	n
blacksmith	4	n	miller	5	n
bodyguard	4	n			

298. Military/Police—related clusters: 98, 200, 258, 401

Word	Importance	Part of Speech	Word	Importance	Part of Speech
army	3	n	squadron	4	n
navy	3	n	troop	4	n
police	3	n	brigade	5	n
air force	4	n	corps	5	n
infantry	4	n	detail	5	n
marines	4	n	legion	5	n
patrol	4	n	regiment	5	n

299. Dissimilarity—related clusters: 5, 27, 252

Word	Importance	Part of Speech	Word	Importance	Part of Speech
change	3	v	adapt	4	v
difference	3	n	contrary	4	adj
different	3	adj	develop	4	v
opposite	3	adj	development	4	n
unequal	3	adj	deviate	4	v
unlike	3	adj	differ	4	v

Word	Importance	Part of Speech	Word	Importance	Part of Speech
diverse	4	adj	vary	4	v
freak	4	n	discriminate	5	v
quirk	4	n	metamorphosis	5	n
reform	4	v	molt	5	v
separate	4	v	temper	5	n
undergo	4	v	transform	5	v
variety	4	n	transition	5	n
various	4	adj			

300. Pursuit—related clusters: 38, 39, 40, 44, 66, 141, 147, 169, 170, 182, 199, 215, 216, 247, 280, 281, 282, 283, 301, 302, 322, 338, 403

Word	Importance	Part of Speech	Word	Importance	Part of Speech
chase	3	v	**track**	3	v
follow	3	v	pursue	4	v

301. Reducing/Diminishing—related clusters: 38, 39, 40, 44, 66, 141, 147, 169, 170, 182, 199, 215, 216, 247, 280, 281, 282, 283, 300, 302, 322, 338, 403

Word	Importance	Part of Speech	Word	Importance	Part of Speech
crumble	3	v	shrivel	4	v
crumple	3	v	wither	4	v
shorten	3	v	compress	5	v
shrink	3	v	condense	5	v
tighten	3	v	corrugate	5	v
diminish	4	v	cramp	5	v
dwindle	4	v	crinkle	5	v
reduce	4	v	wilt	5	v

302. Separating—related clusters: 38, 39, 40, 44, 66, 141, 147, 169, 170, 182, 199, 215, 216, 247, 280, 281, 282, 283, 300, 301, 322, 338, 403

Word	Importance	Part of Speech	Word	Importance	Part of Speech
divorce	3	v	bisect	5	v
separate	3	v	detach	5	v
split	3	v	divert	5	v
disconnect	4	v	ravel	5	v
unwind	4	v			

303. Shapes (General Names)—related clusters: 69, 99, 142, 193, 218, 270, 326

Word	Importance	Part of Speech	Word	Importance	Part of Speech
outline	3	n	profile	4	n
pattern	3	n	skyline	4	n
shape	3	n	contour	5	n
figure	4	n	oblong	5	n
form	4	n	silhouette	5	n
frame	4	n			

304. Exercise—related clusters: 143, 158, 183, 209, 370

Word	Importance	Part of Speech	Word	Importance	Part of Speech
exercise	3	v	somersault	4	n
practice	3	v	sprint	4	v
stretch	3	v	workout	4	n
cartwheel	4	n	threshold	5	n
jog	4	v	yoga	5	n

305. Actions Associated with Disease/Injury—related clusters: 230, 231, 287, 371, 404

Word	Importance	Part of Speech	Word	Importance	Part of Speech
blister	3	n	whiplash	4	n
burn	3	n	wound	4	n
scab	3	n	abscess	5	n
sunburn	3	n	concussion	5	n
cripple	4	v	fester	5	v
infect	4	v	gash	5	n
paralyze	4	v	venom	5	n
poison	4	v	welt	5	n
sprain	4	n			

306. Dark—related clusters: 271, 272, 372, 405

Word	Importance	Part of Speech	Word	Importance	Part of Speech
dark	3	adj	blot	4	n
shade	3	n	blur	4	n
shadow	3	n	darkness	4	n

Word	Importance	Part of Speech	Word	Importance	Part of Speech
fade	4	v	shady	4	adj
gloom	4	n	splotch	5	n
haze	4	n			

307. Natural Catastrophes—related clusters: 90, 226, 375, 406

Word	Importance	Part of Speech	Word	Importance	Part of Speech
avalanche	3	n	emergency	4	n
earthquake	3	n	landslide	4	n
flood	3	n	tragedy	4	n
catastrophe	4	n	blight	5	n
disaster	4	n	calamity	5	n
disastrous	4	adj	crisis	5	n
drought	4	n	ordeal	5	n

308. Jumping—related clusters: 63, 339, 408, 409

Word	Importance	Part of Speech	Word	Importance	Part of Speech
hop	3	v	lunge	4	v
jump	3	v	lurch	4	v
leap	3	v	pounce	4	v
bound	4	v	spring	4	v
coil	4	v			

309. Shellfish (And Others)—related clusters: 32, 35, 64, 65, 70, 82, 95, 117, 155, 188, 189, 194, 310, 341

Word	Importance	Part of Speech	Word	Importance	Part of Speech
lobster	3	n	jellyfish	4	n
shell	3	n	mollusk	4	n
shrimp	3	n	octopus	4	n
snail	3	n	oyster	4	n
starfish	3	n	shellfish	4	n
clam	4	n	stingray	4	n
coral	4	n	squid	4	n
crab	4	n	plankton	5	n
crayfish	4	n	scallop	5	n
eel	4	n			

310. Equipment Used with Animals—related clusters: 32, 35, 64, 65, 70, 82, 95, 117, 155, 188, 189, 194, 309, 341

Word	Importance	Part of Speech	Word	Importance	Part of Speech
collar	3	n	harness	4	n
horseshoe	3	n	muzzle	4	n
leash	3	n	rein	4	n
saddle	3	n	stirrup	4	n
chaps	4	n	yoke	4	n
halter	4	n	bridle	5	n

311. Cruelty and Meanness—related clusters: 43, 45, 55, 291, 292, 293, 312, 313, 378, 379, 380, 381, 416, 417, 422, 427, 428

Word	Importance	Part of Speech	Word	Importance	Part of Speech
cruel	3	adj	fierce	4	adj
mean	3	adj	merciless	4	adj
unkind	3	adj	savage	4	adj
violent	3	adj	drastic	5	adj
cruelty	4	n	ferocious	5	adj
destructive	4	adj	vicious	5	adj

312. General Upset—related clusters: 43, 45, 55, 291, 292, 293, 311, 313, 378, 379, 380, 381, 416, 417, 422, 427, 428

Word	Importance	Part of Speech	Word	Importance	Part of Speech
alone	3	adj	solemn	4	adj
bother	3	v	somber	4	adj
upset	3	v	balk	5	v
depress	4	v	dejected	5	v
disappoint	4	v	disrupt	5	v
discourage	4	v	dour	5	adj
dissatisfied	4	adj	impose	5	v
distress	4	v	infringe	5	v
disturb	4	v	interfere	5	v
frustrate	4	v	molest	5	v
serious	4	adj	sullen	5	adj

313. Doubt and Hope—related clusters: 43, 45, 55, 291, 292, 293, 311, 312, 378, 379, 380, 381, 416, 417, 422, 427, 428

Word	Importance	Part of Speech	Word	Importance	Part of Speech
belief	3	n	disappointment	4	n
doubt	3	n	faith	4	n
hope	3	n	hopeless	4	adj
trust	3	n	optimism	4	n
desperate	4	adj	despair	5	n

314. Lubricants and Fuels—related clusters: 92, 96, 118, 119, 163, 242, 254, 275, 276, 315, 316, 419, 420

Word	Importance	Part of Speech	Word	Importance	Part of Speech
fuel	3	n	petroleum	4	n
gas	3	n	refuel	4	v
grease	3	n	diesel	5	n
oil	3	n	lubricate	5	v
alcohol	4	n	turpentine	5	n
lubrication	4	n			

315. Handles—related clusters: 92, 96, 118, 119, 163, 242, 254, 275, 276, 314, 316, 419, 420

Word	Importance	Part of Speech	Word	Importance	Part of Speech
doorknob	3	n	grip	4	n
handle	3	n	hilt	5	n
knob	3	n			

316. Miscellaneous Devices—related clusters: 92, 96, 118, 119, 163, 242, 254, 275, 276, 314, 315, 419, 420

Word	Importance	Part of Speech	Word	Importance	Part of Speech
dial	3	n	baton	4	n
ladder	3	n	crank	4	n
pedal	3	n	easel	4	n
switch	3	n	fulcrum	4	n
trigger	3	n	platform	4	n
barometer	4	n	pointer	4	n

(Continued)

Word	Importance	Part of Speech	Word	Importance	Part of Speech
pulley	4	n	reel	5	n
spool	4	n	sawhorse	5	n
stepladder	4	n	spindle	5	n
wand	4	n	toggle	5	n

317. Lack of Permanence (People)—related clusters: 56, 94, 111, 203, 204, 205, 206, 227, 330, 343, 344, 382, 432, 444

Word	Importance	Part of Speech	Word	Importance	Part of Speech
guest	3	n	runaway	4	n
stranger	3	n	spectator	4	n
visitor	3	n	tourist	4	n
gypsy	4	n	vacationer	4	n
hobo	4	n	wanderer	4	n
migrant	4	n	boarder	5	n
passenger	4	n	fugitive	5	n
refugee	4	n	vagabond	5	n

318. Vehicles (Snow)—related clusters: 93, 97, 120, 128, 159, 234, 331

Word	Importance	Part of Speech	Word	Importance	Part of Speech
sled	2	n	bobsled	4	n
sleigh	2	n	toboggan	4	n
snowplow	3	n			

319. Titles and Names—related clusters: 53, 71, 112, 138, 248, 256, 279, 320

Word	Importance	Part of Speech	Word	Importance	Part of Speech
name	2	n	trademark	4	n
title	2	n	caption	5	n
nickname	3	n	denomination	5	n
autograph	4	n	dub	5	v
brand	4	n	monogram	5	n
identify	4	v	stigma	5	n
label	4	n	tag	5	n
signature	4	n			

320. Rules and Laws—related clusters: 53, 71, 112, 138, 248, 256, 279, 319

Word	Importance	Part of Speech	Word	Importance	Part of Speech
law	2	n	contract	4	n
rule	2	n	deed	4	n
regulation	3	n	diploma	4	n
charter	4	n	policy	4	n
commandment	4	n	treaty	4	n
constitution	4	n	curfew	5	n

321. Places Related to Meetings/Worship—related clusters: 60, 106, 121, 190, 210, 324, 335, 364, 365, 366, 399, 400

Word	Importance	Part of Speech	Word	Importance	Part of Speech
church	2	n	chapel	4	n
shrine	3	n	convent	4	n
temple	3	n	mission	4	n
capitol	4	n	monastery	4	n
cathedral	4	n	synagogue	4	n

322. Opening and Closing—related clusters: 38, 39, 40, 44, 66, 141, 147, 169, 170, 182, 199, 215, 216, 247, 280, 281, 282, 283, 300, 301, 302, 338, 403

Word	Importance	Part of Speech	Word	Importance	Part of Speech
open	2	v	shutdown	4	n
shut	2	v	ajar	5	adj
gape	4	v	restrict	5	v

323. Durability/Strength—related clusters: 202, 441

Word	Importance	Part of Speech	Word	Importance	Part of Speech
strong	2	adj	sturdy	4	adj
weak	2	adj	fragile	5	adj
delicate	3	adj	makeshift	5	adj
brittle	4	adj	potent	5	adj
durable	4	adj	ramshackle	5	adj
flimsy	4	adj	subtle	5	adj
frail	4	adj			

324. Storage Locations—related clusters: 60, 106, 121, 190, 210, 321, 335, 364, 365, 366, 399, 400

Word	Importance	Part of Speech	Word	Importance	Part of Speech
barn	2	n	storeroom	4	n
shed	3	n	warehouse	4	n
greenhouse	4	n	arsenal	5	n
shack	4	n	hothouse	5	n

325. Objects (General Names)—related clusters: 107, 164, 181, 251, 268, 367

Word	Importance	Part of Speech	Word	Importance	Part of Speech
thing	2	n	substance	4	n
object	3	n	entity	5	n
matter	4	n			

326. Bluntness/Sharpness—related clusters: 69, 99, 142, 193, 218, 270, 303

Word	Importance	Part of Speech	Word	Importance	Part of Speech
sharp	2	n	blunt	4	adj
dull	3	adj	keen	4	adj

327. Things that Are Commonly Measured—related clusters: 13, 15, 18, 19, 28, 33, 73, 130, 373, 374

Word	Importance	Part of Speech	Word	Importance	Part of Speech
angle	2	n	circumference	4	n
diameter	3	n	latitude	4	n
radius	3	n	longitude	4	n
census	4	n	meridian	5	n

328. Lack of Popularity/Familiarity—related clusters: 261, 289

Word	Importance	Part of Speech	Word	Importance	Part of Speech
secret	2	adj	undiscovered	4	adj
private	3	adj	unknown	4	adj
personal	4	adj	anonymous	5	adj
privacy	4	n	solitude	5	n
secrecy	4	n			

329. Growth and Survival—related clusters: 245

Word	Importance	Part of Speech	Word	Importance	Part of Speech
grow	2	v	withstand	4	v
survive	3	v	endure	5	v
bloom	4	v	evolve	5	v
cope	4	v	flourish	5	v
mature	4	v	prosper	5	v
stamina	4	n	tolerance	5	n
survival	4	n	tolerate	5	v
thrive	4	v			

330. Size of People—related clusters: 56, 94, 111, 203, 204, 205, 206, 227, 317, 343, 344, 382, 432, 444

Word	Importance	Part of Speech	Word	Importance	Part of Speech
giant	2	n	pygmy	4	n
dwarf	3	n	runt	4	n
midget	4	n	troll	4	n

331. Vehicles (Work-Related)—related clusters: 93, 97, 120, 128, 159, 234, 318

Word	Importance	Part of Speech	Word	Importance	Part of Speech
tractor	3	n	forklift	4	n
wheelbarrow	3	n	derrick	5	n
barrow	4	n	harrow	5	n

332. Independence and Freedom—related clusters: 211, 228, 278, 294, 295, 350, 351, 385, 386, 387, 388, 389, 429, 433, 434

Word	Importance	Part of Speech	Word	Importance	Part of Speech
free	2	adj	dependent	4	adj
liberty	3	n	independent	4	adj
obedient	3	adj	voluntary	4	adj

333. Writers and Reporters—related clusters: 68, 88, 146, 167, 173, 229, 236, 257, 264, 265, 266, 297, 334, 355, 356, 357, 358, 359, 360, 361, 392, 393, 394, 395, 396, 397, 436

Word	Importance	Part of Speech	Word	Importance	Part of Speech
author	2	n	poet	4	n
speaker	3	n	reporter	4	n
writer	3	n	spokesperson	4	n
critic	4	n	weatherman	4	n
editor	4	n	publisher	5	n
narrator	4	n	scribe	5	n

334. People Who Clean Up—related clusters: 68, 88, 146, 167, 173, 229, 236, 257, 264, 265, 266, 297, 333, 355, 356, 357, 358, 359, 360, 361, 392, 393, 394, 395, 396, 397, 436

Word	Importance	Part of Speech	Word	Importance	Part of Speech
garbageman	2	n	**custodian**	3	n
janitor	2	n			

335. Places Related to Transportation—related clusters: 60, 106, 121, 190, 210, 321, 324, 364, 365, 366, 399, 400

Word	Importance	Part of Speech	Word	Importance	Part of Speech
station	2	n	hangar	4	n
airport	3	n	terminal	4	n
depot	4	n			

336. Organs—related clusters: 75, 76, 80, 115, 140, 157, 160, 191, 213, 437

Word	Importance	Part of Speech	Word	Importance	Part of Speech
stomach	2	n	liver	4	n
heart	3	n	lung	4	n
gland	4	n	bowel	5	n
gut	4	n	diaphragm	5	n
intestine	4	n	ovary	5	n
kidney	4	n	spleen	5	n

337. Characteristics of Rocks/Soil—related clusters: 133, 237, 337, 402, 438

Word	Importance	Part of Speech	Word	Importance	Part of Speech
sand	2	n	powder	4	n
pebble	3	n	barren	5	adj
mineral	4	n	igneous	5	adj

338. Halting Actions—related clusters: 38, 39, 40, 44, 66, 141, 147, 169, 170, 182, 199, 215, 216, 247, 280, 281, 282, 283, 300, 301, 302, 322, 403

Word	Importance	Part of Speech	Word	Importance	Part of Speech
quit	2	v	resist	4	v
stop	2	v	smother	4	v
avoid	4	v	abolish	5	v
barrier	4	n	abstain	5	v
blockade	4	n	barricade	5	n
cancel	4	v	bondage	5	n
cease	4	v	boycott	5	v
clog	4	v	congest	5	v
dodge	4	v	muffle	5	v
extinguish	4	v	prohibit	5	v
halt	4	v	refrain	5	v
intercept	4	v	restrain	5	v
lapse	4	v	retard	5	v
obstacle	4	n	stifle	5	v
obstruct	4	v	terminate	5	v
prevent	4	v			

339. Kicking Actions—related clusters: 63, 308, 408, 409

Word	Importance	Part of Speech	Word	Importance	Part of Speech
kick	2	v	stomp	4	v
stamp	3	v	tramp	4	v

340. Mathematical Quantities—related clusters: 166, 410, 423

Word	Importance	Part of Speech	Word	Importance	Part of Speech
sum	2	n	area	4	n
average	3	n	fraction	4	n
total	3	n	gross	4	n

(Continued)

Word	Importance	Part of Speech	Word	Importance	Part of Speech
maximum	4	n	percentage	4	n
mean	4	n	proportion	4	n
median	4	n	ratio	4	n
minimum	4	n	interest	5	n
multiple	4	n	sine	5	n
percent	4	n			

341. Primates—related clusters: 32, 35, 64, 65, 70, 82, 95, 117, 155, 188, 189, 194, 309, 310

Word	Importance	Part of Speech	Word	Importance	Part of Speech
monkey	2	n	baboon	4	n
gorilla	3	n	chimpanzee	4	n
ape	4	n			

342. Linking Verbs—related clusters: 1, 3, 4, 411

Word	Importance	Part of Speech	Word	Importance	Part of Speech
become	2	v	appear	4	v
seem	3	v	remain	4	v

343. Names that Indicate Permanence for People—related clusters: 56, 94, 111, 203, 204, 205, 206, 227, 317, 330, 344, 382, 432, 444

Word	Importance	Part of Speech	Word	Importance	Part of Speech
pioneer	2	n	puritan	4	n
caveman	3	n	taxpayer	4	n
citizen	3	n	tenant	4	n
alien	4	n	townspeople	4	n
native	4	n	villager	4	n
newcomer	4	n	aborigine	5	n
patriot	4	n	veteran	5	n
pilgrim	4	n			

344. Names that Indicate Fame—related clusters: 56, 94, 111, 203, 204, 205, 206, 227, 317, 330, 343, 382, 432, 444

Word	Importance	Part of Speech	Word	Importance	Part of Speech
star	2	n	idol	4	n
celebrity	3	n	savior	4	n

345. Communication (Information Previously Withheld)—related clusters: 14, 61, 100, 105, 177, 198, 207, 255, 346, 383

Word	Importance	Part of Speech	Word	Importance	Part of Speech
admit	3	v	confide	5	v
tattle	3	v	divulge	5	v
confess	4	v	expose	5	v
reveal	4	v			

346. Recording/Translating Information—related clusters: 14, 61, 100, 105, 177, 198, 207, 255, 345, 383

Word	Importance	Part of Speech	Word	Importance	Part of Speech
record	3	v	interpret	4	v
recording	3	n	score	4	v
video	3	n	translate	4	v
cassette	4	n	decode	5	v

347. Interest—related clusters: 46, 67, 132, 137, 154, 225, 249, 277, 348, 349, 384

Word	Importance	Part of Speech	Word	Importance	Part of Speech
attention	3	n	concentration	5	n
interest	3	n	intrigue	5	n
curiosity	4	n			

348. Procedures and Processes—related clusters: 46, 67, 132, 137, 154, 225, 249, 277, 347, 349, 384

Word	Importance	Part of Speech	Word	Importance	Part of Speech
process	3	n	method	4	n
recipe	3	n	procedure	4	n
routine	3	n	system	4	n

(Continued)

Word	Importance	Part of Speech	Word	Importance	Part of Speech
convention	5	n	maneuver	5	n
function	5	n	technique	5	n
logic	5	n			

349. Beliefs—related clusters: 46, 67, 132, 137, 154, 225, 249, 277, 347, 348, 384

Word	Importance	Part of Speech	Word	Importance	Part of Speech
belief	3	n	superstition	4	n
opinion	3	n	tradition	4	n
custom	4	n	creed	5	n
habit	4	n	doctrine	5	n
ideal	4	n	mythology	5	n
instinct	4	n	philosophy	5	n
practice	4	n			

350. Shyness—related clusters: 211, 228, 278, 294, 295, 332, 351, 385, 386, 387, 388, 389, 429, 433, 434

Word	Importance	Part of Speech	Word	Importance	Part of Speech
bashful	3	adj	meek	4	adj
shy	3	adj	mild	4	adj
coy	4	adj	skittish	4	adj
helpless	4	adj	timid	4	adj

351. Dishonesty—related clusters: 211, 228, 278, 294, 295, 332, 350, 385, 386, 387, 388, 389, 429, 433, 434

Word	Importance	Part of Speech	Word	Importance	Part of Speech
dishonest	3	adj	unfaithful	4	adj
naughty	3	adj	cunning	5	adj
unfair	3	adj	traitor	5	n
mischief	4	n	treason	5	n
mischievous	4	adj	underhanded	5	adj
sly	4	adj			

352. Equipment Used with Water/Liquid—related clusters: 87, 101, 102, 127, 296, 353, 391, 424

Word	Importance	Part of Speech	Word	Importance	Part of Speech
faucet	3	n	nozzle	4	n
hose	3	n	pump	4	n
sprinkler	3	n	spout	4	n
fountain	4	n	hydraulic	5	adj
funnel	4	n	valve	5	n
hydrant	4	n			

353. Moisture—related clusters: 87, 101, 102, 127, 296, 352, 391, 424

Word	Importance	Part of Speech	Word	Importance	Part of Speech
cloud	3	n	dew	4	n
fog	3	n	smog	4	n

354. Characteristics Related to Clothes/Wearing of Clothes—related clusters: 47, 62, 125, 129, 145, 178, 212, 224, 263, 435

Word	Importance	Part of Speech	Word	Importance	Part of Speech
barefoot	3	adj	informal	4	adj
naked	3	adj	nude	4	adj
bare	4	adj	worn	4	adj
bareheaded	4	adj	sheer	5	adj

355. Assistants and Supervisors—related clusters: 68, 88, 146, 167, 173, 229, 236, 257, 264, 265, 266, 297, 333, 334, 356, 357, 358, 359, 360, 361, 392, 393, 394, 395, 396, 397, 436

Word	Importance	Part of Speech	Word	Importance	Part of Speech
boss	3	n	landlord	4	n
leader	3	n	landowner	4	n
owner	3	n	manager	4	n
assistant	4	n	sponsor	4	n
chairman	4	n	superintendent	4	n
director	4	n	supervisor	4	n
foreman	4	n	apprentice	5	n
landlady	4	n	landholder	5	n

356. Occupations Usually Held by Youth—related clusters: 68, 88, 146, 167, 173, 229, 236, 257, 264, 265, 266, 297, 333, 334, 355, 357, 358, 359, 360, 361, 392, 393, 394, 395, 396, 397, 436

Word	Importance	Part of Speech	Word	Importance	Part of Speech
babysitter	3	n	**paperboy**	3	n

357. Discoverers and Scientists—related clusters: 68, 88, 146, 167, 173, 229, 236, 257, 264, 265, 266, 297, 333, 334, 355, 356, 358, 359, 360, 361, 392, 393, 394, 395, 396, 397, 436

Word	Importance	Part of Speech	Word	Importance	Part of Speech
astronaut	3	n	geology	4	n
geography	3	n	inventor	4	n
scientist	3	n	spaceman	4	n
astronomy	4	n	veterinarian	4	n
biology	4	n	frogman	5	n
chemistry	4	n	psychology	5	n
discoverer	4	n	researcher	5	n
ecology	4	n	taxidermy	5	n
economics	4	n			

358. Occupations Associated with Imprisonment/Slavery—related clusters: 68, 88, 146, 167, 173, 229, 236, 257, 264, 265, 266, 297, 333, 334, 355, 356, 357, 359, 360, 361, 392, 393, 394, 395, 396, 397, 436

Word	Importance	Part of Speech	Word	Importance	Part of Speech
guard	3	n	gladiator	5	n
prisoner	3	n	warden	5	n
slave	3	n			

359. Construction and Repairmen—related clusters: 68, 88, 146, 167, 173, 229, 236, 257, 264, 265, 266, 297, 333, 334, 355, 356, 357, 358, 360, 361, 392, 393, 394, 395, 396, 397, 436

Word	Importance	Part of Speech	Word	Importance	Part of Speech
plumber	3	n	mason	4	n
repairman	3	n	mechanic	4	n
carpenter	4	n	draftsman	5	n

360. Legal Professions—related clusters: 68, 88, 146, 167, 173, 229, 236, 257, 264, 265, 266, 297, 333, 334, 355, 356, 357, 358, 359, 361, 392, 393, 394, 395, 396, 397, 436

Word	Importance	Part of Speech	Word	Importance	Part of Speech
judge	3	n	attorney	4	n
lawyer	3	n	counselor	4	n

361. Servants—related clusters: 68, 88, 146, 167, 173, 229, 236, 257, 264, 265, 266, 297, 333, 334, 355, 356, 357, 358, 359, 360, 392, 393, 394, 395, 396, 397, 436

Word	Importance	Part of Speech	Word	Importance	Part of Speech
maid	3	n	housekeeper	4	n
servant	3	n	usher	4	n
butler	4	n	bellhop	5	n
chauffeur	4	n	redcap	5	n
doorman	4	n			

362. Woodlands and Forests—related clusters: 50, 114, 139, 168, 267, 363, 398

Word	Importance	Part of Speech	Word	Importance	Part of Speech
forest	3	n	grove	4	n
jungle	3	n	thicket	4	n
glade	4	n	woodland	4	n

363. Pastures and Fields—related clusters: 50, 114, 139, 168, 267, 362, 398

Word	Importance	Part of Speech	Word	Importance	Part of Speech
field	3	n	orchard	4	n
prairie	3	n	paddy	4	n
battleground	4	n	pasture	4	n
countryside	4	n	vineyard	4	n
meadow	4	n			

364. Structures that Are Manmade—related clusters: 60, 106, 121, 190, 210, 321, 324, 335, 365, 366, 399, 400

Word	Importance	Part of Speech	Word	Importance	Part of Speech
building	3	n	skyscraper	4	n
tower	3	n	structure	4	n
construction	4	n	silo	5	n

365. Factories, Mills, and Offices—related clusters: 60, 106, 121, 190, 210, 321, 324, 335, 364, 366, 399, 400

Word	Importance	Part of Speech	Word	Importance	Part of Speech
office	3	n	sawmill	4	n
shop	3	n	studio	4	n
factory	4	n	windmill	4	n
headquarters	4	n	workshop	4	n
mill	4	n	treadmill	5	n

366. Ranches and Farms—related clusters: 60, 106, 121, 190, 210, 321, 324, 335, 364, 365, 399, 400

Word	Importance	Part of Speech	Word	Importance	Part of Speech
farm	3	n	dairy	4	n
ranch	3	n	plantation	5	n

367. Packing and Wrapping—related clusters: 107, 164, 181, 251, 268, 325

Word	Importance	Part of Speech	Word	Importance	Part of Speech
pack	3	v	bind	4	v
tape	3	v	furl	4	v
tie	3	v	unravel	4	v
wrap	3	v			

368. Failure and Success—related clusters: 58, 72, 243

Word	Importance	Part of Speech	Word	Importance	Part of Speech
fail	3	v	qualify	4	v
succeed	3	v	bumble	5	v
deserve	4	v	bungle	5	v
merit	4	v	muff	5	v

369. Attitudinals (Fortunate/Unfortunate)—related clusters: 30, 31, 285, 431, 439, 440

Word	Importance	Part of Speech	Word	Importance	Part of Speech
luckily	3	adv	happily	4	adv
unfortunately	3	adv			

370. Magic—related clusters: 143, 158, 183, 209, 304

Word	Importance	Part of Speech	Word	Importance	Part of Speech
magic	3	n	astrology	5	n
trick	3	n	gimmick	5	n
stunt	4	n	sorcery	5	n

371. Ailments and Diseases—related clusters: 230, 231, 287, 305, 404

Word	Importance	Part of Speech	Word	Importance	Part of Speech
blind	3	n	stress	4	n
cold	3	n	diphtheria	5	n
deaf	3	n	influenza	5	n
blindness	4	n	malaria	5	n
cancer	4	n	mute	5	adj
croup	4	n	scurvy	5	n
lame	4	n	smallpox	5	n
mumps	4	n	starvation	5	n
polio	4	n	tuberculosis	5	n
rabies	4	n			

372. Actions Related to Light—related clusters: 271, 272, 306, 405

Word	Importance	Part of Speech	Word	Importance	Part of Speech
reflect	3	v	glow	4	v
shine	3	v	lighten	4	v
twinkle	3	v	radiate	4	v
brighten	4	v	shimmer	4	v
dazzle	4	v	sparkle	4	v
flash	4	v	glisten	5	v
glitter	4	v	illuminate	5	v

373. Actions Related to Measurement—related clusters: 13, 15, 18, 19, 28, 33, 73, 130, 327, 374

Word	Importance	Part of Speech	Word	Importance	Part of Speech
measure	3	v	fathom	5	v
weigh	3	v			

374. Devices Used for Measurement—related clusters: 13, 15, 18, 19, 28, 33, 73, 130, 327, 373

Word	Importance	Part of Speech	Word	Importance	Part of Speech
thermometer	3	n	scale	4	n
yardstick	3	n	speedometer	4	n
compass	4	n	gauge	5	n
measurement	4	n			

375. Characteristics Associated with Weather—related clusters: 90, 226, 307, 406

Word	Importance	Part of Speech	Word	Importance	Part of Speech
dry	3	adj	muggy	4	adj
overcast	3	adj	arid	5	adj
sunny	3	adj	sultry	5	adj

376. Products of Fire—related clusters: 78, 220, 414, 442

Word	Importance	Part of Speech	Word	Importance	Part of Speech
ash	3	n	cinder	4	n
smoke	3	n	ember	5	n

377. Chemicals—related clusters: 418, 425, 443

Word	Importance	Part of Speech	Word	Importance	Part of Speech
caffeine	3	n	neon	4	n
helium	3	n	nitrogen	4	n
oxygen	3	n	sodium	4	n
ammonia	4	n	sulfur	4	n
chemical	4	n	carbon	5	n
cholesterol	4	n	chlorine	5	n
compound	4	n	enzyme	5	n
hydrogen	4	n			

378. Guilt and Worry—related clusters: 43, 45, 55, 291, 292, 293, 311, 312, 313, 379, 380, 381, 416, 417, 422, 427, 428

Word	Importance	Part of Speech	Word	Importance	Part of Speech
guilt	3	n	anxious	4	adj
shame	3	n	concern	4	n
worry	3	n	fret	4	n

Word	Importance	Part of Speech	Word	Importance	Part of Speech
humiliation	4	n	tension	4	n
strain	4	n	uncomfortable	4	adj
suspense	4	n	uneasy	4	adj
tense	4	v	anxiety	5	n

379. Irritability—related clusters: 43, 45, 55, 291, 292, 293, 311, 312, 313, 378, 380, 381, 416, 417, 422, 427, 428

Word	Importance	Part of Speech	Word	Importance	Part of Speech
grouch	3	n	gruff	4	adj
grumpy	3	adj	grumble	4	v
rude	3	adj	impertinent	5	adj
disagreeable	4	adj			

380. Excitement and Attention—related clusters: 43, 45, 55, 291, 292, 293, 311, 312, 313, 378, 379, 381, 416, 417, 422, 427, 428

Word	Importance	Part of Speech	Word	Importance	Part of Speech
amaze	3	v	tingle	4	v
excite	3	v	appall	5	v
surprise	3	v	astonishment	5	n
amazement	4	n	ecstasy	5	n
astonish	4	v	hubbub	5	n
awe	4	n	kindle	5	v
disbelief	4	n	marvel	5	v
rejoice	4	v	passion	5	n
thrill	4	v	spellbound	5	adj

381. General Human Traits—related clusters: 43, 45, 55, 291, 292, 293, 311, 312, 313, 378, 379, 380, 416, 417, 422, 427, 428

Word	Importance	Part of Speech	Word	Importance	Part of Speech
skill	3	n	capacity	4	n
talent	3	n	discipline	4	n
attitude	4	n	feature	4	n
attribute	4	n	knack	4	n

(Continued)

Word	Importance	Part of Speech	Word	Importance	Part of Speech
manner	4	n	flair	5	n
personality	4	n	heredity	5	n
quality	4	n	trait	5	n
bearing	5	n			

382. Experience/Expertise—related clusters: 56, 94, 111, 203, 204, 205, 206, 227, 317, 330, 343, 344, 432, 444

Word	Importance	Part of Speech	Word	Importance	Part of Speech
beginner	3	n	source	4	n
expert	3	n	specialist	4	n
ace	4	n	amateur	5	n
genius	4	n	novice	5	n
pro	4	n	veteran	5	n
scholar	4	n	virgin	5	n

383. Promises—related clusters: 14, 61, 100, 105, 177, 198, 207, 255, 345, 346

Word	Importance	Part of Speech	Word	Importance	Part of Speech
promise	3	n	pact	5	n
vow	4	n	plea	5	n
guarantee	5	n	pledge	5	n

384. Definition/Meaning—related clusters: 46, 67, 132, 137, 154, 225, 249, 277, 347, 348, 349

Word	Importance	Part of Speech	Word	Importance	Part of Speech
define	3	v	meaning	4	n
definition	4	n	represent	4	v
interpret	4	v			

385. Lack of Initiative—related clusters: 211, 228, 278, 294, 295, 332, 350, 351, 386, 387, 388, 389, 429, 433, 434

Word	Importance	Part of Speech	Word	Importance	Part of Speech
lazy	3	adj	dormant	5	adj
casual	4	adj	lax	5	adj
idle	4	adj	listless	5	adj

386. Luck and Success—related clusters: 211, 228, 278, 294, 295, 332, 350, 351, 385, 387, 388, 389, 429, 433, 434

Word	Importance	Part of Speech	Word	Importance	Part of Speech
lucky	3	adj	unfortunate	4	adj
successful	4	adj			

387. Stubbornness and Strictness—related clusters: 211, 228, 278, 294, 295, 332, 350, 351, 385, 386, 388, 389, 429, 433, 434

Word	Importance	Part of Speech	Word	Importance	Part of Speech
strict	3	adj	stern	4	adj
grave	4	adj	stubborn	4	adj
ornery	4	adj	obstinate	5	adj
severe	4	adj	perverse	5	adj
sober	4	adj	rigor	5	n
steadfast	4	adj			

388. Spirituality—related clusters: 211, 228, 278, 294, 295, 332, 350, 351, 385, 386, 387, 389, 429, 433, 434

Word	Importance	Part of Speech	Word	Importance	Part of Speech
holy	3	adj	divine	5	adj
religious	4	adj	heathen	5	n
sacred	4	adj	pious	5	adj
spiritual	4	adj	skeptic	5	n
supernatural	4	adj			

389. Caution—related clusters: 211, 228, 278, 294, 295, 332, 350, 351, 385, 386, 387, 388, 429, 433, 434

Word	Importance	Part of Speech	Word	Importance	Part of Speech
careful	3	adj	watchful	4	adj
careless	4	adj	gingerly	5	adj
reckless	4	adj	lax	5	adj
slack	4	adj	painstaking	5	adj
stingy	4	adj	prudent	5	adj
suspicious	4	adj	wary	5	adj

390. Geometric Planes—related clusters: 9, 17, 20, 21, 22, 23, 25, 26, 37, 49, 430

Word	Importance	Part of Speech	Word	Importance	Part of Speech
sideways	3	adj	vertical	4	adj
diagonal	4	adj	broadside	5	n
horizontal	4	adj	lateral	5	adj
perpendicular	4	adj			

391. Water-Related Directions—related clusters: 87, 101, 102, 127, 296, 352, 353, 424

Word	Importance	Part of Speech	Word	Importance	Part of Speech
afloat	3	adv	inland	4	n
ashore	4	adv	offshore	4	n
downstream	4	n	midstream	5	n

392. Food Service Occupations—related clusters: 68, 88, 146, 167, 173, 229, 236, 257, 264, 265, 266, 297, 333, 334, 355, 356, 357, 358, 359, 360, 361, 393, 394, 395, 396, 397, 436

Word	Importance	Part of Speech	Word	Importance	Part of Speech
waiter	3	n	dishwasher	4	n
waitress	3	n	busboy	5	n
chef	4	n			

393. Messengers—related clusters: 68, 88, 146, 167, 173, 229, 236, 257, 264, 265, 266, 297, 333, 334, 355, 356, 357, 358, 359, 360, 361, 392, 394, 395, 396, 397, 436

Word	Importance	Part of Speech	Word	Importance	Part of Speech
mailman	3	n	postmaster	4	n
courier	4	n			

394. Occupations Associated with the Outdoors—related clusters: 68, 88, 146, 167, 173, 229, 236, 257, 264, 265, 266, 297, 333, 334, 355, 356, 357, 358, 359, 360, 361, 392, 393, 395, 396, 397, 436

Word	Importance	Part of Speech	Word	Importance	Part of Speech
cowboy	3	n	cowhand	4	n
cavalry	4	n	deckhand	4	n
cowgirl	4	n	hunter	4	n

Word	Importance	Part of Speech	Word	Importance	Part of Speech
lumberjack	4	n	rancher	4	n
miner	4	n	shepherd	4	n
prospector	4	n			

395. People Who Buy and Sell—related clusters: 68, 88, 146, 167, 173, 229, 236, 257, 264, 265, 266, 297, 333, 334, 355, 356, 357, 358, 359, 360, 361, 392, 393, 394, 396, 397, 436

Word	Importance	Part of Speech	Word	Importance	Part of Speech
customer	3	n	shopper	4	n
agent	4	n	broker	5	n
merchant	4	n	client	5	n
seller	4	n	vendor	5	n

396. People Who Work in Offices—related clusters: 68, 88, 146, 167, 173, 229, 236, 257, 264, 265, 266, 297, 333, 334, 355, 356, 357, 358, 359, 360, 361, 392, 393, 394, 395, 397, 436

Word	Importance	Part of Speech	Word	Importance	Part of Speech
secretary	3	n	receptionist	5	n
clerk	5	n	typist	5	n

397. Occupations Associated with Transportation—related clusters: 68, 88, 146, 167, 173, 229, 236, 257, 264, 265, 266, 297, 333, 334, 355, 356, 357, 358, 359, 360, 361, 392, 393, 394, 395, 396, 436

Word	Importance	Part of Speech	Word	Importance	Part of Speech
pilot	3	n	porter	5	n
aviator	4	n	steward	5	n
driver	4	n	stewardess	5	n
skipper	4	n			

398. Characteristics of Places—related clusters: 50, 114, 139, 168, 267, 362, 363

Word	Importance	Part of Speech	Word	Importance	Part of Speech
desert	3	adj	urban	4	adj
landscape	4	n	wilderness	4	n
mountainous	4	adj	heath	5	n
rural	4	adj	moor	5	n
rustic	4	adj	municipal	5	adj
tundra	4	n	steppe	5	n

399. Medical Facilities—related clusters: 60, 106, 121, 190, 210, 321, 324, 335, 364, 365, 366, 400

Word	Importance	Part of Speech	Word	Importance	Part of Speech
hospital	3	n	mortuary	5	n
clinic	4	n	ward	5	n
morgue	5	n			

400. Monuments—related clusters: 60, 106, 121, 190, 210, 321, 324, 335, 364, 365, 366, 499

Word	Importance	Part of Speech	Word	Importance	Part of Speech
monument	3	n	tomb	4	n
landmark	4	n	tombstone	4	n
memorial	4	n	headstone	5	n
sphinx	4	n	totem	5	n

401. Business and Social Groups—related clusters: 98, 200, 258, 298

Word	Importance	Part of Speech	Word	Importance	Part of Speech
audience	3	n	organization	4	n
assembly	4	n	session	4	n
association	4	n	staff	4	n
committee	4	n	troupe	4	n
company	4	n	union	4	n
conference	4	n	auxiliary	5	n
convention	4	n	commission	5	n
council	4	n	conglomerate	5	n
foundation	4	n	institute	5	n
league	4	n	partnership	5	n
membership	4	n			

402. Actions Associated with Crops/Soil—related clusters: 133, 237, 259, 337, 438

Word	Importance	Part of Speech	Word	Importance	Part of Speech
plant	3	v	sow	4	v
cultivate	4	v	grub	5	n
fertilize	4	v	harrow	5	v
harvest	4	v	tend	5	v
irrigate	4	v	thresh	5	v
plow	4	v	till	5	v

403. Force—related clusters: 38, 39, 40, 44, 66, 141, 147, 169, 170, 182, 199, 215, 216, 247, 280, 281, 282, 283, 300, 301, 302, 322, 338

Word	Importance	Part of Speech	Word	Importance	Part of Speech
force	3	v	pressure	4	n
energy	4	n	propulsion	5	n

404. Germs and Genes—related clusters: 230, 231, 287, 305, 371

Word	Importance	Part of Speech	Word	Importance	Part of Speech
germ	3	n	virus	4	n
bacteria	4	n	microbe	5	n
organism	4	n	septic	5	adj

405. Clarity—related clusters: 271, 272, 306, 372

Word	Importance	Part of Speech	Word	Importance	Part of Speech
invisible	3	adj	murky	4	adj
clarity	4	n	pale	4	adj
dim	4	adj	transparent	4	adj
drab	4	adj	visible	4	adj
dull	4	adj	opaque	5	adj
faint	4	adj	vague	5	adj

406. Clouds—related clusters: 90, 226, 307, 375

Word	Importance	Part of Speech	Word	Importance	Part of Speech
cloud	3	n	cumulus	4	n
cirrus	4	n	thunderhead	4	n

407. Neatness/Sloppiness—related clusters: 186, 187, 253

Word	Importance	Part of Speech	Word	Importance	Part of Speech
neat	3	adj	tidy	4	adj
sloppy	4	adj	prim	5	adj
tangle	4	n	shipshape	5	adj

408. Creeping/Lurking Actions—related clusters: 63, 308, 339, 409

Word	Importance	Part of Speech	Word	Importance	Part of Speech
crawl	3	v	sneak	4	v
creep	4	v	lurk	5	v
prowl	4	v	slither	5	v
slink	4	v			

409. Standing/Stationary—related clusters: 63, 308, 339, 408

Word	Importance	Part of Speech	Word	Importance	Part of Speech
stand	3	v	pose	5	v
posture	4	n	prone	5	adj
recline	4	v	straddle	5	v

410. Branches of Mathematics—related clusters: 166, 340, 423

Word	Importance	Part of Speech	Word	Importance	Part of Speech
math	3	n	geometry	4	n
algebra	4	n	mathematics	4	n
arithmetic	4	n	trigonometry	5	n

411. Semi-Auxiliary Verbs—related clusters: 1, 3, 4, 342

Word	Importance	Part of Speech	Word	Importance	Part of Speech
have to	3	v	had better	4	v
had best	4	v			

412. Events and Dates (General)—related clusters: 179, 413

Word	Importance	Part of Speech	Word	Importance	Part of Speech
event	3	n	occurrence	4	n
affair	4	n	project	4	n
attempt	4	n	situation	4	n
condition	4	n	circumstance	5	n
development	4	n	context	5	n
environment	4	n	enterprise	5	n
experience	4	n	feat	5	n
happening	4	n	incident	5	n
occasion	4	n	instance	5	n

413. Political Events—related clusters: 179, 412

Word	Importance	Part of Speech	Word	Importance	Part of Speech
vote	3	v	nominate	4	v
campaign	4	n	voter	4	n
crusade	4	n	ballot	5	n
elect	4	v			

414. Products Associated with Fire—related clusters: 78, 220, 376, 442

Word	Importance	Part of Speech	Word	Importance	Part of Speech
pipe	3	n	tobacco	4	n
cigar	4	n	wick	4	n
cigarette	4	n	paraffin	5	n

415. Paint—related clusters: 57

Word	Importance	Part of Speech	Word	Importance	Part of Speech
paint	3	n	tint	4	n
dye	4	n	enamel	5	n
stain	4	n	lacquer	5	n

416. Actions Related to Fear—related clusters: 43, 45, 55, 291, 292, 293, 311, 312, 313, 378, 379, 380, 381, 417, 422, 427, 428

Word	Importance	Part of Speech	Word	Importance	Part of Speech
scare	3	v	terrify	4	v
cringe	4	v	wince	4	v
haunt	4	v	flinch	5	v
horrify	4	v	petrify	5	v
startle	4	v			

417. Envy and Jealousy—related clusters: 43, 45, 55, 291, 292, 293, 311, 312, 313, 378, 379, 380, 381, 416, 422, 427, 428

Word	Importance	Part of Speech	Word	Importance	Part of Speech
jealous	3	adj	jealousy	4	n
envy	4	n	possessive	4	adj
grudge	4	n			

418. Electricity and Magnetism—related clusters: 377, 425, 443

Word	Importance	Part of Speech	Word	Importance	Part of Speech
magnet	3	n	radiation	4	n
charge	4	n	microwave	5	n
electric	4	n	radioactive	5	adj
hydroelectric	4	adj			

419. Machines—related clusters: 92, 96, 118, 119, 163, 242, 254, 275, 276, 314, 315, 316, 420

Word	Importance	Part of Speech	Word	Importance	Part of Speech
machine	3	n	mechanical	4	adj
appliance	4	n	apparatus	5	n
clockwork	4	n	contraption	5	n
equipment	4	v	gadget	5	n
hardware	4	n	rig	5	n
machinery	4	n			

420. Vision-Related Equipment—related clusters: 92, 96, 118, 119, 163, 242, 254, 275, 276, 314, 315, 316, 419

Word	Importance	Part of Speech	Word	Importance	Part of Speech
camera	3	n	microscope	4	n
binoculars	4	n	telescope	4	n
lens	4	n	eyepiece	5	n

421. Trees/Bushes (Types)—related clusters: 36, 108, 192, 269

Word	Importance	Part of Speech	Word	Importance	Part of Speech
aspen	4	n	elm	4	n
balsa	4	n	fir	4	n
beech	4	n	hickory	4	n
birch	4	n	locust	4	n
cedar	4	n	maple	4	n
citrus	4	n	mulberry	4	n
cottonwood	4	n	oak	4	n
dogwood	4	n	pine	4	n

Word	Importance	Part of Speech	Word	Importance	Part of Speech
poplar	4	n	eucalyptus	5	n
redwood	4	n	evergreen	5	n
spruce	4	n	hemlock	5	n
willow	4	n			

422. Contentment and Comfort—related clusters: 43, 45, 55, 291, 292, 293, 311, 312, 313, 378, 379, 380, 381, 416, 417, 427, 428

Word	Importance	Part of Speech	Word	Importance	Part of Speech
comfort	4	n	satisfy	4	v
comfortable	4	adj	snug	4	adj
content	4	adj	soothe	4	v
cozy	4	adj	sympathize	4	v
mellow	4	adj	sympathy	4	n
peaceful	4	adj	tame	4	v
pity	4	n	welfare	4	n
relief	4	n	console	5	v

423. Mathematical Constructs—related clusters: 166, 340, 410

Word	Importance	Part of Speech	Word	Importance	Part of Speech
denominator	4	n	rate	4	n
equation	4	n	evaluate	5	v
exponent	4	n	function	5	n
formula	4	n	plane	5	n
identity	4	n	range	5	n
product	4	n	slope	5	n
quotient	4	n	term	5	n

424. Slimy Substances—related clusters: 87, 101, 102, 127, 296, 352, 353, 391

Word	Importance	Part of Speech	Word	Importance	Part of Speech
foam	4	n	slime	4	n
quicksand	4	n	froth	5	n
scum	4	n	goo	5	n
sediment	4	n	muck	5	n
silt	4	n			

425. Atoms and Molecules—related clusters: 377, 418, 443

Word	Importance	Part of Speech	Word	Importance	Part of Speech
atom	4	n	electron	5	n
atomic	4	adj	ion	5	n
molecule	4	n	nucleus	5	n
neutron	4	n	proton	5	n
nuclear	4	adj			

426. Freedom/Lack of Freedom—related clusters: 41, 89, 148, 171, 184

Word	Importance	Part of Speech	Word	Importance	Part of Speech
escape	4	v	release	4	v
flee	4	v	sacrifice	4	v
parole	4	n	surrender	4	v

427. General Names for Feelings—related clusters: 43, 45, 55, 291, 292, 293, 311, 312, 313, 378, 379, 380, 381, 416, 417, 422, 428

Word	Importance	Part of Speech	Word	Importance	Part of Speech
emotion	4	n	mood	4	n
impression	4	n	sensation	4	n
impulse	4	n	sense	4	n

428. Actions Related to Neglect—related clusters: 43, 45, 55, 291, 292, 293, 311, 312, 313, 378, 379, 380, 381, 416, 417, 422, 427

Word	Importance	Part of Speech	Word	Importance	Part of Speech
maroon	4	v	exclude	5	v
omit	4	v	isolate	5	v
overlook	4	v	neglect	5	v

429. Prudence—related clusters: 211, 228, 278, 294, 295, 332, 350, 351, 385, 386, 387, 388, 389, 433, 434

Word	Importance	Part of Speech	Word	Importance	Part of Speech
modest	4	adj	chaste	5	adj
modesty	4	n	discreet	5	adj
sensible	4	adj			

430. Absence/Presence—related clusters: 9, 17, 20, 21, 22, 23, 25, 26, 37, 49, 390

Word	Importance	Part of Speech	Word	Importance	Part of Speech
absence	4	n	present	4	adj
absent	4	adj	unavailable	4	adj
available	4	adj			

431. Attitudinals (Expected/Unexpected)—related clusters: 30, 31, 285, 369, 439, 440

Word	Importance	Part of Speech	Word	Importance	Part of Speech
amazingly	4	adv	typically	4	adv
naturally	4	adv	inevitably	5	adv

432. Financial Status—related clusters: 56, 94, 111, 203, 204, 205, 206, 227, 317, 330, 343, 344, 382, 444

Word	Importance	Part of Speech	Word	Importance	Part of Speech
beggar	4	n	millionaire	4	n
bum	4	n	peasant	4	n

433. Patience—related clusters: 211, 228, 278, 294, 295, 332, 350, 351, 385, 386, 387, 388, 389, 429, 434

Word	Importance	Part of Speech	Word	Importance	Part of Speech
patience	4	n	restless	4	adj
patient	4	adj			

434. Humor—related clusters: 211, 228, 278, 294, 295, 332, 350, 351, 385, 386, 387, 388, 389, 429, 433

Word	Importance	Part of Speech	Word	Importance	Part of Speech
hilarious	4	adj	witty	4	adj
humorous	4	adj			

435. Armor—related clusters: 47, 62, 125, 129, 145, 178, 212, 224, 263, 354

Word	Importance	Part of Speech	Word	Importance	Part of Speech
armor	4	n	shield	4	n
sheath	4	n			

436. Occupations Associated with Money—related clusters: 68, 88, 146, 167, 173, 229, 236, 257, 264, 265, 266, 297, 333, 334, 355, 356, 357, 358, 359, 360, 361, 392, 393, 394, 395, 396, 397

Word	Importance	Part of Speech	Word	Importance	Part of Speech
banker	4	n	teller	5	n
cashier	4	n			

437. Body Systems—related clusters: 75, 76, 80, 115, 140, 157, 160, 191, 213, 336

Word	Importance	Part of Speech	Word	Importance	Part of Speech
circulation	4	n	perspire	4	v
digest	4	n	digestion	5	n

438. Actions Associated with Metals—related clusters: 133, 237, 259, 337, 402

Word	Importance	Part of Speech	Word	Importance	Part of Speech
rust	4	v	tarnish	5	v
corrode	5	v			

439. Attitudinals (Correctness/Incorrectness)—related clusters: 30, 31, 285, 369, 431, 440

Word	Importance	Part of Speech	Word	Importance	Part of Speech
correctly	4	adv	wrongly	4	adv
incorrectly	4	adv			

440. Attitudinals (Wisdom/Lack of Wisdom)—related clusters: 30, 31, 285, 369, 431, 439

Word	Importance	Part of Speech	Word	Importance	Part of Speech
cleverly	4	adv	wisely	4	adv
reasonably	4	adv			

441. Consistency—related clusters: 202, 323

Word	Importance	Part of Speech	Word	Importance	Part of Speech
elastic	4	adj	supple	4	adj
gel	4	n			

442. Insulation—related clusters: 78, 220, 376, 414

Word	Importance	Part of Speech	Word	Importance	Part of Speech
fireproof	5	adj	insulate	5	v

443. Acids—related clusters: 377, 418, 425

Word	Importance	Part of Speech	Word	Importance	Part of Speech
acid	4	n	alkaline	5	adj

444. Names that Indicate Political Disposition—related clusters: 56, 94, 111, 203, 204, 205, 206, 227, 317, 330, 343, 344, 382, 432

Word	Importance	Part of Speech	Word	Importance	Part of Speech
confederate	5	adj	republican	5	adj
democratic	5	adj	tory	5	n
independent	5	adj	whig	5	n

APPENDIX C

This appendix contains the 60 super clusters, along with their related clusters, listed in order of how basic they are.

1. Auxiliary and Helping Verbs: 1, 3, 4, 342, 411
2. Pronouns: 6, 7, 8, 11, 12, 34
3. Cause and Effect: 10, 273
4. Physical Location and Orientation: 9, 17, 20, 21, 22, 23, 25, 26, 37, 49, 390, 430
5. Measurement, Size, and Quantity: 13, 15, 18, 19, 28, 33, 73, 130, 327, 373, 374
6. Time: 2, 16, 24, 29, 52, 59, 79, 83, 126, 144, 233
7. Comparison and Contrast: 5, 27, 252, 299
8. Color: 57, 415
9. Verbal Interactions: 14, 61, 100, 105, 177, 198, 207, 255, 345, 346, 383
10. Animals: 32, 35, 64, 65, 70, 82, 95, 117, 155, 188, 189, 194, 309, 310, 341
11. Importance and Goodness: 58, 72, 243, 368
12. The Human Body: 75, 76, 80, 115, 140, 157, 160, 191, 213, 336, 437
13. Trees and Plants: 36, 108, 192, 269, 421
14. Acquisition and Ownership: 41, 89, 148, 171, 184, 426
15. Parts of Dwellings: 91, 113, 123, 134, 217, 284
16. Vehicles and Transportation: 93, 97, 120, 128, 159, 234, 318, 331
17. Money and Goods: 104, 109, 116, 122, 201, 214
18. Actions Involving Walking and Running: 63, 308, 339, 408, 409
19. Attitudinals: 30, 31, 285, 369, 431, 439, 440
20. Water: 87, 101, 102, 127, 296, 352, 353, 391, 424
21. Sounds and Noises: 84, 103, 156, 165, 175
22. Food and Eating: 48, 51, 74, 86, 124, 136, 153, 162, 174, 176, 208, 222, 232, 246
23. Literature, Composition, and Writing: 53, 71, 112, 138, 248, 256, 279, 319, 320
24. Arts and Entertainment: 54, 77, 239, 244
25. Seeing and Perceiving: 135, 195
26. Clothing: 47, 62, 125, 129, 145, 178, 212, 224, 263, 354, 435
27. Texture, Durability, and Consistency: 202, 323, 441

REFERENCES

Anders, P. L., Bos, C. S., & Filip, D. (1984). The effect of semantic feature analysis on learning disabled students. In J. A. Niles & L. A. Harris (Eds.), *Yearbook of the National Reading Conference: Vol. 33. Changing perspectives in research on reading/language processing and instruction* (pp. 162–166). Rochester, NY: National Reading Conference.

Beck, I., McKeown, M., & Omanson, R. (1987). The effects and uses of diverse vocabulary instructional techniques. In M. McKeown & M. Curtis (Eds.), *The nature of vocabulary acquisition* (pp. 147–163). Mahwah, NJ: Erlbaum.

Beck, I. L., & McKeown, M. G. (1985). Teaching vocabulary: Making the instruction fit the goal. *Educational Perspectives, 23*(1), 11–15.

Beck, I. L., McKeown, M. G., & Kucan, L. (2002). *Bringing words to life: Robust vocabulary instruction.* New York: Guilford Press.

Becker, W. C., Dixon, R., & Anderson-Inman, L. (1980). *Morphographic and root word analysis of 26,000 high frequency words.* Eugene, OR: University of Oregon, College of Education.

Biemiller, A., & Slonim, N. (2001). Estimating root word vocabulary growth in normative and advantaged populations: Evidence for a common sequence of vocabulary acquisition. *Journal of Educational Psychology, 93*(3), 498–520.

Calderon, M., August, D., Slavin, R., Duran, D., Madden, N., & Cheung, A. (2005). Bringing words to life in classrooms with English-language learners. In E. F. Hiebert & M. L. Kamil (Eds.), *Teaching and learning vocabulary: Bringing research to practice* (pp. 115–136). Mahwah, NJ: Erlbaum.

Carroll, J. B., Davies, P., & Richman, B. (1971). *The American Heritage word frequency book.* New York: American Heritage Publishing.

Dunn, M., Bonner, B., & Huske, L. (2007). *Developing a systems process for improving instruction: Lessons learned.* Alexandria, VA: Association for Supervision and Curriculum Development.

Dupuy, H. P. (1974). *The rationale, development and standardization of a basic word vocabulary test* (DHEW Publication No. HRA 74-1334). Washington, DC: U.S. Government Printing Office.

Freeman, Y. S., & Freeman, D. E. (2009). *Academic language for English language learners and struggling readers.* Portsmouth, NH: Heinemann.

Gifford, M., & Gore, S. (2008). *The effects of focused vocabulary instruction on underperforming math students.* Alexandria, VA: Association for Supervision and Curriculum Development.

Graves, M. F. (2006). *The vocabulary book: Learning and instruction.* New York: Teachers College Press.

Graves, M. F., & Slater, W. H. (1987, April). *The development of reading vocabularies in rural disadvantaged students, inner-city disadvantaged students, and middle-class suburban students.* Paper presented at the meeting of the American Educational Research Association, Washington, DC.

Hart, B., & Risley, T. R. (1995). *Meaningful differences in the everyday experience of young American children.* Baltimore: Paul H. Brookes Publishing Co.

Heimlich, J. E., & Pittelman, S. D. (1986). *Semantic mapping: Classroom applications.* Newark, DE: International Reading Association.

Hyerle, D. (1996). *Visual tools for constructing knowledge.* Alexandria, VA: Association for Supervision and Curriculum Development.

Hyerle, D. (2009). *Visual tools for transforming information into knowledge* (2nd ed.). Thousand Oaks, CA: Corwin Press.

Kamil, M. L., & Hiebert, E. F. (2005). Teaching and learning vocabulary: Perspectives and persistent issues. In E. F. Hiebert & M. L. Kamil (Eds.), *Teaching and learning vocabulary: Bringing research to practice* (pp. 1–23). Mahwah, NJ: Erlbaum.

Marzano, R. J. (2004). *Building background knowledge for academic achievement: Research on what works in schools.* Alexandria, VA: Association for Supervision and Curriculum Development.

Marzano, R. J. (2006a). *Preliminary report on the 2004–2005 evaluation study of the ASCD program for building academic vocabulary.* Alexandria, VA: Association for Supervision and Curriculum Development.

Marzano, R. J. (2006b). *Supplemental report on the effects of the ASCD program for building academic vocabulary on students classified as eligible for free and reduced lunch (FRL) and students classified as English language learners (ELL).* Alexandria, VA: Association for Supervision and Curriculum Development.

Marzano, R. J. (2007). *The art and science of teaching.* Alexandria, VA: Association for Supervision and Curriculum Development.

Marzano, R. J., & Haystead, M. W. (2009). *Identifying and classifying basic and advanced terms.* Denver, CO: Marzano Research Laboratory.

Marzano, R. J., & Marzano, J. S. (1988). *A cluster approach to elementary vocabulary instruction.* Newark, DE: International Reading Association.

Marzano, R. J., & Pickering, D. J. (2005). *Building academic vocabulary: Teacher's manual.* Alexandria, VA: Association for Supervision and Curriculum Development.

Marzano, R. J., Kendall, J. S., & Paynter, D. E. (1991). *Analysis and identification of basic words in grades K–6.* Denver, CO: Mid-continent Research for Education and Learning.

McLaughlin, B., August, D., Snow, C., Carlo, M., Dressler, C., White, C., Lively, T., and Lippman, D. (2000, April). *Vocabulary improvement and reading in English language learners: An intervention study.* Paper presented at the Research Symposium on High Standards in Reading for Students from Diverse Language Groups: Research, Practice & Policy, Washington, DC: U.S. Department of Education, Office of Bilingual Education and Minority Languages Affairs (OBEMLA).

Nagy, W. E., & Anderson, R. C. (1984). How many words are there in printed school English? *Reading Research Quarterly, 19*(3), 304–330.

Nagy, W. E., & Herman, P. A. (1984). *Limitations of vocabulary instruction* (Tech. Rep. No. 326). Urbana, IL: University of Illinois, Center for the Study of Reading (ERIC Document Reproduction Service No. ED248498).

National Center for Educational Statistics. (2002). *Public school student, staff, and graduate counts by state, school year 2000–2001.* Washington, DC: Author.

National Institute of Child Health and Human Development (2000). *Report of the National Reading Panel: Teaching children to read: An evidenced-based assessment of the scientific research literature on reading and its implications for reading instruction: Reports of the subgroups.* Washington, DC: Author.

Ogden, C. K. (1932). *The basic words: A detailed account of uses.* London: Landor & Kegan Paul.

Pittelman, S. D., Heimlich, J. E., Berglund, R. L., & French, M. P. (1991). *Semantic feature analysis: Classroom applications.* Newark, DE: International Reading Association.

Stahl, S. A. (1999). *Vocabulary development.* Cambridge, MA: Brookline Books.

Thorndike, R. L., & Lorge, I. (1943). *The teacher's word book of 30,000 words.* New York: Teachers College Press.

Umbel, V. M., Pearson, B., Fernandez, M. C., & Oller, D. K. (1992). Measuring bilingual children's receptive vocabularies. *Child Development, 63,* 1012–1020.

White, T. G., Sowell, J., & Yanagihara, A. (1989). Teaching elementary students to use word-part clues. *The Reading Teacher, 42,* 302–308.

INDEX

Creeping/Lurking Actions cluster, 230
Crookedness/Straightness related clusters, 167
Crops/Soil Actions-associated clusters, 228
Cruelty and Meanness related clusters, 206
Curved and Circular Shapes related clusters, 192
Cutting Tools-related clusters, 144

D

Dairy Products clusters, 109
Dark related clusters, 204–205
Days and Months
    Parts of a Day related clusters, 107
    related clusters, 85
Definition/Meaning related clusters, 224
Dependability and Eagerness related clusters, 201
Descending Motion related clusters, 134–135, 147
Desire related clusters, 200
Destructive Actions related clusters, 182
Dimensionality related clusters, 115–116
Diminishers, related clusters, 80
Directions, related clusters, 79
Direction To and From related clusters, 76
Direct vocabulary instruction
    introductory phase, strategies for, 25–35
    overview of, 23–25
    student-based development of descriptions,
        examples, and illustrations, 35–45
Discoverers related clusters, 218
Disease related clusters, 172
    Action Associated with Disease/Injury clusters, 204
    Ailments and Diseases clusters, 221
Dishonesty related clusters, 216
Dissimilarity related clusters, 202–203
Distances, related clusters, 81
Domains of Work related clusters, 186
Double bubble, comparison phase of vocabulary
    instruction, 50
Doubt and Hope related clusters, 207
Down/Under, related clusters, 82–83
Drawing, Writing, Drawing, and Reading, related
    clusters, 103–104
Drinks related clusters, 150
Dupuy vocabulary criteria, 2–3
Durability/Strength related clusters, 209
Dwellings for animals clusters, 154–155

E

Ears, Eyes, and Nose clusters, 134
Ease and Difficulty related clusters, 168
Eating and Drinking related clusters, related clusters, 93
Electricity and Magnetism related clusters, 232
Electronics related clusters, 194
Emotions related clusters
    Anger clusters, 200
    Caring and Trusting clusters, 95
    Contentment and Comfort clusters, 233
    Cruelty and Meanness clusters, 206

Dependability and Eagerness clusters, 201
Doubt and Hope clusters, 207
Envy and Jealousy clusters, 231
Excitement and Attention clusters, 223
Fun and Joy clusters, 91
General Upset clusters, 206
Guilt and Worry clusters, 222–223
Irritability clusters, 223
Names for Feelings clusters, 234
Pride and Confidence clusters, 195
Sadness clusters, 90
Shyness clusters, 216
Emptiness and Fullness, related clusters, 103
Engines related clusters, 194
English language learners (ELL)
    comparison phase of vocabulary instruction for, 47
    vocabulary instruction needs of, 6–8
    vocabulary notebooks for, 64
Envy and Jealousy clusters, 231
Equipment Used with Animals clusters, 206
Equipment Used with Water/Liquid clusters, 217
Events and Dates clusters, 230
Excitement and Attention clusters, 223
Exclamations, related clusters, 78
Exercise related clusters, 204
Expanding Motion related clusters, 196
Expected/Unexpected clusters, 235
Experience/Expertise related clusters, 224
Explicit metaphors, comparison phase of vocabulary
        instruction, 52–53
Eyes related clusters, 134

F

Fabric related clusters, 150–151
    Linens clusters, 132
Face related clusters
    Facial expressions clusters, 138
    Head and Face clusters, 123
Factories, Mills, and Offices related clusters, 220
Failure and Success related clusters, 220
Fame related clusters, Names that Indicate Fame, 215
Familiarity and Popularity related clusters, 199
    Lack of Popularity/Familiarity clusters, 210
Family relationships clusters, 24–25, 113
Fasteners, related clusters, 111–112
Fear related clusters, 200
    Actions related to fear clusters, 231
Feeling and Striking related clusters, 157–158
Feet
    Legs and Feet related clusters, 106
    Things Worn on Hands and Feet cluster, 99
Fences and Ledges related clusters, 167
Fighting related clusters, 187–188
Financial Status related clusters, 235
Fire related clusters, 168
    Producers of fire clusters, 222
    Products Associated with fire clusters, 231

P

Packing and Wrapping related clusters, 220
Paint related clusters, 231
Pants, Shirts, and Skirts related clusters, 127
Parks and Yards clusters, 134
Parts of a Day, related clusters, 107
Parts-related clusters, 130
Pastures and Fields clusters, 219
Patience related clusters, 235
People related clusters
  General Names cluster, 95
  Groups of Animals/Peoples clusters, 186
  Lack of Permanence clusters, 208
  People Who Buy and Sell clusters, 227
  People Who Work in Offices clusters, 227
  Size of People clusters, 211
Performance and Entertainers related clusters, 146
Periods of Time, related clusters, 93–94
Permanence for People, clusters of Names
    Indicating, 214
Persuasion/Advice related clusters, 185
Physical Traits
  Physical Characteristics related clusters, 184
  Size, 154
Places Related to Learning/Experimentation, related
    clusters, 98
Places to Live clusters, 125
Places Where Goods Can Be Bought/Sold related
    clusters, 165
Plants and Flowers related clusters, 191–192
Poems and Songs, related clusters, 94
Police related clusters, 202
Political Disposition, Names clusters
    indicating, 237
Political Events clusters, 231
Political Groups related clusters, 159–160
Popularity related clusters, 199
  Lack of Popularity/Familiarity clusters, 210
Positive Information related clusters, 116
Prepared Foods related clusters, 126–127
Prepositions
  basic instruction in, 31
  student-developed concepts, 40–41
Presentation of Information clusters, 98–99
Pride and Confidence related clusters, 195
Primary auxiliary verbs, 75
Primates related clusters, 214
Procedures and Processes clusters, 215–216
Productive vocabulary, defined, 1–2
Promises related clusters, 224
Pronouns
  basic instruction in, 33–34
  indefinite, 87
  interrogative, 76
  reflexive pronouns, 75–76
  related clusters, 75–76

relative pronouns, 77
  student-developed concepts, 42–43
Protection/Incarceration, Places Related to,
    clusters, 119
Prudence related clusters, 234
Publication Types related clusters, 180–181
Public Officials related clusters, 190
Pulling and Pushing related clusters, 152
Pursuit related clusters, 203

Q

Questioning related clusters, 150

R

Ranches and Farms related clusters, 220
Reading
  basic vocabulary used in, 2–4
  Literature types clusters, 134
  Writing, Drawing, and Reading, related
      clusters, 103–104
Receiving/Taking Actions related clusters, 137
Receptive vocabulary, defined, 1–2
Recording/Translating Information clusters, 215
Recreation and Sports clusters, 152
  Equipment related clusters, 141–142
  Places related to Sports/Entertainment, 155
  Recreational Events and Festivals clusters, 151
Rectangular/Square Shapes clusters, 135
Reducing/Diminishing related clusters, 203
Reflexive pronouns, 75–76
Relationship markers
  addition, 75
  concurrent action, 74, 79
  contrast, 84
  subsequent action, 83
Relative pronouns, 77
Religious and Clergy related clusters, 190
  Places Related to Meetings/Worship
      clusters, 209
Reptiles/Mythical Animals related clusters, 108
Review and refinement phase of vocabulary
    instruction, 24–25
  games, 57–60
  give-one, get-one activities, 54–55
  roots and fixes, 55–57
  strategies for, 54–60
Right and Wrong, related clusters, 104–105
Rocks and Jewels related clusters, 175
  Rocks/Soil characteristics clusters, 213
Rodents related clusters, 154
Rooms, related clusters, 111
Roots and fixes, review and refinement phase of
    vocabulary instruction, 55–57
Root words, identification of, 2–4
Royalty and Statesmen related clusters, 148
Rules and Laws related clusters, 209